THE MAGNETISM OF ANTARCTICA

THE ROSS EXPEDITION 1839–1843

JOHN KNIGHT

Whittles Publishing

Published by
Whittles Publishing Ltd,
Dunbeath,
Caithness, KW6 6EG,
Scotland, UK

www.whittlespublishing.com

Printed and bound by CPI Group (UK) Ltd, Croydon, CR0 4YY

CONTENTS

PART TWO

PART THREE

FOREWORD

My great, great, great grandfather, Sir James Clark Ross was a revered seaman, scientist and an exceptional leader whose courage and curiosity were key to him being chosen to pioneer expeditions to explore the unchartered waters of the Arctic and Antarctic regions.

Roald Amundsen was to say of Ross in 1912:

> Few people of the present day are capable of rightly appreciating this heroic deed, this brilliant proof of human courage and energy. With two ponderous craft - regular 'tubs' according to our ideas - these men sailed right into the heart of the pack, which all previous explorers had regarded as certain death ... These men were heroes - heroes in the highest sense of the word ... A man who'll be remembered as one of the most capable seamen the world has ever produced and a votary of science to whom Antarctic scientific exploration owes so much.

The magnitude of preparing, never minding executing and completing, a three-year expedition to an unchartered frozen continent would be a formidable task today – even in an engine-powered vessel with all the technical navigational and communication tools available. To do it 180 years ago in a sailing ship is unfathomable.

James was the most experienced of all the 19th century Arctic officers and was often considered the first authority on all matters relating to Arctic navigation, so it's not surprising he was chosen to lead the expedition to Antarctica. His foresight combined with his fastidious attention to detail meant the ships were built to endure the rigours of the journey and a comprehensive crew of trusted, able seamen with a broad array of expeditionary experience complemented the criteria to accomplish such a pioneering voyage of discovery. As Amundsen intonated, James paved the way for future scientific explorers. His achievements in magnetism, the extensive data he recorded on the climate, the ocean, ice and landscapes, as well as the extensive botanical and ornithological collections exceeded all expectations.

I am privileged to have a signed first edition copy of the two volumes of *Voyage to Southern Seas* he authored in 1847 which contain all the detailed information he collected. It's definitely not bedtime reading material - more of a record and resource; and not having a seafaring bone in my body, I've found it hard to comprehend, which is probably why I've still not yet read them in their entirety. I know I should, but I need a more captivating 21st century style of writing that recreates the reality of the people, skills and mindset of everyone involved in successfully pulling off such a heroic task.

Thankfully there are polar expedition enthusiasts who love nothing more than immersing themselves in copious volumes of narrated facts. John Knight's avidity has culminated in a collection of 600 books which he's absorbed over the years. As a prolific reader of the mind, body and soul genre books myself, I recognise the urge to transpose what one has gleaned from numerous sources and write a book that has everything in one place so the reader is inspired with as big a representation of the subject as is possible. John has ingeniously weaved facts about the ships, the craftsmen, the crew and the experiences encountered during the expedition into a book that binds the magic of an heroic journey between the covers of *The Magnetism of Antarctica*. He has used his strengths from a lifetime as an engineer to design and structure complex information into creating a compelling book that brings this historic event to life. This helps the reader to understand the individuals and institutions of a particular period in time and so the objectives, strengths, choices and circumstances all create a coherent whole.

James was an adept seaman with a fascination for magnetism which undoubtedly underpinned the reason he thought his lifestyle was his birthright – what he was born to do because it felt like a natural extension of who he was. He must have been an extraordinarily inspirational leader to have maintained the morale and keep an entire crew alive for four winters while stranded in the Arctic and three consecutive years travelling to and from Antarctica. His exemplary conduct and phenomenal finds were honoured with a knighthood in 1844 and a doctorate of common law by Oxford University in 1845. I have no doubt that he would have had the same qualities of patience, respect, trust and integrity that my father and grandfather had – both true gentlemen in my eyes.

I had the privilege of taking my own voyage of discovery to Antarctica in February 2016 by kind invitation of Heritage Expeditions - thankfully in a vessel that was a far cry from being ponderous or tub-like! I saw many of the 89 landmarks James named and was privileged to be taken on a special excursion with my uncle, James Hood Ross, to Possession Island which was the first place James Clark Ross landed. We were prevented from landing on the shore due to the volume of floating ice, so we perilously posed for photos on a large piece of ice a few hundred metres away, holding a flag emblazoned with the Ross family crest to commemorate the day when two generations of Rosses returned 175 years later to metaphorically repossess the island. It was a surreal and emotional experience reconnecting to my roots and being in the place for which I was actively involved in campaigning for marine protection. Just six months later, the wreck of HMS *Terror* was found at the bottom of an Arctic bay and in late October the Ross Sea became the first marine protected area in Antarctica.

Dreams are the essence of what life is all about. Imagine if the crews of HMS *Erebus* and HMS *Terror* had given up hope during the unrelenting storm on the night of 12th March 1842 – a tireless heroic act in and of itself that James recorded in the *Voyage to the Southern Seas*.

> … I should commit an act of injustice to my companions if I did not express my admiration of their conduct on this trying occasion throughout a period of twenty eight hours during any one of which there appeared to be very little hope that we should live to see another; the coolness, steady obedience and untiring exertions of each individual were every way worthy of British Seamen.

Imagine if all those involved in protecting the Ross Sea had given up. Imagine if John Knight had not dreamt of crafting *The Magnetism of Antarctica*. We would not be privy to such a unique account that comprehensively captures the magnitude of the historic exploration of Antarctica.

Philippa Ross BSc(Hons) Psych.Adv.Dip.Ed
Human Ecologist

PART ONE

THE EXPEDITION

1 THE BEGINNING

THE WHYS, WHATS AND WHEREFORES OF A SUCCESSFUL EXPEDITION

All well-organised expeditions have a starting place, a target and hopefully a finishing line. This expedition was to be a classic example of a project that achieved all it set out to do, and much more besides. HMS *Erebus* and HMS *Terror*, having set out from Chatham Royal Naval Dockyard in September 1839, crossed the finishing line in September 1843, when after four years away from England their crews were discharged on arrival at Woolwich.[1] Their target is the subject of the story that we are about to uncover.

Chatham was always busy with ships preparing to sail to destinations across the world. In the 18th and 19th centuries it had become the largest Royal Naval dockyard in the country. Its pre-eminence had been brought about by the proximity of one of England's arch-rivals across the intervening North Sea, the Netherlands, and its connections to other European countries, notably Spain, both of them with strong Catholic ties. Ever since the first Elizabethan age these two countries had constantly threatened war against England. This was because England was predominantly Protestant at the time and there still lingered the hatred and suspicion that had manifested itself over the preceding decades between the two branches of Christianity. There were of course other strategic reasons for Chatham's importance, such as the Thames estuary just up the coast, carrying so much trade into and out of England, together with the proximity of London, the capital city and seat of government.

Chatham had built up a strong reputation for constructing ships of all classes, and when overhauls and repairs needed to be executed, Chatham had the necessary docking facilities as well.

According to historical records the site extended to 400 acres, and at its peak employed as many as 1,700 men. All manner of crafts and skills were required to carry out the construction

---

1 Now in London, but then in Kent.

Chatham Royal Naval Dockyard, from a painting by Joseph Farrington in 1790.

of a ship; it is amazing today to look back at the immense variety of workmen required to make up the labour force employed in a shipyard: carpenters, sail and rope makers, spinners, blacksmiths, coopers and caulkers, all busy carrying out their trades, together with anchorsmiths, plumbers, block-makers, sawyers and draymen. All these men worked in teams led by a supervising officer, the shipwright. Then in the offices there were draughtsmen and storemen, and clerks to ensure a smooth supply of technical and logistical support. Other staff would be employed to ensure the buildings, slipways and dry docks were kept in good repair; and then there was finally the man at the top, the commissioner, who sent in daily reports to the Admiralty on the progress made on ships in for overhaul and refitting or under construction.

The site of the Royal Naval dockyard at Chatham, on the banks of the Medway estuary only a few miles from the open sea, would of course have brought the saltiness of the seaside wafting in. Your nostrils would also have been alerted to the other distinctive smells that would have pervaded the scene: smoke from the relatively new steam-driven tugboats operating around the harbour basin, and the blacksmiths' forges and furnaces where they would be manufacturing metal components for the repair work being carried out on any ships in for refitting. Discarded food and other waste materials, mostly untreated sewage, that had found their way into the water and started their cycle of decay, topped up with horse manure along the wharves, would have made their contribution to the odour present during a warm summer's day, but the sweet aroma of the woodyard could be savoured for the brief time spent admiring the huge stacks of the various timbers that a naval dockyard would require in the course of the construction work: timber still held sway as a building material at this time, but the use of cast iron and forged steel was gaining the upper hand, much as plastics and manmade fibres have replaced many metals today.

Chatham Docks in their early years.

The sounds of the activity going on would have made it difficult to hear a friendly word – or a curse if you happened to stand in the wrong place for an instant – especially when dockworkers were shouting instructions to the sailors operating the derricks. The squeal and clatter of the cartwheels as cargo and supplies were hauled from place to place, and the horses' hooves grinding against the cobbles of the quay, would set your teeth on edge. As you passed by any of the blacksmiths' workshops your ears would be assailed by the ring of hammers on anvils. Even so, with all your senses alerted you would have time to observe the activity taking place in the dry docks where ships were being serviced, and from the vantage point of the wharves there was always the possibility of seeing a new ship under construction on the slipways.

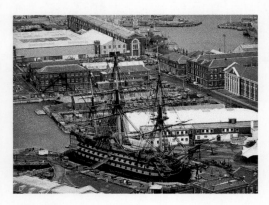

HMS Victory, *berthed in Portsmouth Harbour.*

By 1838 the yard had a history dating back over 200 years and, having superseded Portsmouth in its capacity to repair and build naval ships, had become the largest builder of warships amongst all the Royal Navy's dockyards. It might be surprising to you to learn that Chatham could boast of having built more of the ships that fought at the Battle of Trafalgar than any other yard. Nearly a quarter of the entire English fleet, including HMS *Victory*, had started their lives on the slipways in the Medway area.

It has to be remembered that for nearly two centuries Britain really did dominate world trade and its trading routes. Our navy oversaw the world's seas, and could be relied upon to deal ruthlessly with any attempt by another nation or privateer to interfere with British commerce.

After the Battle of Waterloo the Second Peace Treaty of Paris in 1815 saw the final overthrow of Napoleon and the start of his second exile, this time to St Helena, far away in the southern Atlantic Ocean. Now there was to be a period of relative peace for Britain. There were always hotspots around the world, though, the most violent of these being the war against the young, up-and-coming United States of America, which had taken advantage of Britain's forces being tied up in Europe. With French support – the French had seen this as an opportunity to reassert their influence in what had been taken from them by the British colonial expansion in the late 18th century – the Americans had been intent on expanding into Canadian territory, but with a strong defence it was rebuffed.

Generally speaking, however, Britain could rest on its laurels from 1815. So the Royal Navy had to find new uses for the hundreds of ships and thousands of officers and men at its disposal. Sir John Barrow, the second secretary to the Admiralty, the most powerful man dealing with naval affairs, saw an opportunity in the opening up of new routes to markets that had been virtually closed to British entrepreneurs and manufacturers during the Napoleonic wars.

This was how the United Kingdom entered into the realm of exploration; up until then exploration had been carried out mainly by private enterprise: speculative merchants hoping to steal a march on their rivals in the rush to win new markets for themselves. Now, however, the tide had turned and during Barrow's sojourn at the Admiralty exploration of the globe would be driven by the Royal Navy. The search for the North-west Passage began in earnest with the despatch of Captain John Ross in 1817. This was followed by William Parry's expedition, launched a couple of years later, and so it went on right through to the Franklin disaster in 1848 – and even after that the ships looking for traces of Franklin's men carried on surveying the region.

Part of this newfound need to explore the remote regions of the world brought about the mounting of an expedition to Antarctica. In 1838. James Clark Ross was asked to take the search for new lands to the opposite end of the world. He would achieve this by using two ships especially adapted for this sort of exploratory work: HMS *Erebus* and HMS *Terror*.

Both ships were ex-Royal Naval bomb vessels and their massively strong construction lent them to the task that was being organised. The main criterion was, of course, that they would be strong enough to withstand three years of working in or near the pack ice that they were likely to encounter. To that end the hulls of both ships were strengthened enormously, and it was Chatham Naval Dockyard that carried out the refits.

Erebus, built in 1826 at Pembroke Dock, had been designed by the naval architect Sir Henry Peake. Her main statistics were: a gross weight of 370 tons, a length of 105 feet a width of 28 feet and a draught of about 14 feet. Her original armaments included two mortars for bomb delivery, and fourteen cannons. Her consort, *Terror*, had also been designed by Sir Henry Peake but had been constructed at Bideford, in north Devon. *Terror* was 50 tons lighter than *Erebus* and a little shorter and not quite so wide or deep, but was still capable of delivering two mortar bombs at a time, and had a number of cannons. Both vessels were crewed by 64 men, including an officer complement of 15 and the captain. Due to the varied nature of the mission they were about to undertake, the ships carried a good selection of boats – nine for each vessel, all told. These ranged from a pinnace, the largest, to four cutters, two whaleboats and finally a couple of small dinghies. They were all propelled by sail or oars depending on the circumstances, and because of their range of sizes they could carry out anything from small expeditions of their own to conveying just the captain on visits to other ships anchored nearby or going ashore.

In early 1828 *Erebus* undertook her first commission, patrolling in the western Mediterranean. Her main duty was to intercept Barbary pirates operating out of north African ports and capturing merchant vessels. The pirates were not just interested in the cargoes; they also captured the crewmen, who would be sold as slaves, and the officers, who would earn the pirates a ransom. The requisitioned vessels were an additional source of revenue to them.

Erebus operated in the Mediterranean for two years, but on her return to England was laid up and was only brought back into service in order to be prepared for this expedition. She was then towed to Chatham to begin the refit that would prepare her for the rigours of the voyage ahead.

Terror had had a more adventurous life; her first action was between 1813 and 1814 when she was involved in the American War, as it was known. After her return home she was despatched to join *Erebus* in the Mediterranean. but whilst crossing the Bay of Biscay was severely damaged in a storm and had to be towed back to England.

In 1836 Captain George Back had her modified for his attempt to find the elusive Northwest Passage: from Hudson's Bay (as originally named) through the Foxe Basin towards what had become known as the Fury and Hecla Strait. It was hoped that this could be navigated as a possible exit that would lead directly to the Arctic Ocean and so avoid the tortuous route through the archipelago north of the Canadian mainland. But *Terror* was beset by ice in Hudson's Bay, and it was only by superb seamanship after her release that she was sailed back across the Atlantic to be beached at Lough Swilly on the west coast of Ireland. After she was repaired, she suffered the same fate as *Erebus*: laid up until selected for the Antarctic expedition.

The refitting of the two exploration ships proceeded with some degree of haste so that they would be ready to set sail before the end of September 1839. This would give them time to arrive in the southern hemisphere in the summer season while exploring their way to Tasmania, where they hoped to spend their first southern winter.

Chatham Royal Docks, where the modifications were to be carried out, had itself been undergoing a major overhaul during the previous two decades. The Medway could now be cleared of silt using a steam-powered dredger. This improved the access up the river for sailing ships, especially the larger ones that were now being built for the navy. Steam power was also utilised to pump water out of the new dry docks, built of granite instead of the wooden piles that had been traditionally used. The old dry dock system had relied on the rise and fall of the tides; when the tide rose, a ship would be manoeuvred into the dock whose wooden gates would then be wedged closed; then when the tide fell the ship would be left high and dry, supported on wooden braces.

The granite for the rebuilt docks came down the North Sea on barges from Aberdeen where it had been quarried, and although initially very expensive it provided a much stronger and longer-lasting solution to the almost perennial problem of replacing damaged and rotten timber pilings. The new docks were dug out several feet below the low tide level, and the entrances were designed to create a double barrier to the rising tide. Wooden gates formed the inner barrier, and a caisson was deployed to create an outer barrier. The steam pump could not only keep the lock between the gates and the caisson free from any water leaking in but could also pump out the deeper part of the dock, which lay below the low tide mark.

The designer of these vastly improved dry docks was George Parkin, the master shipwright at Chatham, and his design was implemented by John Rennie, one of Britain's leading engineers. The work spanned nearly 20 years, but by the time that *Erebus* and *Terror* were brought in for their massive refit three of the docks had been converted and they even had the luxury of wooden roofs, enabling the workforce to work throughout the year. These granite docks have stood the test of time and have been retained as part of the Historic Dockyard Museum that maintains the now redundant dockyard and runs it as a working museum.

No 3 Dry Dock at Chatham Royal Dockyard, much as it would have looked at the time of the expedition (with of course the exception of HMS Ocelot, the last submarine built there, in 1962).

The modifications carried out to both vessels were mainly to strengthen their already strong hulls; remember they had been built to stand the great stresses imposed by launching their mortar bombs. The launch pads set deep into the hulls had to be removed, and the large hatches were replaced with decking, creating space to store the nine boats that were to be carried aboard each ship.

The ships' bows and sides were strengthened externally by a layer of English elm planking 6 inches thick right down to the keel, where Canadian elm was used. The hull was then sheathed in copper sheets. This would help to protect the timbers in two ways: first it reduced the risk of attack by marine growth and the shipworm prevalent in the warmer waters they would sail through to reach the Antarctic, and secondly the copper would reduce the friction at or below the waterline as the ship passed through the icefields.

More planking was fitted to the internal walls of the hull; this was applied in several layers, each layer mounted diagonally to the layer beneath, and all the layers were caulked in the hope of sealing the hull against any damage sustained. Bulkheads were strengthened, again to withstand the ingress of water and reduce the risk of flooding spreading through the whole of the lower portion of the ship. In polar exploration, damage to the ship's hulls was a very real risk and this was to become evident when the two ships entered the ice-packed seas that surrounded the great southern continent. No less than six pumps were supplied to each ship. Four of them, known by the designer's name, Massey, consisted of two endless chains running over upper and lower pulleys, which supported blades mounted along their length and held at right angles to them, much as an escalator is constructed. The chains were suspended within two metal tubes that ran down into the bilges. The top pulley could be manually rotated so that the chains would descend down one tube, and after they had passed over the bottom pulley would be pulled back up through the other tube in a continuous motion. At the bottom, the two tubes were held apart and into this space each blade could scoop up a quantity of water. On the upward cycle the water would be retained between the blades and the bore of the tube, and as each blade reached the top of the return leg of the tube the water would discharge over the ship's side. This efficient system extracted an almost continual flow of water.

There is a very informative appendix in Volume I of James Clark Ross's two books about the modifications carried out at the Chatham dockyard under the supervision of Mr Rice. He lists all the alterations that took place to the two ships, using terms such as: penstocks (flood gates to allow water to reach the pump well), limber boards (removable boards stopping rubbish getting into the pump well), quarter galleries (windows across the stern of ship), thwartship bulkheads (partitions placed between holds), crutches and sleepers (stiffening brackets and timbers laid lengthwise to withstand the shock of impacts as from ice) and many

327

APPENDIX, No. I.

MEMORANDUM OF THE FITTINGS OF H. M. SHIP EREBUS,
BY MR. RICE, OF CHATHAM DOCKYARD.

THE ship is fortified externally by solid chock channels, the spaces between the channels being similarly fitted, tapering at the extremities, so as to form an easy curvature in a fore and aft direction; the side is doubled with six-inch oak plank under the channel, increasing to eight-inch at the wale, which is three feet broad; from thence, through a space of five feet, the doubling diminishes to three inches in thickness, of English elm, and the remainder of the bottom to the keel is doubled with three-inch Canada elm. The quarter galleries are removed, and the quarter pieces and stern strongly united by planking; all rails and projections being carefully avoided.

The knee of the head being removed, the bow is terminated by fittings or thick bolsters, leaving no projections at the stern. Braziers, or thick copper, is substituted for that ordinarily used, extending along the body at the line of flotation, and entirely covering the bow down to the keel.

Within-board, the spaces between the bands at the floor heads, &c., are fitted in with six-inch oak plank; the entire surface in the hold being caulked, two thicknesses of 1½ inch African board are then worked diagonally over the bands, &c. at right angles to each other, each layer being also caulked. The thwartship bulkheads of the fore, main, and after holds are wrought diagonally of two thicknesses of 1½ inch African board at right angles to each other, the

Y 4

upper ends rabbetting into the lower deck beams, and the lower ends into four-inch plank, wrought upon the doubling. The bulkheads are caulked on both sides, and rendered water-tight. The wing bulkheads are similarly wrought. The limber boards are likewise caulked down and doubled by a fore and aft plank. Penstocks are introduced in the limbers at the bulkhead, allowing a communication, when required, from one compartment to another, leading to the well. The fore hold is provided with two common pumps, to work on the weather deck; and the well is furnished with four of Massey's excellent pumps.

The bow, internally, is fortified with a solid mass of timber eight inches moulded, canting from abreast the foremast to the stemson, square to the body. Between the upper and lower decks, and also between the lower and orlop decks, thick shelf pieces are wrought, terminating under the transom abaft, and meeting at the middle line at the deck hooks forward.

The central planks of the weather deck are six inches thick, laid fore and aft; the remainder of the deck is wrought double; the lower planks, three inches thick, are laid fore and aft; the upper planks, three inches thick, diagonally, having fearnaught dipped in hot tallow, laid between the two surfaces. The beams of this deck are connected by pointers, or diagonally-lopped carlings, from the catheads forward.

Additional crutches and sleepers have been introduced abaft, and diagonal trusses worked between the chocks under the lower deck beams. The ship is otherwise very strongly built, having diagonal iron riders, iron hooks and crutches in the bow, and iron sleepers abaft.

Filling timbers have been introduced in the stern, with an inner transom, kneed to the stern post and ship's side, double-planked inside and out, thus rendering the counter as strong as the bow, to meet the shocks which the extremities are most likely to encounter in the ice.

Chatham,
19th September, 1839.

Instructions issued to Chatham Dockyard for strengthening Erebus and Terror.
Copied from James Clark Ross's book, A Voyage of Discovery and Research.

more. In short, virtually every structural timber was strengthened not by a single extra piece of seasoned wood but at least two and in some cases several layers. Wrought-iron brackets were added, or replaced existing wooden ones. The decking timbers and cross-braces were fortified, too, in order to help hulls withstand severe nips from encroaching ice floes.

Whilst the ships were being overhauled other modifications were added; one in particular was a basic central heating system called the Sylvester, after its inventor. It was known from previous polar expeditions that condensation caused a lot of problems, especially in the cabins and the living quarters of the ships, and this system could be described as a heat exchanger. Using tubing and metal ducting, warm air could be passed around the ship and fed through vents into the various living and sleeping areas. The hot air was generated by a metal jacket built around the galley stoves, and the heat given off by the stoves was retained within the attached ducting. Using the principle that hot air rises, a flow of warm air would make its way along the ducts and so draw in replacement air from below the kitchen range. This would allow the warm air to dissipate throughout the ship and at the same time utilise the otherwise wasted hot air generated by the cooking range.

In *Terror*, the Sylvester system replaced a hot-water-based arrangement that had been fitted before her abortive trip under the captaincy of Captain George Back; his remarks about its usefulness were apparently very disparaging.

All the old standing rigging was taken down and replaced with new, as were all the sails, sheets and anchor chains; a complete overhaul of all the running gear was implemented.

The two ships were to be absent from Britain's shores for a period of at least three or possibly four years, and although provisions could be obtained en route it was felt necessary to provide the bulk of the stores from the outset in case of unforeseen events. By this time in the history of polar exploration the navy was beginning to understand how to keep the crews healthy, but another three-quarters of a century was to pass before it was realised that a balanced diet containing the essential vitamins was needed to keep illness at bay. One advantage that Ross's expedition had over other polar ventures was that if all went to plan his two ships would be making calls at ports along the way where the crew could be fed fresh provisions to relieve the onboard diet of the salt meats, ship's biscuit and tinned and pickled vegetables that formed the basis of meals on most long voyages.

The naval authorities were clearly coming to terms with the health and welfare of the sailors; there was a realisation that poor-quality food and the lack of strict controls over its management were directly connected to the health and well-being of the men, especially those that embarked on long voyages. It was not unusual for a ship to be away from her home port for three or four years. For expedition ships, this could mean isolation from fresh food for many months at a time, leading to outbreaks of scurvy. Despite the awareness of its prevention by lime juice, the disease was at that time not fully understood and once it had set in there was no known remedy. So the Admiralty had put in place a strict code of practice which suppliers of food were expected to adhere to, but as with all regulations these were often circumvented if there was any extra profit to be made. For instance although flour was issued only from mills that were government owned or controlled, and the bread supplied had to be made from flour processed by these mills, this did not stop unscrupulous suppliers from slipping in quantities of old stock.

After the invention of canning food in the early 19th century, tinned meats and vegetables were supplied to the naval authorities. It turned out, however, that only the smaller tins were useful; food in larger cans turned out to have a very limited shelf life, probably because the cooking process had failed to fully eliminate the harmful bacteria that would have been present at the outset of the cooking cycle. And then, even when the food had been successfully cooked and sealed, the cans were subject to rusting and damage due to incorrect handling or stowage. The food in a can with any sort of perforation would soon become contaminated, so inadequately trained cooks could unwittingly subject their comrades to food poisoning. Such was the delicate balance between the new technology and the desire to improve the victualling lot of sailors and keep them in robust health on these long voyages.

Despite all the logistical problems the larders of both ships carried an impressive array of foodstuffs. A short résumé of the supplies can be garnered from the list in Ross's account of the expedition; it contained items such as 3½ tons of cooked mutton, nearly 8 tons of beef, over 3 tons of veal and ox cheeks, and a selection of concentrated soups and gravy. Vegetables in tins, as well as a store of fresh carrots, parsnips, beetroot, onions and turnips, were added by the commissariat. Pickling had long been known as a way of preserving food, and this meant the inclusion of pickled walnuts, onions and cabbage. Another item that was taken and that other later explorers would have been advised to make use of was over a ton of cranberries, although the benefits of these truly antiscorbutic fruit was not realized at the time. Lime juice is not mentioned in the list but it can be assumed that a number of casks would have been present in the manifest.

Regulations concerning the supply of food and drink aboard all Royal Naval ships were overhauled in 1824 and written orders were given to each ship detailing the rations that were to be carried. A daily ration for a seaman would normally consist of a pound of fresh meat and bread, half a pound of fresh vegetables, a gallon of beer and a few ounces of sugar, cocoa and tea. As mentioned above, when the fresh supplies were used up the basic rations would be resumed. So the ship's larder would also stock raisins, currants, suet and wine – and, most importantly for a sailor, a good quantity of rum.

The opportunity of stocking up with fresh supplies was always taken, and a number of stations around the world, in places such as Madeira, the Canary Isles, St Helena and Cape Town, could furnish these essentials. Watering, of course, always took place when the opportunity arose, even when food supplies could not be obtained.

The naval authorities, learning from the experience gained by sending ships to the Arctic, also supplied a selection of warm woollen clothing for the men, to cope with the rigours of the extremely cold environment they were headed towards. In the ship's slops chest would be items for crew members who wore out or lost any of their clothes. Normally, the value of any items supplied would be deducted from the men's pay packets at the end of a voyage, the exceptions being on the death of the sailor or the total loss of the ship; but on this expedition it would appear that the winter clothing issued came gratis of the Admiralty, another indication of its preparedness to maintain a healthy crew at all costs.

Despite the improvement in the health of the crews, one factor in particular was still overlooked. This was the conditions under which the men lived. On the smaller naval ships the crew's quarters were so low in the ship that it was impossible for them to open any air vents on the sides for fear of seawater pouring in. The only way to bring fresh air down into the men's quarters was by opening the hatches on the decks – and in stormy weather even this practice risked heavy seas cascading down into the lower decks. The concept of a forced air supply to the below decks quarters where the men lived and slept had not yet been invented. n addition, in all naval ships a sailor had little more than 18 inches in which to sling his hammock, bringing his body into contact with those of his neighbours as they slept, so when any contagious disease struck, the crowding would rapidly turn this into an epidemic, decimating a crew. Tropical stations were particularly prone to this problem, yellow fever, typhoid and malaria being the worst diseases.

By 1840 personal hygiene had become a more important matter, and the officers would order the hammocks to be brought out on deck for cleaning; the bedding had to be changed, and the sailors were instructed to launder their clothes, at least twice a week. Washing and bathing were supervised to ensure there were no laggards.

Pay, which had traditionally been given only when the voyage was completed and the crew were paid off, was modified so that an allowance could be drawn for shore leave whilst away from the home port. A strict record of the monetary withdrawals was kept to ensure that a man always stayed enough in credit to cover on return to base any losses he might have incurred during the voyage.

Drinking water, traditionally stored in wooden casks or barrels, did not retain its freshness for more than a couple of weeks. The build-up of algae tainted the water to the point where it became repulsive and virtually undrinkable. The introduction of iron water tanks helped enormously and reduced the pollution. But even the metal tanks had their own problem, in that as the water was drained off the rusty sediment at the bottom of each tank would be agitated by the ship's motion, resulting in an unpleasant brownish deposit in the water. Lead plumbing was introduced to help with this problem, but of course at the time nobody knew of the detrimental effects of lead on the brain and body. The use of lead pipes and tanks is thought to have been one of the causes of the Franklin expedition's demise, but not before well over 100 years had elapsed was this investigated.

With very limited personal storage space below decks, the sailor would usually have a wardrobe consisting of a woollen or canvas cap, even the broad, flat-brimmed hat that is a such a familiar sight in pictures of sailors of the Victorian age. A jacket, single- or double-breasted, could be waist length or longer, and was made out of a heavy woollen serge. A sailor's trousers, made of canvas or linen (not cotton as this was too expensive), came to just below the knees, and were of a loose fit so as not to restrict movement when their wearer was aloft. The sailors' shirts would, like their trousers, be of linen or canvas, or sometimes Osnaburg, a flax or jute-based material which probably came from Germany. Shoes had a square toe, which meant they would fit either foot, but they were dispensed with when working aloft, and sometimes on deck as well. Stockings, made of knitted wool or stitched pieces of cotton cloth that could be replicated by the sailor whilst on board his ship, came in handy. Nearly all the crew members wore a neckerchief, or kerchief, round their neck or in their hair. Whichever way they were worn, their primary use was not decorative but to wipe sweat or water from hands and face to help avoid slipping whilst working.

A typical gundeck aboard a Victorian warship, showing how the crew were dressed.

Although the officers wore a fairly standard range of uniforms with insignia denoting their rank, the common seamen had to wait until well into the 19th century before their attire was deemed to be important enough to bring in some regularity about how they looked. Earlier than this they would have been expected to come fully clothed or resort to the slops chest to buy what they needed. A few captains might finance the crew's apparel if they were wealthy enough and were concerned about appearances. This practice was, however, usually reserved for the crew of the captain's gig or when visiting officers were received aboard. It was in the late 1850s that standardisation for all ratings came in, and blue seemed to have been the preferred colour.

The other items essential for life on board included most notably a hammock, or sometimes two to allow a change of bedding, especially when the sailor was wet through after his watch. As there was so little room for storage a canvas holdall would be used instead of a wooden trunk to keep the sailors' possessions together – and woe betide any thief. A woollen blanket and pillow, together with needle and thread for repairing his garments, were essential items of the sailor's kit, as was one of the most important tools that he would carry aloft, a sheath knife, to free tangled rigging or sails; the knife would be buckled to the waistband behind him, so he could easily reach it with either hand.

The captain and his fellow officers had long had the privilege of wearing a decent uniform. In fact, they had at least two distinct uniforms: one for day-to-day wear whilst working the ship, and the second set, their dress uniform, would enable them to present themselves in all their resplendent attire for functions ashore or when paying their respects to the Admiralty or other senior officers. This basic system is still used in all branches of the armed forces.

How naval uniforms developed; these are from a few years after this expedition: right: ordinary seaman, far right: able seaman, lower right: lieutenant, far lower right: captain.

By the time that Captain Ross and his deputy, Commander Crozier, were ready to sail from Chatham the dress code for officers would include a white shirt under a waistcoat; on top of these would be a double-breasted jacket boasting brass or gold buttons. The cuffs would have matching buttons on them. The most striking aspects of the jacket were the epaulettes and tasselled braids mounted on each shoulder. The size and splendour of these would be enough for any sailor to instantly identify the officer's rank.

2 TARGETS AND INSTRUCTIONS

ROYAL SOCIETY AND ADMIRALTY ORDERS

Now begins the story of two of the most famous ships ever to set sail from our shores: Her Majesty's Discovery Ship HMS *Erebus* and her consort, HMS *Terror*, under the overall command of Captain James Clark Ross, with Commander Francis Crozier sailing in *Terror*. They were headed for the virtually unknown great southern continent, Antarctica. The year was 1839, and they were not expected back to British shores until 1843.

This expedition was to be the first official government-sponsored foray into the distant Southern Ocean since James Cook had, nearly 70 years earlier, ventured south of the Antarctic Circle, the imaginary line that at the time [2]encircled the globe at 66°33'46.7". The primary object of this 19th-century expedition was scientific; the study of global magnetism which it was hoped would provide the answers to one of the outstanding problems of the day relating to navigation; how to accurately determine a ship's position and draw up reliable charts. Such charts would benefit the commercial interests of British shipping in carrying out the worldwide trade that the burgeoning industrial growth of England was clamouring for.

The Royal Society having been consulted at length, had agreed to become involved with the voyage; it is only fair to say that it was its influence that had projected the enterprise from not just one of exploration but to what was probably one of the most solidly scientific expeditions ever launched. As well as the study of magnetic fields, other investigations would prove equally important to the scientific community: the natural historical and biological specimens brought back took months of painstaking cataloguing to complete. Each ship had on board two specialists to organise the collections. In *Erebus* these were a young Joseph Hooker, assistant surgeon, and the ship's surgeon, Robert McCormick, who took every

---

2 It moves; at the time of writing it's at approximately 66°33'48.9".

opportunity of going ashore and exploring to find anything that grew or moved. They were ably assisted by their counterparts on *Terror*, Surgeon John Robertson and his assistant, David Lyall. Hooker, who would go on to become one of the most highly regarded scientists of his era and a close friend of Charles Darwin, succeeded his father in taking charge of Kew Gardens, and was eventually given a knighthood.

As the time approached for departure Ross received two sets of instructions, one from the Admiralty and the second from the Royal Society. The Admiralty set came with the formal heading:

> By the Commissioners for executing the office of Lord High Admiral of the United Kingdom of Great Britain and Ireland.

This set of instructions took about 1,700 words to relay the full extent of what was required of Ross and his two ships.

The Royal Society added a dissertation around three times longer. The first sentence is a fine example of the careful wording used:

> The Council of the Royal Society are very strongly impressed with the number and importance of the desiderata in physical and meteorological science, which may wholly or in part be supplied by observations made under such highly favourable and encouraging circumstances as those afforded by the liberality of Her Majesty's government on this occasion.

On looking at the requirements of the two sets of instructions in a little more detail, it becomes apparent that the officers of both ships, although not well versed in most of the aspects of the sciences that they would be asked to be involved in, were required to keep detailed records, and that this would involve many off-duty hours writing up the readings and records taken during the expedition.

Great emphasis was put on the co-ordinated recording of magnetic readings from the various observatories that were going to be set up during the journey south. The scientific establishment in Europe, under the guidance of the two prominent German scientists Carl Friedrich Gauss and Wilhelm Weber, had devised a system of measuring the horizontal intensity of the Earth's magnetic field.[3] This followed numerous field trials carried out in Germany and other, mainly European, countries and it was hoped that a similar set of results in the southern hemisphere taken as the two ships ventured towards Antarctica would confirm that magnetic variations that took place in the north were mirrored in the south.

---

3 It would be too complicated to explain in detail this natural phenomenon, except to say that in geometric terms the Earth's magnetic forces act in three dimensions best described as the X, Y and Z axes. The magnetic forces can be measured as components of the three axes i e. XY, XZ and YZ, all of which change from place to place on the Earth's surface, and which affect the swing or dip of a compass needle.

The ships were supplied with the latest equipment for the various branches of investigation that the scientists hoped to look into. To this array of instrumentation was added a comprehensive stock of containers and preservatives for the collection of flora and fauna they would amass. The ships' officers were also going to take seawater samples from differing depths, testing them for salinity and temperature. Wire cables would allow the lowering of the cleverly designed sampling jars to bring the samples up from known depths and the same cables could be used to lower a weight until it reached the seabed, enabling a record to be kept of variations in the ocean depth and, in an early version of gravity coring, using a cleverly designed hollow in the weight, to bring up samples of the seabed itself. Ocean currents were monitored by comparing dead reckoning[4] with more accurate measurements of the ship's course once her position had been fixed.

The magnetic instruments on board enabled the officer responsible to record the variations in magnetic density, using Gauss and Weber's method of calculation. Deflections of the compass needle downwards and the amount of swing that the needle indicated away from the true south were noted, using the highly sensitive apparatus supplied by the Royal Society.

Amongst all the requirements set out in the Admiralty's orders were several cautionary notes: the ships should be kept in contact with one another as much as possible, and a series of rendezvous stations should be set up to fall back on in the event of separation. The officers on both ships were to carry out the scientific work and they were to frequently exchange their results so as to minimise any errors occurring. They were not to enter into hostilities with other vessels even if it were known that Great Britain was at war with another nation. (Both ships carried a dozen or so cannon, but these were for signalling, to help them keep in contact during inclement weather, or for any other peaceable consideration.) Additionally, both commanders would have been provided by the British government with a letter of indemnity explaining that they were on a voyage of discovery, and as such could claim neutrality; this was common practice amongst most European nations. Another important recommendation was for the ships to withdraw from any ice which could trap them for the duration of the southern winter. Although both ships had been strengthened substantially there were no contingency plans in place to mount any rescue operation, and the safe return of their ships and their crews was no doubt uppermost in the Admiralty's mind. Both Ross and Crozier were seasoned Arctic navigators, but retention in the ice for a winter would seriously jeopardise the whole expedition. Ross had in fact been marooned in the Arctic for four winters between 1829 and 1833 while on an expedition under the command of his uncle John Ross. His ship, the privately owned *Victory*,[5] had been trapped in the ice of Prince Regent Inlet to the north of the Canadian mainland, and despite repeated attempts to gain their freedom the party had eventually abandoned their ship and taken to their boats. Against all the odds they were eventually picked up by a passing whaling ship. It was during that expedition that James

4 DR is based on a vessel's compass heading and her speed through the water, and cannot include the errors induced by drift and current.

5 Not the famous ship of the line at Trafalgar, but an ex-Mersey ferryboat.

The rescue of Captain John Ross and his crew in the Arctic in 1833 by Isabella *under Captain John Humphrey. But in the Antarctic, there would be no possibility of such a rescue.*

Clark Ross had sledged to the North Magnetic Pole, and his ambition on this new expedition was to locate the South Magnetic Pole.

The role of the Royal Society would become more apparent when the ships returned home with their results, and to prepare for this the society set up several sub-committees, each comprising members with expertise in the scientific fields to be investigated.

From the point of view of the officers on the two ships, the easiest subjects were meteorology and physics, as these were closely related to their knowledge of running the ship and navigating it; for the other subjects the surgeons and their two assistants would be in charge. Ross and Crozier were keen to see that the scientific nature of the expedition lacked for nothing when it came to putting the ships' companies at the disposal of the scientists. Some of the landings that were carried out on the remote and inhospitable shores they encountered only became possible due to the skills of the seamen delegated to the task. It is not within the scope of this book to delve into the complexity of the observations, samples and records taken, but suffice it to say that they formed one of the largest sets of data ever brought back by a single expedition.

By the 15th century all the major land masses on the planet apart from the Antarctic had been colonised by humans. The dramatically lower sea levels of the last great Ice Age had allowed hunter-gatherer groups to gain access to the Americas as they followed the quarry they lived off. In the case of Australia, only small, simple canoes were required to transport people southward across the straits from the islands of what is now Indonesia. Later, the many islands dispersed across the breadth and width of the three great oceans of the world would be reached by daring crews aboard fragile craft such as rafts and canoes fitted with sails. These islands would also act as stepping stones to other shores such as New Zealand and Greenland. Greenland was, in fact, exceptional in that the Inuit had managed to work their way eastwards from Asia to Canada and on, whereas the Vikings sailed westward from Iceland many centuries later, unaware of the presence of the Inuit. The Vikings subsequently visited Labrador and sailed down the east coast of North America for hundreds of miles, returning to Greenland without the aid of any navigational aids apart from stars and a crude form of compass.

Examples of scientific instruments typical of the expedition: Top left: chronometer. Top right: sextant. Bottom left: dip circle. Bottom right: theodolite.

Ever since ships have sailed out of sight of land their commanders have needed to determine their positions as accurately as possible. For many centuries navigation by the stars and the sun held sway, but the further people ventured into the unknown the more they felt in need of a surer way of determining their position. This led to all sorts of devices, such as the backstaff, the astrolabe, the cross-staff and the quadrant. Finally came the sextant and all its variants, culminating in the last quarter of the 18th century when Jesse Ramsden, an instrument maker of considerable skill, produced a sextant of great accuracy, probably the pinnacle of this instrument's design. Combining this with the successful trials that had been carried out by the James Cook on the chronometer, and the knowledge that emanated from the likes of the Ross expedition about the Earth's magnetic field, mariners were now armed with the means to determine with a greater degree of accuracy than ever before their courses across the oceans of the world.

Developments in cartography would see the drawing of the lines of latitude and longitude. These are so familiar to us today that not a second thought is given to them, but the division of the Earth's surface into sectors and segments by a series of imaginary lines spaced out in an accurate pattern and projected onto charts was a major step in map-making. In conjunction with an accurate way of determining time, a course could now be plotted on any chart that would ensure the ship could be steered to its destination with a great deal of accuracy.

Throughout the Ross expedition the crews constantly measured and recorded ocean currents and tidal rises and falls, and kept a strict record of distances travelled using the logs trailed behind the ships to measure their speeds and distances, eventually to bring home a mass of information that would be correlated into tables for the use of future voyagers. Not only would the expedition tabulate the readings taken whilst they were at sea but observatories would be built on land to provide even more accurate measurements of magnetic variations. With this requirement in mind, part of the cargo loaded at the outset would have been all the wooden building materials necessary to construct the observatories, which were to be erected on St Helena, at Cape Town, on Kerguelen Island in the southern Indian Ocean, Hobart in Tasmania, and possibly Sydney. At least one officer, with a couple of crew members to assist him, was taken aboard at Chatham to man each observatory after it was commissioned, to be repatriated to Britain after the expedition was concluded.

Other nationalities, including the Americans and the French, had been preparing to send expeditions to Antarctica. One of the French expeditions had been led by Jules Dumont d'Urville. He had joined the Napoleonic navy aged 17 but for the first few years he and most of the other French sailors had been trapped in port by the Royal Naval blockade, lifted only after the defeat of Napoleon at Waterloo. During d'Urville's years of enforced inactivity he turned his attention to studying languages; he eventually became so proficient that he mastered not only English and German but at least four more, including Ancient Greek and Latin.

With the restoration of the monarchy in France (King Louis XVIII had spent his exile in England) the French navy was again able to sail freely from its bases, and Dumont d'Urville found himself aboard a survey ship carrying out hydrographic work among the islands of the Mediterranean. During this period he visited the Greek island of Milo, and the story goes that while he was ashore he was shown the statue of Venus. The statue, correctly identified by d'Urville as a valuable antiquity, was bought by the French government and now resides in the Louvre Museum.

Between 1822 and 1836 he took part in several voyages across the oceans of the world, and despite worsening health he persuaded the king of France to authorise him to lead an expedition to the South Magnetic Pole. With two ships, *Astrolabe* and the slightly smaller *Zélée*, he had set out in September 1837, a full two years before Ross could hope to sail. To Ross's utmost annoyance, d'Urville's plans were near-identical to his own; the frustration must have been hard for Ross to bear.

D'Urville, in command of *Astrolabe*, headed south. One of his aims was to better the furthest south set by James Weddell, a target that d'Urville was not, as it turned out, able to achieve. When Ross, with his vast knowledge of travelling in polar seas and even overwintering, eventually set out from Chatham his ships would be fully stocked with an abundance of suitable clothing and rations that would keep his crews free from scurvy – but not so with the Frenchman; once he had left the temperate zones, where fresh provisions could be obtained, his crews would be subject to the traditional rations of salt meat and ships biscuit, which soon led to the onset of scurvy.

Even so, they eventually reached the perimeter of the frozen continent and carried out a surprising amount of accurate survey work. In the process they had a brief sighting of an American exploration vessel, *Porpoise*, captained by Charles Wilkes. The sighting was very brief, however, as *Porpoise* turned and disappeared into the fog without so much as a signal.

The French expedition ships Astrolabe *and* Zélée, *on the expedition led by Lieutenant Jules Dumont d'Urville.*

As the health of d'Urville's two crews became manifestly worse he had no alternative but to head for Hobart. On his return to France, made painful by the knowledge that he had lost a son to cholera during his absence, he was promoted to admiral and given a number of awards by geographical societies. Then, not long after his return he and his family were travelling by train when the engine was derailed and the firebox split, setting alight the wreckage and killing many people including d'Urville and the remaining members of his immediate family.

He is credited with seeing for the first time a penguin now known as the Adélie, which he had named after his wife. The French territorial claim in Antarctica, Adélie Land, was also named after her.

The Congress of the United States of America, meanwhile, had been prodded into action by a swell of public demand for the country to support the sealers, the spearhead of American activity in the islands of Antarctica. The men had wiped out the seals in their hunting grounds, and new grounds needed to be found to restore the lucrative business. It was common knowledge, as well, that several European powers were about to descend on Antarctica in an effort to seize a portion of this new continent for their countries' benefit.

The American Charles Wilkes was not the first or even the second choice to lead this new enterprise; after all, his expertise was cartography and hydrographics. Despite his limited experience of command he took charge of the largest of the six ships in the flotilla – *Vincennes*, *Peacock*, *Porpoise*, *Relief*, *Flying Fish* and *Sea Gull* – as they departed in August 1838 from Hampton Roads on the east coast of Virginia. They sailed down to Madeira, called at Rio de Janeiro and rounded Cape Horn after visiting Tierra del Fuego, before proceeding up the Pacific coast of South America passing Chile and Peru, where *Sea Gull* was lost with all hands.

Then, passing through some of the Pacific Island groups, they eventually reached Sydney before, in December 1839, Wilkes committed his ships to the turbulent voyage to Antarctica. After charting the frozen edge of this vast new continent for some 1,600 miles, he set out for home, completing a circumnavigation of the world and running up a total distance of 87,000 miles.

As he had lost two of his ships and the crew of one of them – in all, 28 men had lost their lives in the enterprise – he was court-martialled on his return. He was acquitted of both losses, however, and of another case relating to the alleged massacre of about 80 islanders in Fiji following the death of two of his seamen. What he did suffer, though, was the indignity of being found guilty of the extreme punishments he had meted out to the men under his command.

Some of his discoveries were to be brought into doubt by Ross and other navigators, including Captain Robert Falcon Scott; Ross sailed right over a location where Wilkes had claimed to have found land. Nevertheless, when Wilkes died at the age of nearly 80 in Washington in 1877, he had risen to the rank of rear admiral.

3 JAMES CLARK ROSS AND FRANCIS CROZIER

THE EXPEDITION'S COMMANDERS

Rear Admiral Sir James Clark Ross, to give him the full title he earned at the end of one of the most illustrious careers that the navy had ever seen, was born in 1800, and at the age of 12 he entered the Royal Navy. He served under his uncle, John Ross, on the first of many expeditions to find the North-west Passage. The culmination of his active naval career would be his involvement in the searches for the missing Franklin expedition in 1848. Between 1812 and 1848 he participated in six Arctic voyages and his penultimate one to Antarctica. He died peacefully at his home in Aston Abbots, Buckinghamshire, on 3 April 1862, just short of his 60th birthday.

His uncle, Captain John Ross, had sailed to the Arctic in 1818 with two ships. His flagship, HMS *Isabella*, was accompanied by HMS *Alexander*, whose captain was Lieutenant William Parry. Two other ships set sail at the same time, HMS *Dorothea*, whose senior officer was Captain David Buchan, supported by HMS *Trent* under Lieutenant John Franklin. Whilst *Isabella* and *Alexander* were to proceed westwards in search of the fabled North-west Passage to the Pacific, *Trent* and *Dorothea* would head due north towards Spitsbergen to seek a way across the Polar sea to reach the Pacific Ocean to the Pacific. Neither group succeeded in its mission, but lessons were learnt.

Isabella and *Alexander* suffered a substantial delay caused by the seas between Greenland and Canada remaining frozen for longer than usual in 1818. Once on the Canadian side of the Davis Strait the two ships slowly made their way northwards, passing several inlets still full of the previous winter's ice. Finally they came to Lancaster Sound and found it ice-free. Ross proceeded into the sound with caution. Then one of the most controversial mistakes ever made in Arctic exploration took place as they ventured further into the unknown and uncharted Lancaster Sound. The officer of the watch at the time reported land ahead, but due to the misty conditions this was not immediately confirmed. However, as the mist cleared for a short period Ross saw for himself the mountains ahead, and immediately ordered the ships to retreat and resume their southerly journey. Ross named the mountains after John Croker, first secretary of the Admiralty.

Upon his return to England later in 1818 there took place a considerable discussion as to the validity of the sighting. Lieutenant Parry maintained that it had only been some sort of mirage and eventually persuaded the second secretary of the Admiralty, John Barrow, to allow him to send a second expedition to disprove the existence of this range of mountains.

John Ross was promoted to full captain, but was then put on half-pay and virtually forgotten by the Admiralty. This was seen by him as a snub for his failure to determine the reality of what he claimed to have seen in Lancaster Sound. He defended himself vigorously by issuing pamphlets and writing numerous letters to members of the Admiralty and other influential people, but he did not stand much of a chance against the obduracy of John Barrow.

Meanwhile, Midshipman James Clark Ross accompanied the newly promoted Captain Parry as they set off in 1819 aboard HMS *Hecla* with HMS *Griper* as consort. Again, the ice off the west coast of Greenland proved a stumbling block, but eventually the obstruction was overcome and the two ships arrived off the entrance to Lancaster Sound. As they penetrated further into the sound there was no mist – and no range of mountains in sight to prevent further exploration. Westwards they sailed, and eventually they reached 110°W. At this point they were the first to cross the line where the Admiralty had declared they would award a bounty of £5,000. Their furthest west was achieved at 112°51', and as no further progress was possible that season they turned back a few miles to winter on Melville Island, in a place they called Winter Harbour. Attempts to progress further west the following season proved futile because of the ice, and the ships turned for home, arriving at the beginning of November 1820.

Young Ross had gained further valuable experience of working a ship through icy and treacherous seas. It was to be over 80 years before this farthest west was bettered, when Roald Amundsen achieved it by sailing right through the North-west Passage for the first time, between 1903 and 1906.

In addition to gaining sailing experience in some of the most dangerous seas in the world Ross also began a lifelong interest in global magnetism. Aboard *Hecla* had been Captain Edward Sabine, an officer in the Royal Artillery. He was a leading expert in the study of magnetism, and young Ross soon showed his aptitude for scientific subjects by helping Sabine with his experiments. Their good relationship continued for the remainder of Ross's career.

William Parry, with this most successful of all Arctic missions under his belt, was asked to pursue another journey of discovery. So, in 1821 he once more sailed to the Arctic. Midshipman Ross had shown a great deal of promise on his earlier voyage and he found himself once more selected by Parry to travel to the Arctic.

Their aim this time was to penetrate into Hudson Bay as far north as possible to seek out a way of connecting up with Point Turnagain. This was the point that Franklin and Richardson's

Hecla *and* Fury, *Fury class bomb vessels almost identical to* Erebus *and* Terror. *Original painting held at the National Maritime Museum, Greenwich.*

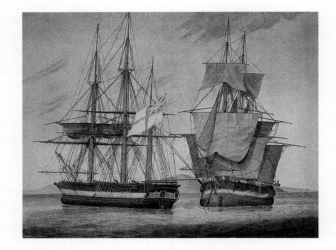

land expedition had reached in 1820, travelling eastwards along the Canadian coastline in birchbark canoes. Sailing conditions for Captain Parry in 1821 were not the best, however, and a winter harbour was selected so that his two ships, *Fury* and *Hecla*, could resume the search the following summer. Whilst frozen in for the winter, several land sorties were carried out during which they encountered a group of Inuit who told them of a channel to the north that would lead them to another sea. So the following sailing season the ships progressed further north to spend a second winter, and as they explored away from their winter base they located the strait they had been told about by the Inuit. Unfortunately, their luck had run out as they found it impassable due to a vast accumulation of ice. It was time to turn for home and a well-earned respite.

Young James Clark Ross was beginning to make a mark for himself, and on the expedition's return to England he found he had been promoted to the rank of lieutenant. He had found a niche for himself as well, with a budding interest in natural history; a newly discovered species of bird was named after him, the Ross gull.

In 1744 the government had set up a £20,000 reward for the first expedition to complete the passage through to the Pacific, but this time there was not going to be a winner and it would have to wait many years – until, indeed, the Franklin search was at its height – before a claim was made for the money. The claimant was Captain Robert McClure with his crew in HMS *Investigator*, and they were recognised as the first to complete the North-west Passage.[6] More about this story can be found in Part Three, under *Investigator*.

The next step in Ross's career came shortly after his return from the Hudson Bay exploit. He volunteered to sail once more with Captain Parry, in 1824; also on this venture was

---

6 Many years later it was established that the accolade should in fact have gone to the members of the Franklin expedition who had managed to struggle as far as the Back River before succumbing to scurvy. They were thus the first to join up with the extent of earlier discoveries and hence complete the North-west Passage.

Midshipman Francis Crozier, a friend Ross had made on the earlier expedition. The plan this time was to attempt to find the passage by exploring Prince Regent Inlet, first seen during Parry's 1819 expedition. *Griper's* lacklustre performance on Parry's Hudson Bay expedition led to her being replaced by *Fury*. The two ships would convey them up the west coast of Greenland and across the Davis Strait into Baffin Bay to the entrance of Lancaster Sound. On the south side of this sound was located Prince Regent Inlet. But they were again delayed by ice whilst crossing from Greenland, this time for nearly eight weeks, before they finally broke clear. They arrived at the entrance to the inlet and proceeded south. With the lateness of the season and the sea already starting to freeze over it became paramount to find a suitable wintering harbour. They chose their winter refuge on the eastern coast of the inlet, and named it Port Bowen. They welcomed 1825 in the hope of greater success; freeing themselves from the clutches of their winter abode they set off once more, but the wind drove the ever-present pack ice against both ships, forcing them towards the shore. *Fury* was driven ashore, and when she was refloated it was evident that she had sustained too much damage to continue. The decision was made to beach her again, and heave her down[7] to assess the possibility of carrying out repairs. It became clear that the damage was so severe that Parry summoned both ships companies and announced that with immediate effect they would prepare *Hecla* for a return to England and abandon any further exploration. They sailed for home the next day, 26 August 1825, leaving *Fury* to her fate, stranded on the desolate shore.

The stores left on the beach where *Fury* had been abandoned were quite considerable, and in 1830 John Ross was to make use of them when he and James Clark Ross and their men were trapped after the destruction of their own small ship, *Victory*.

Although the Prince Regent Inlet expedition was unsuccessful, Parry, continuing to enjoy the favour of the Admiralty's second secretary, was delegated to put together an expedition for an attempt on the North Pole.

Lieutenant James Clark Ross again sailed north with Parry, this time as his second in command. They were accompanied by another lieutenant, the newly promoted Francis Crozier. The surgeon was Robert McCormick, and in the ship's company were Edward Bird and Thomas Abernethy. These four men would join Ross in the Antarctic

The objective this time was to reach the North Pole by sailing as far north as possible then walking over the sea ice. Parry had again chosen *Hecla*, but this time there was to be no consort. Parry knew that he needed *Hecla* to be settled into a safe harbour as early in June as possible for the expedition to take advantage of the frozen seas north of Spitsbergen. The expedition sailed up the coast of what was then known as West Spitsbergen, accompanied by numerous whaling ships heading for their hunting grounds. As the whaling fleet settled to the tasks before them *Hecla* soon found herself beset by pack ice and it took nearly three weeks before she was free to pursue her course. Released from the ever-present ice she skirted around it and was able to sail further north, to locate the few islets that lie to the north of the main archipelago, where Crozier would later place caches of supplies for the retreating

---

7 Also called 'careening': all the stores and removable objects are unloaded, then the ship is winched over sideways so that the hull can be inspected.

polar party. A good anchorage, however, still eluded them, and it was only as they retraced their route that one was finally selected, on the shores of Sorgfjorden, on the north-eastern corner of West Spitsbergen. The plan, once the expedition members were on the ice, was to pull two small boats, each mounted on a sledge with wheels, using teams of reindeer. But it would appear that little experimentation had been carried out as to the plan's viability; the wheels immediately sank into the surface and the reindeer failed to provide the traction required of them. Finally, the explorers resorted to fitting home-made skis to the boats, and the men hauled them instead. With *Hecla* safely ensconced and Crozier left in charge of her, the exploring party, under the command of Captain Parry accompanied by Lieutenant Ross, could start their trek towards the North Pole. The first part of the journey was by small boat, until they met the polar ice. They adopted a routine of travelling during the colder hours of the day, resting as the sun approached its zenith; this reduced the effort required to cope with thawing ice.

Each day sights were taken to establish the progress they were making, and although the officers did not share this information with the men it soon became evident that the distances they were making were well below what had been envisaged. Worse, what they did not realise until nearly too late was that the ice was drifting southwards nearly as fast as they were battling northwards. After five weeks, Parry calculated they had travelled just 170 miles, which left them still over 500 miles from their objective, the Pole, with the return journey still to tackle. He made the only decision possible; they retraced their steps to *Hecla*. One small crumb of comfort was that they had stood at the furthest north ever achieved, and their record stood for 50 years.

This was to be the last time that James Clark Ross sailed with Parry, and it was in fact to be Parry's last foray into the frozen wastes of the Arctic. From now onwards he would sit behind a desk at the Admiralty as hydrographer of the navy.

James Clark Ross's next assignment came in 1829, when he resumed his association with his uncle, John Ross, who had been actively seeking support for a private venture to explore in the Arctic regions. His previous foray having, as mentioned earlier, ended ignominiously with the débâcle of the imaginary Croker Mountains episode, he wanted to put that behind him. But unfortunately, the Admiralty had a long memory and was not prepared to back him, especially when he had put forward the innovative idea of using steam propulsion to assist a sailing ship. He finally got the backing of Felix Booth, a gin manufacturing magnate, who contributed nearly £20,000.

With James appointed second in command, *Victory* set sail from Margate towards the end of May 1829, victualled for three years. Almost at once the steam engine began to show its propensity for trouble, and the regularity of its breakdowns did not augur well for a trouble-free passage to the Arctic. *Victory*'s sailing capability also left some doubt as to the success the expedition might achieve.

More problems had to be overcome before Ross could turn the head of his ship into the open ocean on the first leg of the journey to Greenland and Lancaster Sound. Part of his plan had been to take a second ship, crewed by whalers. Hopefully they would catch sufficient whales and the cargo of whale oil would help to defray the costs of the expedition. But unexpectedly the captain and crew of the second ship refused to co-operate, giving the reason for their virtual mutiny as the lateness of the season and fearing getting trapped in the ice for the winter. With no resolution in sight to the impasse, Ross cut his losses and proceeded. He did however have the use of a 16-ton sailing ship – a yacht, basically – lent to him by the Admiralty. This, it was decided, could accompany *Victory* only if it could be towed.

Little by little they made headway and reached Greenland by the middle of July that year. *Victory* crossed the Davis Strait and sailed into Lancaster Sound on 6 August, still with the yacht in tow. Reflecting on his earlier voyage Ross senior could only enter a note into his log that he was still sure that even if it had not been mountains that he had seen then it surely must have been a frozen aspect that caused him to turn about and sail south.

Both the Rosses were keenly aware that William Parry had lost one of his expedition's ships in Prince Regent Inlet, and that it was to this same waterway that they were now headed. They located the stores left behind by *Fury*, but of the wreck itself there was no sign. Fortunately the stores were still intact and there was no evidence of any Inuit interference with the stockpile of what would become life-saving supplies. They helped themselves, replenishing food already consumed, and noted what other useful items remained. Time was now of the essence, so they sought and found a suitable winter harbour. The steam engine had finally caused them so much frustration that John Ross ordered its removal, and it was unceremoniously dumped ashore.

Winter quarters in the Arctic were nothing new to most of the officers and crew, and despite the waning daylight several small land trips were made. It was on one of these that James discovered a narrow, but frozen, channel which, cutting across Boothia Peninsula (the northernmost point of the Canadian mainland), turned its northern tip, Somerset Land, into an island. This channel could be the link they sought to proceed westwards the following summer – but the prospect never materialised. The summer of 1830 brought only temporary release from the ice and, having only made 3 miles to the north, they prepared for a second winter there. Trapped for a further season, James continued his exploration and travelled further south and west. His turning point this time was what would eventually be established as King William Island, but on this occasion he assumed it to be part of the mainland and consequently called it King William Land.[8] As the spring of 1831 progressed into May more exploring took place. To travel over the frozen surfaces, they would employ a sledge harnessed to the six dogs given to them by the governor of Holsteinsborg (now Sisimiut) in Greenland, driven by an Inuit, Ikmallik. James was confident he could find the Magnetic North Pole, and set out accordingly, armed with the instruments that would enable him to locate its exact position. James Ross left the ship on 15 May 1831, accompanied by his uncle, as far as the west coast of the Boothia peninsula, when they parted company; John returned to the ship for more supplies while James struck northwards along the coast towards the area where he was sure he could locate the Magnetic Pole. On 1 June 1831 he reached his objective, and recorded the geographical location as 70°5'17" N, 96°46'45" W. Taking nearly a month to complete his journey, he and his

---

8 Ironically, this was where the doomed Franklin expedition would finish up, and where none of the search parties ever thought to look for its doomed members.

companions retreated to the ship in good order using the depots his uncle had laid down for them. This was an achievement that would prove of far more importance scientifically than the attainment of the North Pole when (and if) that was accomplished by the American explorer Robert Peary 78 years later.

As a third winter loomed with *Victory* still icebound, Captain John Ross wrote in his log, 'To us, the sight of the ice was a plague, a vexation, a torment, an evil and a matter of despair.' He made plans for the following spring, when the party would abandon *Victory* and sledge or sail the ship's boats across the frozen sea to reach the open ocean to the north and seek help from a passing whaler – if they could attract its attention. But even this part of the evacuation did not go to plan, and a fourth winter had to be spent at the Fury depot. They built a marquee made out of sail canvas covering a wooden frame all of it encased in snow blocks for insulation. The first man died on 10 January 1832; this was followed a year later by the first scurvy-related death. Other crew members were struggling with the same affliction, but the expedition now had the good fortune to kill a couple of bears, and sealing and fishing became more productive. During the first two winters they had been able to procure fresh meat and fish from visiting Inuit, but after the expedition moved camp the visits stopped, probably due to the migratory life style that the Inuit maintained.

In summer 1833 the explorers managed to take to their boats at last, and made good headway northwards, away from their frozen camp on Fury Beach. By 16 August they had found their way to the extreme northern point of Prince Regent Inlet, and proceeded eastwards in their frail ship's boats towards Admiralty Inlet which they had passed way back in 1829, four long years before.

On 26 August they caught sight of a sail on the horizon, but disappointment took hold as the ship turned away while still well out to sea, and they lost sight of her. Fortune was on their side, however, and a second sail was sighted; this time the ship held her course and the crews of the three little boats saw the ship lower one of her boats and turn towards them.

The rescue ship turned out to be *Isabella*, which had been John Ross' first command in the Arctic when he had made that fateful error about the imaginary Croker Mountains; she had been built for the sealing trade and her main asset was her strengthened hull. The Admiralty, well aware of this, had secured a lease on her for Ross's 1819 expedition. When *Isabella* returned to England after the Croker Mountains affair, she resumed her career as a sealer – and in summer 1833 rescued the John Ross expedition.

The expedition had been away for four and a half years, and all aboard had been given up for lost. The ecstatic reception given the uncle and nephew team after their arrival in England reached its climax as they were granted an audience with King William IV. Furthermore, the Admiralty was persuaded that it had a responsibility to pay the wages of *Victory*'s crew as recompense for the hardships they had endured and in recognition of the exploring work they had accomplished during their enforced entrapment in the ice.

James Clark Ross received a posting for one year to serve aboard HMS *Victory* in Portsmouth and was promoted to post captain. Following his 12-month sojourn on HMS *Victory* the Admiralty offered him a position carrying out a magnetic survey of the British Isles, for which he was uniquely qualified, and which he accepted. Before he could complete his work, however, another catastrophe loomed: the early onset of an extremely severe winter in 1836 had resulted in the entrapment of many whaling ships in the Davis Strait. Ross immediately offered his services to lead a rescue attempt. He travelled to Hull, supervised the readying of HMS *Cove*, and set out on the rescue mission in January 1837. But despite the supreme effort of all involved in getting the vessel prepared in time, his efforts came to nought: all but one of the whalers managed to gain their own release, as he was to find out on his return to England.

The naval career of Captain Francis Rawdon Moira Crozier, RN FRS FRAS, followed a pattern very similar to that of James Clark Ross. Crozier had been born in Banbridge, County Down, in what is now Northern Ireland. His father was known locally as a successful businessman and a wealthy landowner, so Francis's upbringing would have been in a fairly affluent household.

In 1801, five years after his birth, the Act of Union was passed, creating the United Kingdom from the four countries that comprise the British Isles: England, Wales, Scotland and Ireland. This entity was to last until Southern Ireland gained its independence in 1922.

In Crozier's home town there is an imposing monument to him. He is standing on an octagonal plinth surmounted on eight pillars and at its base are four polar bears guarding him with snarling countenances.

Left: Captain James Clark Ross, painted by John Wildman in 1834. The original is held by the National Maritime Museum, Greenwich. Upper left: Commander Francis Crozier's statue in Banbridge, Co Down. Upper right: the plaque dedicated to him in the parish church.

He joined the navy in 1810 at the age of 14 by travelling down to Cork to sign on to his first vessel. She was HMS *Hamadryad*, a 34-gun frigate captured from the Spanish navy in 1804. The first voyage for him was across the Atlantic Ocean as part of a flotilla escorting British merchant ships carrying manufactured goods to North America. The next ship he joined was HMS *Briton*, patrolling the coast of Portugal and the Bay of Biscay. At this time Napoleon was at the height of his powers and as he was receiving vital supplies from a sympathetic United States of America and other countries, the British government was desperately trying to blockade the Spanish ports to cut off this source of valuable material, including bullion from Spain's colonies in South America.

In 1814 he was promoted to midshipman when orders came through that *Briton* was to proceed to the East Indies via Cape Horn; but her journey was interrupted by new orders which diverted her to Rio de Janeiro. After leaving Rio *Briton* forced her way round Cape Horn and on to Valparaiso, and then after a period for the crew to recuperate after the Horn, they sailed on northwards to Lima. From there they sailed out into the Pacific, accompanied by HMS *Tagus*, to try and locate an American raiding ship that was interfering with British shipping in the vicinity of the East Indies. But despite a wide search the marauder slipped away undetected.

On the homeward journey they thought they had discovered a new uncharted island, but it turned out to be Pitcairn. This was only the second time that a vessel had put into the island since the mutineers from *Bounty* had settled on it in 1789. Although the authorities in England had been made aware of the location of Pitcairn Island, they had never followed up the information.

The story of the mutiny had reverberated around Britain when Captain Bligh returned home. He and 17 of the original 18 men that had been cast adrift had survived an epic open boat journey of 3,500 miles from Tahiti to Timor in the then Dutch East Indies. By the time of *Briton*'s visit all but one of the original mutineers had either died or been murdered, leaving just one of them still alive, along with the Tahitian women they had taken with them. Today the island is populated by some of the descendants of the original mutineers.

On his return to Britain Crozier gained his mate's certificate in 1817, ensuring his continuation of employment in the navy – but now, in peacetime, opportunities for advancement were few and far between. He spent a short time aboard HMS *Dotterel* in 1818, and in 1821 he was selected to be part of Parry's expedition to try for the second time to find the North-west Passage. This was to be attempted by sailing north through Hudson Bay, and it was also to be the first time Crozier sailed with James Clark Ross, both of them midshipmen at this point. This attempt too, however, was thwarted by impenetrable ice in a channel named after the two ships, *Hecla* and *Griper*. The expedition had been away for nearly three years, and the journey back to England took nearly two months.

After Parry's return from this Hudson Bay adventure he was given a third chance to seek the North-west Passage, and Midshipman Crozier enlisted as a member of his crew. Yet again, the ice brought this third foray to an abrupt halt and, as mentioned earlier, resulted in the abandonment of *Fury*. All the men were ferried back to Britain aboard *Hecla*. The two voyages and three winters of exploration spent in the Arctic had hardened Crozier to the life of an explorer, and when Parry was instructed to attempt the North Pole, Crozier volunteered once more, now as a lieutenant. When the time came for Parry to set out across the frozen ocean from Spitsbergen towards the Pole, he left the command of *Hecla* to none other than the up-and-coming explorer Francis Crozier. He was also tasked with laying down three depots of food to support Parry and Ross on their retreat.

On the expedition's return in 1827 Crozier was paid off and spent several years as a first lieutenant – but on half-pay. He spent his lay-off period studying for his future promotion, and with his early education found absorbing all the information relatively easy. His one consolation at this otherwise humdrum stage in his career was the invitation extended to him to become a member of the Royal Astronomical Society in recognition of his work connected with astronomy and navigation that he had pursued whilst in the Arctic.

In 1831 Crozier's father died, and it coincided with an opportunity for him to resume his naval career, although the prospects were not nearly as exciting as his previous three commissions. HMS *Stag*, an Andromeda class frigate with an armament of 46 guns, was being despatched to the waters of the Bay of Biscay for routine patrol work, but at least Crozier was once again at sea and on full pay again. *Stag*'s first commander was Captain Troubridge, a naval aide-de-camp to the king. Troubridge was superseded by Captain Nicholas Lockyer, and he and Crozier completed the commission, which terminated in 1835. He again found himself on half-pay, and at nearly 40 years old his prospects were not looking very bright. The emergency involving the whaling fleet in the Davis Strait brought a request from his long-time friend James Clark Ross for him to be second in command of *Cove* on her rescue mission.

Ross would never forget the assistance that Crozier gave to him in preparing the rescue attempt, nor the way he helped handle *Cove* as she was battered by a raging gale, which eventually forced her to retire to Stromness in the Orkneys for some major repairs before they could resume their mission. Ross could see that his long-time friend was struggling to advance his career, and wrote several letters to the Admiralty proposing that Lieutenant Crozier should be promoted. Success! Crozier's promotion to commander came through in January 1837, and when the opportunity came in 1838 to prepare *Erebus* and *Terror* for the proposed expedition to the Antarctic, Ross again called on Crozier to supervise the fitting-out of the two ships, ready for the following year. Additionally, Crozier was offered the command of *Terror* for the four-year voyage of discovery.

The Antarctic expedition was followed two years later by an even greater opportunity for Captain Francis Crozier; one that, however, confounded the polar experts of the time and would continue to do so for many generations to come. It was the fateful Franklin expedition. It is of course well known that all the members of the expedition perished in a part of the Canadian Arctic that tragically nobody thought of looking in. So Crozier's name was posthumously engraved in the Hall of Fame for polar explorers.

Apart from his statue in Banbridge, his lasting legacy can be found in other parts of the world where geographical features are named after him. There are four islands: two in the Arctic, another between Greenland and Ellesmere Island and the fourth in the Antarctic.

There is also Cape Crozier, where Scott's expedition located the emperor penguin colony made famous by the exploits of Edward Wilson and his two companions. Then there is a river and a channel in the Canadian Arctic bearing his name. Crozier Point can be found in Spitsbergen, and to cap them all there is even a crater on the Moon named after him.

Captain James Clark Ross had chosen his officers and key crew members with great care. Whenever possible he selected men with a proven track record in polar exploration; those he did not know usually came with a high recommendation from fellow officers. Francis Crozier was to become the most senior of the outstanding men that Ross selected.

4 SETTING SAIL: TO MADEIRA AND THE ATLANTIC ISLANDS

UNDER SAIL AT LAST, AND THE FIRST STORM SEPARATES THE SHIPS

In September 1839 *Erebus* and *Terror* proceeded down the Medway out of Chatham Naval Dockyard towards Gillingham, where the crew received three months' double pay. This was a tradition for all exploring ships' crews at the commencement of a voyage.

In addition, the families of men away from home for extended periods could receive a house-keeping allowance from the sailor's pay through an allotment system set up by the navy. The sailor could also take out a limited cash sum to spend on shore leave in foreign ports. All these transactions would be dutifully recorded in a dedicated ledger kept aboard the ship, and then when the ship returned to its home port all the debts for allotments, shore leave, clothing, to-bacco and mess bills would be deducted before the sailor saw the rest of his hard-earned money.

The two ships were towed out by a steam tug. Then came two important procedures at the start of any voyage: establishing that the chronometers were set to Greenwich Time, and swinging the ships. The latter allowed the navigator to check the accuracy of his compass at the four cardinal points, north, east, south and west. Any variations would be noted; the most likely cause of any such inaccuracies would be the iron components built into the ship on her construction or during a refit, and these variations would now be taken into account when reading the compass on voyage.

Not many ships under sail alone would be able to set out on the date prescribed, and so it was with this pair of ships as they made their tentative way down to Margate. Five days later they were still delayed there, but eventually, on 30 September 1839, they were bearing away to sea. The pilot was put ashore at Deal. This would be the last contact with a home port for nearly four years.

When the two freshly painted, three-masted ex-bomb ships of Her Majesty's Royal Navy eased into the Channel on that first morning of their epic voyage their officers were all smartly dressed in their braided uniforms and the crews looked clean and tidy scaling the rigging and trimming the spanking new sails that were starting to billow out with a fair, following wind. *Erebus* pulled slightly ahead of *Terror* as they both heeled slightly to the pull of the sails, bestowing on their men the feeling of freedom that lies at the heart of every sailor on the start of a voyage.

The Isle of Wight was visible on the starboard bow on the third day of the voyage, and the wind had freshened and stiffened. By the evening there was a shift in wind direction and strength, but by signalling to one another the captains agreed to press on down the Channel rather than seeking shelter at this early stage. The main drawback to sailing in conditions such as these was the low freeboard they had due to the vast quantity of stores in the holds. Until they could lighten their loads there was always the possibility of a large wave breaking over the decks, potentially causing extensive damage.

Four days into the voyage they drew abreast of the Lizard, heading away from the English coast, bound for Madeira; but by the next morning neither ship was in sight of her partner. Even at this early stage it was becoming apparent that under certain wind conditions *Terror* could not hold her station with *Erebus*. The two ships were to lose sight of one another on a number of occasions during the expedition, and on this occasion, having pre-arranged their rendezvous stations along the way, they would meet again on arrival at Funchal on Madeira.

Terror had shortened sail as the weather worsened, but the slightly more seaworthy *Erebus* continued to take advantage of the gustier wind. On entering the Bay of Biscay both ships experienced a strong sea, with large rollers from the Atlantic breaking onto their starboard bows. In trimming the sails of *Terror* three seamen were caught unawares as the ship pitched and the flying boom on which they were working dipped into the sea, but they held on and quickly regained the deck.

Cape Finisterre having been rounded, the ships made their separate ways down the coast of Portugal to its most southerly point, Cape St Vincent, and then they set course across the open Atlantic to make their first landfall at Madeira.

Terror was now a couple of days behind *Erebus*, but notwithstanding that, she was making good the mileage at her best rate. At the start of the third week into the voyage there was a combination of light winds but still a fairly heavy headswell, making the ships uncomfortable to work on. The weather had stayed dry up till now, but by the third Saturday both ships experienced a freshening gale, bringing rain for the first time.

On the morning of 20 October the lookout aboard *Erebus* called out that land had been sighted; Funchal was now only a matter of hours away. The weather had settled down to a steady north-easterly and a much-reduced swell, and sailing was once again a pleasure. *Erebus* dropped her anchors in the Bay of Funchal, and the English consul, Mr Stothard, was the first person that Ross sought out as he stepped ashore. Stothard, having expected the two ships, had prepared a number of facilities that would enable them to carry out the first of the many magnetic observations required of the voyage, and to check the accuracy

Funchal in about 1860, showing the bay where
Erebus *and* Terror *anchored in 1839.*

of their chronometers. The officers of *Erebus* went ashore several at a time, and apart from the important work of taking observations they were free to explore the sights that the island had to offer. The crew were also given a limited amount of shore leave but were under strict instructions to return to the ship by nightfall.

Meanwhile, on the evening of 22 October, as *Terror* was still making her way further south towards Madeira, the men on board were witness to a most unusual display in the sky. Far to the north-west the sky took on a crimson aspect such as none of the watchers had ever seen before. It did not seem to be anything to do with a sunset, because it occurred too far to the north of where the sun would set and they were probably too far south for it to have been a glimpse of the Aurora Borealis – which anyhow is not normally crimson. So, there was no plausible explanation; but what did transpire was that the same effects were seen by the men of *Erebus*, nearly 200 miles away on Madeira. Their experience was noted down in more detail by Ross, who recorded the times and even the angle that the effect reached up into the sky, the maximum height it attained being 43 degrees. The colour started off pale pink and only gradually deepened to the crimson sky witnessed by those aboard *Terror*. Ross became aware of the unsettling effect it had on the local populace, who were speculating on the possibility of it being the fiery effect of some distant volcanic eruption. Madeira itself was of course the result of some cataclysmic eruption many centuries before, as were the majority of the islands this expedition would visit.

Although Madeira is less than 35 miles by about 14 it is capable of generating its own weather. Around Funchal the mornings are the best time to explore because as the sun climbs and starts to heat up the land it draws moisture into the sky, creating clouds by the afternoon. Due to the prevailing winds these clouds build in density and move southwards as the day progresses.

Four days after *Erebus* arrived at Funchal *Terror* dropped her anchor nearby, and the two groups of sailors were again united. There were several exchanges of visitors and the usual chance to talk over the journey so far, including the strange atmospheric phenomenon. They agreed that it wasn't a volcanic eruption, otherwise *Terror* would have experienced some sort of tidal wave[9] so the conclusion was that it must have been a freak sighting of the Aurora Borealis.

---

9 We now know that in the open ocean a tsunami (then called a tidal wave) can be undetectable amid the regular swells, only revealing its true size on approaching shallower water. And to the north-west of Madeira lies the mid-Atlantic Ridge, which irregularly but frequently produces eruptions along its length.

Nossa Senhora do Monte, Funchal.

The commanding officers of the two ships planned to resume their voyage at the end of October, but in the meantime there were the magnetic readings to take, and some of the officers were keen to explore the island. The island's volcanic origin, however, made it very difficult to gain much data on the Earth's magnetic field; the rock caused so many variations in the compass readings, both in the dip of the needle and the direction, that the results would ultimately prove valueless.

Robert McCormick had been invited by one James Muir, an English resident who ran a store, to take part in a pony trek with some local guides. McCormick and several other officers were to be given the chance to climb the highest point of the island, the 1,860-metre Pico Ruivo.
The accompanying group consisted of John Robertson, *Terror's* surgeon; Lieutenant Eardley Wilmot (one of the two Horse Artillery officers assigned to the expedition to help run the observatory to be set up near Cape Town); Mr Muir and two others, making a party of six. Their guides would travel on foot most of the way. They would be away for nearly three days and would cover about 50 miles, not much of it on level ground.

They set off on 25 October from Mr Muir's premises and headed up the steep road that led into the hills above Funchal. As they neared the top, they passed the island's most prominent church, Nossa Senhora do Monte (Our Lady of the Mountain). The route they followed can still be traced on a map of Madeira; the details of the trek can be found in the book that McCormick wrote after his return from the expedition. Their first halt was at Camacha, where today there is a flourishing basket-weaving industry, and as they resumed the journey they came to a view point from where the whole of the eastern peninsula, Ponta de São Lourenço, could be seen. Its magnificent sweep of coastline came into view and the vista extended across the sea towards the neighbouring island of Porto Santo and the barren rocks of the Ilhas Desertas.

The track now led directly north to a high point in the landscape, San Antonio-de-zaza, where they could look down upon the coast towards their next resting place, Porta de Cruz. Today it is more of a small holiday village, as is the next village they passed through, Faial, but when McCormick and his group were there they were both fairly active little fishing ports. Turning inland the group travelled through a region that was well known in Madeira for the vineyards it boasted; they were owned by a Senhor Luiz, and the guides had arranged for the group to stop overnight at his nearby inn.

From here they gained their first sight of Pico Ruivo. Their path the next morning was up through a steep, rock-strewn valley which according to McCormick was devoid of bird life but could boast a variety of plant life including blackberries, broom, furze and azure blue hydrangeas. At the top of the climb up the valley, which took most of the day, they spent the night at a remote inn.

The next morning was pleasantly cool and the party made a very early start, intending to reach the summit before the heat of the day wearied their horses and guides too much. They made the summit by 7.30 a.m., and lingered a while to take in the views. Their first stop on the way down was at another remote little inn, in the hamlet of Cruzinha at the head of a small valley. The food consisted of small loaves of coarse dark bread and a drink of very sour wine, much the same as at the other tavernas they had visited.

The highest mountain in Madeira, Pico Ruivo, climbed by Robert McCormick, the surgeon aboard Erebus.

Ever the explorer, McCormick – who had of course been with James Clark Ross in the Arctic – had left a note, dated 26 October 1839, under a small cairn on the summit of Pico Ruivo, stating that he and others had visited that spot and were from the exploring party aboard *Erebus* and *Terror*.

The final leg of the journey was completed during the early morning, and the group enjoyed a good breakfast at Muir's residence.

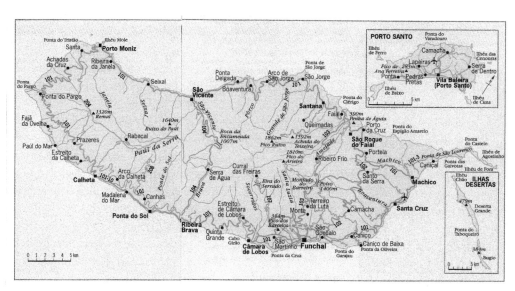

Madeira, showing Camacha, Porto Santo (upper inset), Ilhas Desertas (lower inset), Porto da Cruz, Faial and Pico Ruivo.

McCormick's next adventure was to go by boat along the coast to the east of Funchal to try and reach the extreme eastern end of the Ponta de São Lourenço. On the way they passed Santa Cruz, a small village on a bay of the same name.[10] He had hoped to find evidence of fossilised trees that he had been told about, but in the event they turned out to be just encrusted remains of vegetation caused by a peculiarity in the chemical nature of the soil.

On Saturday night the weather looked ominous, and Ross gave the order to ready both ships for an early departure the next morning, 31 October.

Sailing together for the first time since leaving the Channel, the two ships would next call into Santa Cruz de Tenerife in the Canary Islands. The main purpose of this visit was not so much scientific as expediency: they needed to despatch their mail and reports to London. This was done during the expedition as and when possible, so that in the event of a disaster at least some of their records would be secure.

Ross would have been impatient to proceed, but there was just enough time for McCormick, going ashore with the mail, to venture inland to explore for a few short hours.

The jetty drew a comment from him in his book that this was the place that Admiral Nelson had received the injury that resulted in his arm being amputated. In 1797 the English fleet had been intent on carrying out an assault on Tenerife, at the time under Spanish rule – and Spain was an ally of France. The English saw it as strategically important to their sea route to India and had made several attempts at landing near to Santa Cruz, only to be repelled by the Spaniards. Although one party managed to reach the town square their boats had been discovered and destroyed by the Spanish, and they had to negotiate a retreat. Meanwhile Nelson was making his third attempt at securing a beachhead when he received a direct hit in his right arm; the musket ball passed right through the limb. His men evacuated him to HMS *Theseus*, where the surgeon carried out the amputation. A year later he was back in action, securing the defeat of the French navy at the Battle of the Nile, and in 1801 he again proved victorious at the Battle of Copenhagen.

Ross's expedition was in fact to stay in Santa Cruz for over two more days due to lack of wind. Finally, it picked up sufficiently to allow the ships to bear away. Their destination would be the Cape Verde Islands, and in particular the island of St Jago (or Santiago). Here they hoped to set up an observatory to continue the work started in Madeira. The archipelago lies off the west coast of Africa at 16°N, the same latitude as the Senegal/Mauritania boundary. At the time of the expedition the islands were a Portuguese possession, having been discovered in the middle of the 15th century. They were colonised a few years after their discovery and when the slave trade was at its height in the 17th and 18th centuries the descendants of those colonists prospered.

Sailing conditions proved excellent and with no more than a fair wind and a good set of sails the two ships had no difficulty in keeping company with one another. The sea was so calm that a cow that had been brought aboard *Terror* whilst they were in the harbour at Tenerife was slaughtered and some of it sent across to *Erebus*. As they pursued their course the

---

10 The modern-day airport of Funchal juts out into the sea just past Santa Cruz.

ships passed through an area of sea that was dense with flying fish. These were being chased by a school of dolphins and in their haste to escape quite a number landed on the ships' decks. This was to form the start of the natural history collection that would continue throughout the next four years.

At night the sea was bright with bioluminescence. This was also seen by Charles Darwin during his HMS *Beagle* voyage. He described it as follows: -

> While sailing in these latitudes one very dark night, the sea presented a wonderful and most beautiful spectacle. There was a fresh breeze, and every part of the surface, which during the day is seen as foam, now glowed with a pale light. The vessel drove before her bows two billows of liquid phosphorescence, and in her wake, she was followed by a milky train. As far as the eye reached, the crest of every wave was bright.

As *Erebus* and *Terror* neared the intended anchorage in the bay that formed the natural harbour of St Jago the crew were sent aloft to shorten sail, and at a signal from the boatswain the anchors were dropped. Ross and Crozier climbed down into the boat that was being readied, and the crew pulled for the shore. The objective of the visit was to secure permission from the governor to erect a small observatory for the necessary series of magnetic readings. Other officers took the opportunity of being rowed ashore and ventured into the interior of the island. McCormick had visited this island a few years before, and one of the features he wanted to see again was an enormous baobab tree growing in a small valley. The baobab is a native of Africa and how this one arrived on the island nobody seemed to know, but it was a particularly fine example and when Ross saw it he estimated the trunk was at least 38 feet in circumference.

Amongst the two crews were the detachments of marines nearly always present on Royal Naval vessels; their main function was to protect any parties sent ashore where an inhospitable reception might take place, and of course should the ship be threatened by unwelcome visitors their presence would act as a deterrent. On *Terror* the sergeant in charge was William Cunningham, who had under his direct command a corporal and five privates. In addition to his official duties he kept a private journal of the day-to-day events as they unfolded. From his entry for 16 November he had obviously been ashore; he described the buildings that the inhabitants lived in as huts rather than houses constructed with stone walls, their roofs thatched with straw or leaves. They all had mud floors and no windows, so the only light that penetrated came through the open doorway. Most of the inhabitants were 'of a coloured extraction' and he surmised they were probably former slaves. Good wine could be bought for one shilling a bottle, as could 120 oranges.

These island visits had of course a secondary, but no less important, purpose to their scientific one: to secure a supply of fresh meat and vegetables for the benefit of all on board the two ships.

Having arrived on St Jago on 15 November they set sail again for their next destination, St Paul's Rocks, on Wednesday 20th.

'Porto Praya on the island of St Jago in the Cape Verde Islands', painted by William Alexander in about 1800.

For the next few weeks another set of recordings were to be taken, this time to try and establish how and where the trade winds were formed. It was hoped that hourly measurements of the barometric pressure, air temperature and sea surface temperature would assist in this investigation. The science of wind patterns around the world is too complex to enter into here, but suffice it to say that in 1839 the trade winds were a well-known and well-used feature of the Atlantic and Pacific oceans, and generations of sailors had made use of them without fully understanding their complicated nature. Ross hoped to gain at least some knowledge of them, and the data he collected was to be used to that end.

From time to time the usually reliable trade winds fail, and then the ships enter an area described as the variables, which can result in brief torrential rain and generally squally conditions. Such was the fortune of our explorers as they approached their next destination, St Paul's Rocks. From the first sighting, they spent the best part of two days before they were able to make a safe run in. A complication was the presence of a substantial ocean current that bore them to the leeward of the rocks, and this had to be contested the next morning before the boats could be lowered and allow a landing to be attempted.

The rocks are as remote from the nearest land as it is possible to be. They are over 500 miles from any other land, and lie almost on the equator. As with the Cape Verdes, it was the Portuguese that had discovered them. The discovery was not exactly planned, however, as the ship *São Paulo* came to grief when she struck them. Her crew having been rescued by her consort, *São Pedro*, the incident gave rise to the name Arquipélago de São Pedro e São Paulo. British mariners renamed it St Paul's Rocks.

In 1921 Sir Ernest Shackleton, leading his *Quest* expedition to the Antarctic, made a landing on the rocks. They recorded the animal life they found there and it corresponded very well with that of McCormick's observations in 1839: the sea around the rocky group fairly swarmed with sharks, and the rocks themselves were home to a vast horde of small crabs. There were only two types of birds nesting there during both visits; boobies and noddies. Landing also caused both expeditions a problem, in that there were no beaches, so the boats had to be manoeuvred as close to a rocky outcrop as possible and as the swell lifted a boat the men had to leap across the gap. Even so, Ross managed to transfer some equipment onto the rocks and take some magnetic readings. Once Ross and his team were back on board and had set sail, they sent a depth gauge down on a 500-fathom line – and even though this was just a mile away from the rocks it did not reach the ocean bed, such was the depth from which St Paul's Rocks had emerged aeons before.

Sailing conditions after leaving St Paul's Rocks continued to be favourable for the next two weeks that it took to cover the intervening distance to Trinidade Island. One feature of the voyage during this leg down the Atlantic enabled Ross to establish the position of what he termed the Magnetic Equator.[11]

The effect being registered on both ships simultaneously confirmed the measurements, and Ross noted the latitude as 13°45'S. He continued taking magnetic readings by criss-crossing several times to the north and south of the line he had just found before resuming the voyage south.

Trinidade lies over 700 miles east of the Brazilian mainland, and like most of the remote island groups in the Atlantic it had been discovered by the Portuguese, in 1502. Another similarity it bears to the other islands is its volcanic origin.[12] McCormick gave close inspection to the samples he took from the main island and came to the conclusion that although they were not volcanic he could think of no other way that the islands had been formed. The most outstanding feature is the Nine Pin Rock[13] which stands over 850 feet high. In 1895 Great Britain briefly took control of the little group, but when Brazil gained independence from Portugal the island group was transferred to Brazilian control.

Before they could reach these rocks there was the little matter of crossing the equator. This inevitably entailed the traditional ceremony held whereby King Neptune and his assistants came aboard each ship in turn and the unfortunate men who had not been this far south before were subjected to what can only be described as an attack on their persons. It began by being lathered with a revolting concoction made from kitchen waste, old grease and feathers, being shaved by Neptune's helpers and then ducked in a makeshift pond. After the fun, both crews were awarded an extra tot of grog and the rest of the evening was given over to a typical sailor's party of dancing, music and generally making merry.

As Tuesday 17 December dawned the lookout signalled land to the south, and soon after 7 a.m. the ships dropped anchor in a sheltered bay. A couple of boats were lowered to seek a safe landing place. Ross, Crozier, McCormick and Hooker were among the group of curious visitors who wanted to explore this barely known piece of terra firma. It took a while for the boats to reach a small cove in the lee of the main island and here the intrepid explorers had to plunge into the shallow surf to gain a foothold on dry land – and then all too soon for the scientists, the decision was made to retreat to the ships and make the most of the dwindling daylight to resume their journey. The information that they brought with them from England regarding what they might expect to find on the island left them rather disappointed; they had hoped to find wild goats and pigs, but apart from one goat no sign of any other introduced animal was found. They did however leave behind a cockerel and two chickens from the menagerie they had brought out from England.

It took the two ships from 17 December until 31 January to cross the intervening ocean to gain a view of St Helena. They experienced fair weather and foul, at one stage the seas rising to the

11 Now known as the aclinic line: the imaginary line around the world where, due to the equal attraction of the north and south magnetic poles, the needle of a compass has no readable dip either way. The gradual movement of the magnetic poles makes the line move a bit, too; for its location in 2015, see https://upload.wikimedia.org/wikipedia/commons/d/de/World_Magnetic_Inclination_2015.pdf .
12 Curiously, when Darwin visited it in *Beagle*, he noted that it was not of a volcanic nature.
13 Ninepins is an early variant of skittles and bowling.

point where the decks were awash. Christmas Day was calmer, and the two crews enjoyed a full celebratory meal, albeit for most of them the meat was of the tinned variety; they had obviously run out of the fresh beef taken aboard in the Cape Verde Islands. McCormick records, however, that he and the midshipmen he entertained for lunch that day had roast turkey followed by plum pudding! A week later all hands were summoned on deck, and extra grog and a double helping of more tinned beef was served out to celebrate the coming of the New Year of 1840.

From being becalmed on 3 January they had to endure a squally day on the 4th. As they proceeded there was the constant need to find the time to heave to in order to check the depth of the ocean and test its temperature and salinity at various depths. Under these sailing conditions the two ships were having no difficulty in keeping abreast of one another, facilitating the duplication of the tests they carried out and immediate verification of the results.

Ross in his book states that their progress was comparatively slow on this leg of their journey – from Trinidade to St Helena is something over 1,370 nm (~2,540 km) as the albatross flies – they made only about 23–24 nm per day. Understandably, using weights on cables to test depths of as much as 2,400 fathoms (approx. 4,400 metres) was a time-consuming occupation.

They sighted St Helena on 31 January, and as they approached they could see a number of merchant ships lying at anchor in the harbour, giving them the feeling of having arrived at somewhere important after those barren groups of rocks.

St Helena was one of the places chosen before they departed from England where a permanent observatory would be erected. The island was under British jurisdiction so there were not too many formalities to be dealt with and the governor, Lieutenant-General Middlemore, had been made aware of their impending arrival. Middlemore was in fact the first governor of the island since its transfer from the Dutch East India Company. He had been sent out in 1836 to represent the British government, and as his brief was to drastically reduce the expenses incurred in running the island his arrival heralded the beginning of a very austere period in the island's history, which reflected very badly on the way the British government was viewed by the islanders. Most of the ex-employees of the East India Company had to resort to appeals directly to Britain for financial assistance. These appeals fell mainly on deaf ears, with the comment from the British authorities that the priority was to look after only civil servants employed directly by Britain and everybody else would have to make do. This autocratic decision saw many families emigrating to the Cape of Good Hope Colony as a direct result of the poor pecuniary situation that they found themselves in. None of the writers of the accounts of Ross's expedition appear, however, to have been aware of the difficulties experienced by the inhabitants of the island – strange, as in 1840 the hardships were at their peak.

Around this time slavery was being gradually reduced in some parts of the world, and St Helena became a receiving centre for the unfortunate captives rescued from slavers. They were usually in pretty poor health when they were disembarked, and they had to be cared for before being sent on to the West Indian Islands – but as free servants, not as slaves. Some stayed on St Helena and were eventually employed as local servants or labourers. The slave ships captured were brought into the harbour at Jamestown and broken up so that they could never be used again in the repulsive trade.

Ross did not take long to ascertain that the island's inherent magnetic properties would make the observatory very unsuitable for the main purpose that they had come here for, but there were other useful measurements that could be recorded. The island's strategic position meant that a weather station here would provide vital information for shipping passing up and down the Atlantic; India could only be reached by ships rounding the Cape

Longwood House on St Helena, built to house Napoleon Bonaparte during his exile after the Battle of Waterloo. He died here and was buried nearby.

of Good Hope, as could the ever-increasing trade to Australia and the emerging markets provided by it and New Zealand; even Britain's Pacific island colonies were better served by this passage than by Cape Horn.

The observatory was to be built close to Longwood House, which had been erected for Napoleon Bonaparte. In 1840 his body was still buried on St Helena and his tomb could be visited, but there was neither name nor epitaph to indicate who had been interred there. After a long series of meetings, the British finally allowed his remains to be transferred to France and towards the end of 1840 his coffin was brought back to Paris where he was given a state burial.

Meanwhile, McCormick found time to visit Napoleon's tomb on St Helena; he was more than pleasantly surprised at the tranquillity of the setting and even spent time sketching the scene. He described his impression thus:

> An extensive command of prospect around, presenting a pleasing, rural, peaceful appearance, which, on a fine sunny day, with the birds singing, as was the case when I saw it, with the bold rugged hills of the Flagstaff and the Barn, and glimpses of the sea between altogether forms a fine background to the picture. From every bearing the three plain slabs, beneath which repose the remains of, perhaps, the greatest man the world ever saw, girt round with their bristling wooden palisades, and enclosed by a green sward encircled by trees, the tomb itself in the sequestered nook forming the extremity of the valley, produced on my mind, at first glance, the most striking and impressive effect of any scene my eye ever before rested upon.

Later, McCormick and others, including Sergeant Cunningham, made the effort to climb the 650 steps up to the military observatory on the top of Ladder Hill. From the top of the hill the post commanded a view in every direction of upwards of 100 miles. No wonder the military had built their observatory on this prominence.

On the island at this time there were stationed two military detachments, one from the Royal Artillery and the other from the Royal Engineers; they speedily took on the responsibility of erecting the wooden observatory building that had been carried in sections from England. Lieutenant Lefroy, who had accompanied it, started to set up the instruments that he and his assistants would be using during their stay on the island.

Ross and Crozier allowed their crews some shore leave, stocked up on some essential fresh supplies including livestock, and of course watered the ships. There was at the time of their visit an ex-naval ship, *Arachne*, soon to depart for London with her cargo, and her captain was entrusted with the two exploration ships' up-to-date logs and their mail for England. In addition McCormick sent home a large packing case of specimens that he and Hooker had accumulated.

5 CAPE TOWN AND BEYOND

SAILING THROUGH THE ROARING FORTIES TO KERGUELEN ISLAND

On 9 February 1840, the day they said farewell to St Helena and all the helpful people of the island, it is interesting to note that Cunningham went ashore on 'duty'; one of the sailors had apparently deserted, and Cunningham went in search of him. I can find no further reference to this incident, but I do know that the sailor was not apprehended before *Erebus* and *Terror* set sail, because according to a researcher of Cunningham's diary the name of the miscreant was recorded as one Tilden Taylor, the young gentlemen's (i.e. midshipmen's) steward aboard *Terror*. He had signed on at Chatham, and his home town was recorded as Milton in Kent. Studying the muster list, I found his record was terminated on 9 February 1840, the day the expedition sailed. Interestingly, in the 1841 census, a certain Tilden Taylor appears in it as a baker. His age tallies with that of the missing man when the ships departed, so he seems to have returned to England and settled down to a life ashore! Later censuses do not show anyone of this exact name, so what the future held for him is unknown. Enquiries are ongoing.

A good spread of sails was soon billowing aloft and, helped by a stiff breeze, both ships set a course for Cape Town. As St Helena lies at 16°S, Cape Town, at 34°S, is considerably further south. The voyage took from 9 February until 15 March – and this time *Terror* arrived before *Erebus* by nearly three days. Just as the company aboard *Terror* were starting to get concerned for her safety *Erebus* sailed in and dropped her anchors. The ships had lost contact with one another just four days after leaving St Helena, and the seas, which had picked up considerably as they made their way southwards along the African coast, had caused them considerable difficulty. Ross reports in his journal that *Erebus* had encountered a fairly strong northerly current of much colder water which created very misty conditions, making navigation difficult. Not wishing to close with the land while visibility was restricted, he sensibly held back and took a course further out than *Terror*'s. This accounted for *Erebus*'s delay in reaching port. Despite the ordeals the ships' officers had experienced on this leg of the voyage they all maintained a series of depth, temperature and salinity records.

In 1840 Cape Town had only just become a municipal authority with the power to set its own laws, but the British had been in command there since the end of the Napoleonic wars, when France and her former ally, the Netherlands, had ceded all rights to the Cape Colony in exchange for a one-off payment from Britain. In 1836 the Boer settlers, wishing to be free of British domination and administration, had started their famous trek inland and to the north to set up the Orange Free State and the Transvaal. So the members of our expedition, arriving in 1840, would have witnessed at first hand the fledgling stages of what was to become South Africa as we know it today.

The port area was of great importance to the British Empire, as it provided a major naval servicing and provisioning post for ships making their way to India and back. It was this feature that *Erebus* and *Terror* hoped to take advantage of. The harbour, Simon's Town, is about 20 miles from Cape Town, the colony's capital. Today Simon's Town is the base of the South African Navy.

The two most senior British military officers at Cape Town were Rear Admiral George Elliot and Lieutenant-General Sir George Napier, and it was to these two men that Ross and Crozier paid their first calls to seek the help they needed to set up the observatory.

Having received the requisite permissions to erect the wooden building and restock their ships, the two commanders could spend the next few weeks relaxing and enjoying the company of the top echelon of the town's citizens.

Cape Town actually had its own observatory but although this was for astronomical, rather than magnetic, purposes, its superintendent was only too willing to make available his services for the benefit of the expedition. As mentioned earlier, Lieutenant Eardley Wilmot and three soldiers, who had travelled out aboard *Erebus*, were to be left here to manage the additional facility until the end of the expedition.

The stay at Simon's Town lasted just three weeks, sufficient time to complete and commission the observatory and restock the two ships before they headed out once more on their voyage of discovery.

Before they left South Africa McCormick and Robertson headed inland to climb Table Mountain. They set off at 4 a.m., meaning to reach the top before the sun became too hot. They were disappointed to not see much of the country's wildlife but did at last reach the summit. From here McCormick recalls in his book that they could see right across towards Cape Town, and that as they walked round the plateau at the top of the mountain the naval base came into view in the other direction. They carried on into Cape Town after completing their descent of the mountain; on the way back to Simon's Town they visited the newly erected observatory and saw Wilmot setting up his apparatus.

Getting back to the ships would, however, prove very troublesome. They had hired a chaise for the 20 or so miles to Simon's Town, and having left their departure until past 8 p.m. decided to try and cross a sandy bay as a shortcut. But in the twilight the wheels sank into quicksand and they had to put their shoulders to the chaise to heave it out. While they were

Left: Cape of Good Hope observatory as printed in the London Illustrated News of March 1857.

Below: Plaque at the British Hotel in Cape Town with the record of Ross's visit in 1840. The original hotel has been replaced, and renamed the Clarence.

THE ANTARCTIC EXPLORERS

THE BRITISH HOTEL

HOSTED THE MEMBERS OF THE FOLLOWING HISTORIC ANTARCTIC EXPEDITIONS

SHIP	LEADER	YEAR
Erebus & Terror	James Clark Ross	1840 &1843
Challenger	George Nares	1873
Discovery	Robert Scott	1901
Gauss	Erich von Drygalski	1903
Terra Nova	Robert Scott	1910

Erected by Simon's Town Historical Society and
R + N Master Builders - 2011

trying to accomplish this, the horse became entangled in its harness, which finally broke. With no help immediately available and not wishing to remain out all night they managed to manhandle the chaise out of its immediate difficulty and drag it the last bit of the journey back to Simon's Town. By now all chance of returning to their ships had evaporated, so they rousted the landlord of a local inn out of bed and he very kindly put them up for the night. This was the last of their forays into the countryside, and a few days later the two ships set out on the next part of their voyage. They would return three years later to pick up Wilmot and his aides.

By the next morning the two ships had lost contact with one another again due to a sharp squall just as they reached the open sea. Their next landfall was scheduled as either Marion Island or Prince Edward Island, just a short distance away to the south-east. The days it took them to arrive at these two islands were again spent in the usual measurements of depth, temperature and salinity. Ross was also interested in any ocean currents that could be detected, and fully expected to locate the one that he had experienced as his ship had sailed southwards towards Simon's Town. They did not find it, and he supposed that it was probably caused by cold water welling up nearer to land from some depths further south. The depth of water for a considerable distance as they sailed south showed that there was a huge shoal area, which Ross referred to as the Agulhas Bank. This vast raised portion of the seabed is where the colder Atlantic Ocean meets its much warmer neighbour, the Indian Ocean. A number of ships had come to grief over the years in this part of the ocean, and Ross and Crozier would have been aware of this danger. After taking the observations they required they headed further south. At this juncture, both ships were still out of touch with one another.

The wind had failed *Erebus* on two consecutive days in the middle of April, and this was followed by what Ross describes as the heaviest rain he had ever experienced. He states in his book:

> It came down literally in sheets of water, accompanied by very violent squalls from various quarters, alternately with perfect, but almost momentary calms … Heavy thunder and the most vivid lightning occurred during this great fall of water which lasted for more than ten hours, it required the utmost vigilance by the officers and crew to manoeuvre the ship during the rapid changes both in the strength and direction of the wind.

Compare the notes written by Cunningham aboard *Terror* for the same four days of April, and you would not believe they were on the same basic course. *Terror* experienced a calm period on the 12th followed by fine light winds on the 13th, and under very fine sailing conditions she was making about 7 knots. During the 14th and 15th the wind did become stiffer but apart from a mention of close-hauling the sails and having some rain there is nothing to suggest in his notes the ferocity and quantity of rain that *Erebus* had to endure.

On 15 April the surface temperature of the sea fell dramatically by at least 12°F (~7°C), and Ross surmised that they might be approaching some ice, especially when the wind veered to the south and the air temperature dropped by 9°F (~5°C). As it transpired, they did not meet any ice, and by 21 April, just one week after the torrential rain that had assailed them, they were within sight of Prince Edward Island, between 46° and 47°S. It would be a day later that *Terror* first picked out the profile of this same island; neither ship could see any suitable landing place, and as they had not planned to stop here both sailed on past the two islands that formed the group. Their real goal was the Kerguelen Archipelago, but Ross had been prevailed upon for humanitarian reasons to detour to the Crozet Islands where a small group of men employed in the sealing trade had been landed nearly a year before. They had not been visited in the meantime and their representative at the Cape was concerned about their welfare. Ross had brought food and clothing and some other supplies to see the sealers through the coming winter. It was at this juncture that, due to the sudden drop in temperature, the crew of *Erebus* were issued with warmer clothing .

They first sighted the islands on 26 April but it took the best part of a week to establish contact with the sealers, and even then it was the sealers who rowed out their small boat and clambered aboard *Erebus*. Ross described them as being 'more like Esquimaux than civilised beings'; their clothes were soaked in blubber and the smell emanating from them was most offensive. The leader of the group, a Mr Hickley, told Ross that they had experienced such bad weather that they had not been able to venture out in their boat for over five weeks. All of the sealers appeared to be in good health, probably because they lived on a diet of fresh meat obtained from the 'sea elephants' (elephant seals) they were catching and their success with fishing along the rocky shoreline.

Erebus sailed along most of the coastal strip of Possession and East Islands that formed part of the Crozet Archipelago, which was surveyed as she progressed. The findings entered into the ship's log showed that there were virtually no safe harbours that could be used by a sailing ship of their size, and having completed the errand they had been asked to perform they prepared to make sail. Ross had hoped to meet up again with *Terror* whilst near these islands, but by 1 May, still not having seen his consort, he gave the order to set sail and proceed towards the Kerguelen Islands, where they hoped to set up another of the string of stations for taking magnetic readings. Their stay at Kerguelen was to last for several weeks, so it would be important to make contact again with *Terror*, to make sure all was well with her.

Terror had missed out on the torrential rain that *Erebus* had been subjected to, but between 23 April and 4 May she went through some severe gales herself, with mountainous seas. During this period the crew made visual contact with Prince Edward Island, noting snow on the higher peaks, but the ship does not appear to have come too close to it and sailed on towards the Kerguelen group. Whereas Ross only saw one small lump of ice, Crozier and his officers in *Terror* saw several icebergs sailing majestically along. There was no denying the fact that the weather was getting considerably colder.

On the same day, Friday 1 May, that *Erebus* set course from Prince Edward Island, *Terror* sighted new land on her leeward bow. Orders were given to close-reef the main topsail and storm staysail but despite this precaution the crew had to endure massive seas breaking over the decks, soaking those who were reefing the staysail. As daylight came the ship's company were treated to the first sight of the sun for over a week, and could establish their bearings more accurately. The island, Kerguelen, turned out to be their destination, and their home for the next six weeks – but making a landing on it would be another matter altogether.

Towards the northern end of the island was a bay that had been named Christmas Harbour by none other than Captain James Cook, although the island group itself had been discovered in 1772 by a French explorer who went by the exotic name of Yves-Joseph de Kerguélen-Trémarec. He had returned to France thinking he had discovered a vast land that would turn out to be a fertile region suitable for growing all sorts of desirable crops and which could also contain treasures such as gold and valuable minerals, including coal. But his second visit a couple of years later brought him nearer to the truth. The island is sometimes referred to as Desolation Island.

The heavy weather continued throughout the weekend and even into Monday, but as it abated slightly all sign of land disappeared. Hurricane force winds tore into *Terror* for most of Tuesday but at least the land was back in view. Crozier was, however, forced to keep the ship clear of the land and the next day, realising that the storm had carried her past the entrance to the bay that they were seeking, he turned her back; this time the island was seen across the starboard bow. Christmas Harbour came into sight, but the risk of entering it as the weather stood was a daunting prospect, and caution prevailed until the next morning.

Lying at anchor a mile or so offshore and with a calmer sea, they sent in a boat to reconnoitre before committing the ship. On the approach to the bay they found a particularly dangerous-looking reef at its entrance that would have to be negotiated. Saturday 8 May gave them the first hope of sailing into the bay that would become their home for quite some time, but even now the weather thwarted them. Several more days of patient tacking passed when finally, on the morning of 13 May, after another sally towards the bay entrance and numerous tacks across the mouth, they managed to reach the relative calm of the harbour.

After all this time apart, the two expedition ships were together again. *Erebus* had managed to enter Christmas Harbour a day ahead of *Terror*.

It turned out that Ross and his men aboard *Erebus* had by this time experienced the same sort of conditions , and on *Terror* Cunningham recorded the brief appearance of another vessel on 8 May, but no contact was possible between *Terror* and what must surely have been *Erebus*.

On 7 January 1874 another British vessel of discovery, HMS *Challenger*, slipped into Christmas Harbour and let go her anchors not far from the spot where *Erebus* and *Terror* had been anchored 34 years earlier. She had sailed from Simon's Town and like Ross's two ships had made an attempt to land on Crozet, but had been driven away by the seas smashing onto the rocky coasts.

On board *Challenger* was one Lieutenant Lord George Campbell, who wrote a book based on the diaries he kept and the constant flow of letters that he sent home to his friends and relatives during the three years *Challenger* was at sea. It would seem that *Challenger* made a relatively easy entry into Christmas Harbour, and Campbell's immediate observation was to recall Captain James Cook's visit nearly 100 years before, when he had dubbed the place Desolation Island. Campbell went on to describe the anchorage in more detail:

> Kerguelen Island is a gloomy looking land certainly, with its high, black, fringing cliffs, patches of snow in the higher reaches of the dark coloured mountains, and a grey sea fretted with white horses surrounding it. To right and left of the harbour's entrance are perpendicular, table topped, lava cliffs, covered on the top with green moss. On the left an oblong-shaped block of cliff is separated by a deep cut from its neighbouring cliff, of which it once formed a part; in this detached bit is a colossal arch, 150 feet in height, and 100 feet

Christmas Harbour in Kerguelen Island, painted by Joseph Dayman, the mate on HMS Erebus.

at the base – a grand freak of nature. The harbour narrows to 500 yards some distance from its head, towards which it gradually tapers, ending in a sandy beach. As we lie at anchor on our left, towering 1,000 feet above us is an enormous rounded mass of black basalt, which has burst through rock of older formation and there remained. On our right is a steep slope, covered with moss and grass, traversed occasionally by horizontal bands of Trap-rock, and capped by a peak of grey rock – an old volcano – 1,300 feet high. Ahead, rising from the beach, the mossy slope continues, while beyond and right and left, are bare brown hills.

Thousands and thousands of penguins are sitting along the southern shore – all of the crested kind – the sulphur-crested, and another, a new one to us, with a golden crest extending across the head. These are nesting among the clumps of moss growing on the steep banks above the black rock-shores; and water all around is alive with them, jumping and splashing everywhere.

Campbell seized the opportunity to make his way ashore and marvelled at the abundance of wildlife, which included two species of penguins, ducks by the hundred, bull sealions and their mates, and many, many sea birds. The noise and smell were overpowering. He was in the habit of taking his gun with him and like McCormick before him blazed away at all and sundry. Duck was soon on the menu, and kept the ship supplied while *Challenger* was at anchor over the next couple of days. Then they sailed further south along the coast before entering another protected bay called Betsy Bay, probably named after some sailor working on the sealers that frequented Kerguelen. It was here that Campbell came across a poignant reminder of how fragile life was in those remote places. A group of seven graves with roughly hewn headstones marked the resting place of whalers who had lost their lives whilst trying to catch a whale by harpooning it from an open boat. Once they had hooked on, they would then be towed along waiting for the great beast to tire itself out and at last fall within range of other men with harpoons to deprive it of its life. At some stage in the grisly chase the whale had probably come up for air so near the whaler's boat as to overturn it and cast the men into the sea, where they must have rapidly perished in the freezing waters of the Southern Ocean, whether or not their boat had been destroyed.

The coastline of Kerguelen consisted of a whole series of large inlets on the same lines as the fjord region of Norway, caused by the same relentless gouging by the glaciers of many millennia earlier. *Challenger* spent the remainder of January visiting a number of these inlets

HMS Challenger *in Royal Sound, Kerguelen Island, in 1873 during her round-the-world voyage of discovery, painted by Steven Dews.*

and carrying out a running survey as she progressed along the coast. On the last day of the month she returned to Christmas Harbour and sailed around to the west coast where the sealers that they had contacted earlier assured them that at least one glacier still reached the sea.

Challenger's visit in January proved, unsurprisingly, to be far more amenable regarding the weather than that experienced by Ross's men when they were there in May and June 1840. In fact, Campbell concluded his diary for their stay, reflecting that he had enjoyed his visit.

Ross and Crozier from time to time gave names to various geographical features that they discovered, and here on Kerguelen Island they called the reef at the harbour entrance Terror Reef. Ross had discovered a shallow area in the sea as *Erebus* approached the island, which they named the Erebus Bank – and the natural arch at the entrance to the bay they called Arched Rock.

Christmas Harbour is circular and so it appeared to be safe wherever the wind came from, but to make sure, the two crews spent most of the first day warping and manoeuvring their vessels as close to the shore as possible before securing them for the duration of their stay. The main reason for getting them close in was to facilitate the unloading of all the building materials that would be required to construct the next observatory.

Throughout the expedition Sundays were usually set aside to carry out a simple divine (i.e. Christian) service and allow the crews some recreation time, and so it was on this occasion.

The Toronto Observatory in Canada, painted in 1852 by William Armstrong.

Then the next day and for several days following most of the men were employed in the task of erecting the observatory. They had to complete it by 29 May because that was a Term Day. Several such term days had been pre-planned so that the observations from the many different stations in various parts of the world could be synchronised. This was part of a plan by several countries, including France and Germany, to gain a larger picture of the magnetic variations that were known to occur from time to time.

A short quotation from Ross's first volume has some relevance here:

> It happened most fortunately to be a time of unusual magnetic disturbance, so that our first day's simultaneous observations proved the vast extent and instantaneous effect of the disturbing power, whatever it might be, affecting the magnetometers at Toronto in Canada and here at Kerguelen Island, nearly antipodal to each other, simultaneously and similarly in all their strange oscillations and irregular movements, and thus immediately afforded one of the most important facts that the still hidden cause of magnetic phenomena has yet presented.

This comparison with Toronto was of course only possible when all the results had been collated after the expedition arrived home, but it does show the lengths they had gone to in order to achieve a comprehensive data base for future scientific research.

While the observatory was being prepared, McCormick and Hooker spent most of their time exploring the harbour area and up into the surrounding hillsides, noting the bird life, vegetation and geological structure of the island. McCormick even discovered some fossilised tree trunks, which he measured at 7 feet in diameter. On one occasion he even took one of the sailors to try and bring a substantial sample back to the ship, but the terrain proved too difficult for them to carry the bulky and quite heavy wood. The next day he returned to the spot where the tree trunk lay and this time, even with the help from two sailors, it again proved too difficult to remove so he had to content himself with several much smaller examples.

The weather on the island was proving most depressing with an almost constant sea mist that dampened everything outside including the enthusiasm of those exposed to it but McCormick did not really let that get in the way of his exploring rambles. Most days he could be found out on the hillsides, gun in hand, picking off a few local ducks for the table or seeking out samples of the other birds for whom this island had until now been a safe home.

Having ventured all the way round Christmas Harbour, McCormick volunteered to lead a boat party out of the bay and sail round the coast for several miles to explore the neighbouring Cumberland Bay. Accompanying him on this trip would be Lieutenant Charles Phillips from *Terror*. The two officers had marshalled a crew of three men from each ship to handle the boat, and on 2 June an early start was made, some stars still shining in the pale dawn sky, and the weather for once promising a fine start. They rowed passed the Arched Rock at about 7 a.m., and took a compass bearing before turning along the coast to locate Cumberland Bay.

With their change in direction the wind became favourable, and they shipped their oars and hoisted the small sail, which carried the boat rapidly towards the new bay. Entry into the bay did not prove too difficult, nor did finding a suitable landing place. They had come about 10 miles since departing from Christmas Harbour, and taking once more to the oars they gained the head of the bay.

McCormick was fascinated by the inquisitiveness of the shags that inhabited this bay. They followed the progress of the boat, swooping down towards it, as they had obviously never before seen human beings. They hovered above the boat as it was being rowed along and several times one of the sailors would take a swipe at them with his oar, bringing one down with each blow. These unfortunate birds would finish up by supplementing the explorers' first evening meal.

Reaching the top of the bay they were able to run the boat up onto a sandy beach not far from a small stream trickling down from the high ground that surrounded the bay. The bay was estimated to be 12 miles long, and by 7 p.m. that first evening they were securely set up for cooking their supper and preparing for a good night's sleep in the blanket bedrolls they had brought with them.

The following morning the plan was to head inland and attempt to cross the relatively narrow part of the island, to bring them to the opposite coast. The higher ground that they had to negotiate proved a stumbling block, however, and because of its boggy nature and with the heavy camping equipment they had brought with them they came to a premature halt. McCormick was, however, determined to complete the crossing, and taking just one of the men and discarding their camping gear, the two left the others to retrace their steps, and pressed on across to the other side of the island. Mist enshrouded the view when they arrived and not wishing to be out for the night without any tent or means of protection should the weather become inclement, they beat a retreat and caught up with the others. Now with darkness creeping up on the party and the weather deteriorating all the time it was essential that they find a suitable resting place because they would have to spend the night out on the fells.

Supper consisted of the several ducks that McCormick had managed to shoot, together with pea soup that formed part of the rations they had brought with them. In the morning they resumed their way to the sandy beach, and after gathering together the natural history samples that had been collected and loading the boat with them and their camping gear, they rowed back up the bay towards the entrance. Several times, however, they took detours and carried out some more exploration of a local nature, and in the end these detours were to last for two days; McCormick was constantly being drawn to unusual features in the landscape and of course the boat would have to be beached while he examined them. His curiosity knew no bounds, and for a naval surgeon he was remarkably well informed about all aspects of geology and nature in general.

Finally, they were able to proceed towards the bay entrance but now the weather overtook them and they spent an uncomfortable night in the boat. They had taken a stock of provisions with them to last at least ten days and these were being supplemented with the aid of the gun. They spent the night of Friday 5 June on a sandy beach close to the boat, which they had pulled up nearby, and after a short ramble by McCormick first thing in the morning they launched the boat back into Cumberland Bay and, taking advantage of the fresh breeze, pursued a course that would bring them to the bay's entrance. The sea crossing back to Christmas Harbour threatened to be a rough one, but with the strategic use of oars and sail to take advantage of any variances in the wind they drew level with the harbour entrance and by 4 p.m. had pulled down its length, to reach *Erebus* where she lay at anchor. Ross was at the observatory, and McCormick went to report that he and his team had returned safely. The party had been away for four days.

The members of the expedition that had been left on board the two ships had endured some very poor weather including snow showers and hail. The wind always seemed to be present, and the period that the expedition spent here seems to have been quite a strain on their patience. The accounts that were written at the time and later certainly reflect on the period as one everybody would rather forget.

All the rain had created a fine display of cataracts and waterfalls cascading down off the cliffs that surrounded the bay. Even with the two ships lying only about 40 or 50 yards off the shore it wasn't uncommon that the short crossing ashore and back would be barred by the foulest of weather.

June turned into July and still the weather dominated their existence. One of the biggest problems they had was trying to keep warm and dry. Worse, every time a party went outside there was the certainty that a change of clothing would be required as soon as they gained the sanctuary of the lower decks or their cabins. There were only limited opportunities to dry their clothes, and this made for a very uncomfortable lifestyle

After the short exploration of Cumberland Bay, Ross sent out an order on 8 July for another boat expedition to be organised. This time *Erebus'* first lieutenant, Edward Bird, was to leave with two boats departing from Christmas Harbour as soon as the arrangements could be made and the weather allowed. Their brief was for one of the boats to carry out an examination of White's Bay and the other to return to Cumberland Bay. McCormick and Phillips were to lead the Cumberland Bay party and resume where they had left off on their first visit. Bird and his team were given the job of carrying on past Cumberland Bay to reach White's Bay. But the day after the order was given Bird reported sick.

Cunningham wrote in his journal that Lieutenant Edward Bird from *Erebus* had reported sick on 8 July, and McCormick noted that he would have to be very diplomatic in the way he informed Captain Ross of his first lieutenant's indisposition; McCormick had long thought that Bird had not really had his heart in the expedition.

Cumberland Bay and its geography were quite complicated, judging by a look at the map of Kerguelen. Neither Ross nor Cunningham wrote in any detail about the various groups' experiences except to say they were carrying out survey work. There is however a long entry in McCormick's book about the second Cumberland Bay trip. He certainly was very active during his explorations into the countryside on both sides of the bay. His notes contain an amazing amount of information, and his zeal for the work in hand displays the traits of a very driven person.

There were some ridges in the landscape, bounded by higher land; on his previous visit this had led him to believe that by crossing this feature he would possibly be able to look down into White's Bay. To prove this theory, he took with him as an assistant Edward Fawcett, the boatswain's mate.[14]

The two boats returned to the ships' anchorage in Christmas Harbour 12 days after their departure, and although both the crews were severely strained as a result of the continuing bad weather they at least had not suffered any casualties.

Above: Joseph Dalton Hooker, painted by George Richmond in 1855.

Right: Chart of the 1839 to 1843 Ross expedition.

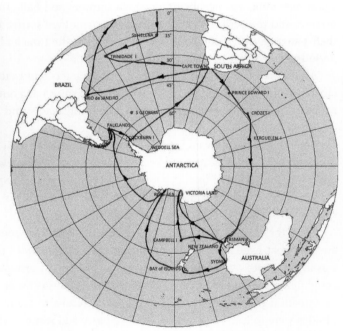

14 Fawcett was later to sail on the ill-fated Franklin expedition to seek out the North-west Passage, and would lose his life along with all its other members. In 1879 an American search party led by Lieutenant Frederick Schwatka was looking for evidence of the Franklin expedition near King William Island off the coast north of Canada when they came across a small wooden board with brass tacks hammered into it, making the initials L.F . Could this possibly have been E.F. for Edward Fawcett? The search party thought it might have been, from a bunk board. They recorded the place where the piece of wood was found as being O'Reilly Island, and this has turned out to be fairly close to the underwater site of the recently discovered *Erebus*.

Joseph Hooker had been given a whole list of 'must haves' by his father, with a request to send home seeds of the plant that most epitomises this island, the Kerguelen cabbage. Hooker senior then wrote to his son reporting that the seeds would not germinate, or when they did, they were dismal plants doomed to failure. Joseph responded that he had successfully grown the plants even aboard the ship and could not understand his father's failures.

Hooker spent many hours searching for samples of the plant and insect life on Kerguelen, but what really caught his attention was the existence of many varieties of mosses and lichens which thrived on the hillsides. Some of these were still embedded in snow and ice, and it was difficult for him to procure any samples; hacking with a suitable metal instrument released some of them but of course damaged the minute structures. He eventually devised a way round the problem by sitting on the sample until it thawed sufficiently to enable him to gently extract the small tuft of vegetation, and add it to his growing collection. His fascination with lichens and mosses, or cryptogams as they are known,[15] went back to his earlier rambles at home as a boy. Even though they do not produce flowers they still provide a colourful display in shades of red, orange, lilac and yellow as they cling to boulders and rock faces on the hillsides.

The distribution of plants across the vast expanses of the Southern Ocean with many hundreds of miles between land masses and other island groups would pose Hooker one of his most serious challenges, and on his return home he frequently corresponded with Charles Darwin and other eminent botanists of the time, to establish a solution to this phenomenon.

---

15 A cryptogam is a plant that does not flower but reproduces itself by spores distributed by the wind or insects and animals. The classification includes ferns and algae.

6 NEXT STOP: HOBART, TASMANIA

TWO TRAGIC ACCIDENTS, A WELCOME REUNION AND BREAK

The stay at Kerguelen was concluding, and the last few observations were completed by 13 July, when the observatory was shut down and dismantled and brought back on board. The sails were checked over and replaced where necessary. Once they had cleared the decks of stores that had been brought aboard they were nearly ready to sail on the next stage of their journey. The ships were swung to re-establish the compass bearings, and on the morning of Monday 20 July they hauled up the anchors and turned towards the harbour entrance with reefed topsails starting to billow for the first time in over six weeks. Cunningham had no remorse at leaving what he described as 'a land I have no particular anxiety to ever visit again'. *Terror* and *Erebus* maintained a steady 7 knots as they cleared the bay entrance and the reef named after *Terror*. Heavy seas were running as they fought their way further from the island, and now they were hopefully bound for Van Diemen's Land (now Tasmania).

One week had elapsed when, on the morning of Tuesday 28 July just as day was breaking, *Terror* was having to cope with a breeze that had strengthened into a gale, and the lookouts reported that *Erebus* had disappeared from view. The hatches were battened down and the main topsail and storm staysail had to be close-reefed. By 1 p.m. the ship was hove to. Resuming their course the next day, they again raised a small amount of sail but the ship rolled to such an extent that her gunwales were at times awash.

Erebus had been displaying blue lights from the masthead and firing cannon to try and keep in touch with her consort. Knowing that *Terror* was a slower vessel *Erebus* kept reducing the amount of sail set, but struggled to keep head into the wind each time. At one stage there was on the deck so much water – which amounted to many tons and could have destabilised the ship – that the only way to allow it to escape was to knock out the gun port covers. So Ross, knowing his friend, Crozier to be an excellent sailor, gave the command to proceed on their journey and *Erebus* carried on alone.

On the afternoon of 30 July, a most unfortunate mishap occurred aboard *Erebus*. Several hands were aloft trimming and setting sails when John Roberts, the boatswain, was hit by the staysail sheet as the ship lurched in response to a severe gust, lost his footing and fell overboard. Action stations was signalled and the ship brought about. Two boats were put into the water and the crews quickly pulled back to the spot he had plunged into, but despite a prolonged search no sign of him could be found. That wasn't the end of the rescue attempt, either, because as the two boats headed back to the safety of the ship the one furthest away was swept by a large wave which washed four crew members into the sea. Fortunately, the outcome of that event at least was not so disastrous, and with the aid of the first boat the four men were quickly pulled to safety. They were soon aboard *Erebus* and a change into drier clothes and a hot drink soon put them to rights.

Several hours had been lost due to the rescue – and then, just as dusk was settling in, the lookout spotted an iceberg some distance off. With darkness nearly upon them it was yet another difficulty to deal with. However, they rose to the challenge and avoided it.

The islands of Prince Edward, Crozet and Kerguelen all lie approximately between the 40th and 45th lines of latitude and by sailing parallel to them Ross was able to take numerous magnetic readings to supplement those taken at the three island groups.

As the distance from Kerguelen grew, the weather for once held its breath and allowed them to put aloft a good spread of canvas. They were soon looking out for their first sight of land since 20 July. It would appear from their logs that *Terror* must have overtaken *Erebus* because *Terror*'s record of land sighted comes at least three days before Ross notes his sighting of the Australian coastline.

Hobart was only about 300 miles further to travel, but now the seas rose under the influence of a gale force wind; one wave crashed on board, breaking up one of the ship's boats and washing overboard quite a lot of items that had been stored in it. On 14 August *Terror* entered the River Derwent, and now the worst part of the outward voyage would soon be at an end. Two days after the pilot came aboard he guided her to a safe anchorage. Then on the 17th *Erebus* came into view and dropped anchor nearby. The next morning both ships were warped further upriver, to a location more convenient for access to the new observatory when it was built.

Ross and Crozier were given a very warm welcome by the governor, Sir John Franklin, and his family. Although there was nearly a generation gap between the two officers and Sir John, this was easily bridged by their common interests: polar exploration and in particular the North-west Passage. Franklin had been on the retired list for a number of years when he was offered the position of governor-general to Van Diemen's Land. Earlier in his naval career he had been at the heart of an overland exploration for the North-west Passage. You might not associate land exploration with the navy but of course most of the officers were experienced navigators and this qualified them for the work in hand over civilians of any occupation, or even army personnel.

Twice in the early 1820s Franklin had led overland expeditions into the virtually unknown regions of the northern Canadian mainland to reach the Arctic Ocean, and then he and his companions had travelled along the coastline in specially constructed shallow-draught boats, mapping as they went along. In addition to these two unique expeditions he had also taken part in two other exploits: the first of these had been directed towards finding a way through the frozen Arctic Ocean towards the North Pole; and the second was one of the earliest attempts to seek out the North-west Passage, a project which had become so synonymous with the Royal Navy of the early 19th century. At the time of the meeting between these three men none of them would have guessed that Sir John would ultimately travel to the Arctic one more time for what should have been the final attempt to complete the sea route through the islands of northern Canada and so claim for England the glory it had so long sought, and for themselves the accolade of discovering the North-west Passage. Even more coincidental was the fact that the two ships he would command were just then at anchor within sight of his residence, Government House. His ship would be *Erebus* and it would be the lot of newly promoted Captain Crozier to sail in *Terror*.

By the time of his death in 1847 Franklin's naval career had spanned nearly 50 years from the time when he had first gone to sea from his home in the small market town of Spilsby in rural Lincolnshire. Here in the marketplace stands one of the memorials erected in his memory to mark the town's association with one of England's best-known sailors. The search for his lost expedition was never successful in terms of finding any survivors, and innumerable searches have been carried out over the years to try and ascertain the causes of the catastrophe. Only one written record was ever found; this had only a very limited amount of information on it, and even that was open to different interpretations.

Finally in 2014 the first of the two missing ships was discovered on the seabed: *Erebus*, Franklin's command ship. Two years later and in a different location, the wreck of *Terror* was located. The two wrecks are in a far better state of preservation than anyone would have thought possible, and ironically the two sites, although many miles apart, were not too far from positions that had been known to the local Inuit populations. When the two ships were abandoned on 22 April 1848, there were just 105 men still alive out of a total starting complement of 129, Sir John being among the deceased. This would have left Crozier in overall command. *Terror* was found not too many miles from where she had been abandoned, and *Erebus* had drifted, or possibly been sailed, some miles further south; but at the time of writing the two wreck sites are kept secret to avoid any disturbance by treasure seekers, and information as to what might be found has yet to be disclosed.

Back to August 1840: in preparation for the arrival of the Antarctic expedition in Tasmania, Franklin had been hard at work getting all the materials together for the main observatory, which, at 48 feet long by 16 feet wide, would be quite commodious. It had, of course, to be constructed without any ferrous metal components. He had at his disposal the convict labour that was readily available around that time; a total of nearly 200 men had been busy cutting and preparing the timber, and once the site had been selected, they were set to work on the footings. The building site chosen, on solid sandstone, would not cause deviation in the magnetic instruments. According to the archive records the construction work was completed in nine days, which meant that on the next term days, set for 27 and 28 August, it could be co-ordinated with other stations located in various parts of the globe including those set up in Cape Town and St Helena.

As each station was commissioned a set of the instruments Ross had brought was allocated to it. The two ships also carried identical sets, and this would enable them to participate in the term days whilst away from Hobart. The primary interest for the expedition was the magnetic observations and the following instruments are recorded in Ross's book: a declination instrument, a horizontal and a vertical force magnetometer, a dip circle, a transit with an azimuth circle and two chronometers.

Magnetic forces all round the world are governed by the Earth's magnetic field and lines of force. These vary across the globe and can be measured and plotted on charts. It was hoped that sending this expedition to the southern hemisphere to set up and maintain magnetic observatories would enable the scientists involved in these strange phenomena to compare the results already obtained in the northern half of the Earth. The German scientist Carl Friedrich Gauss and other leading experts of the period had predicted that the southern hemisphere would be virtually a mirror image of the northern sector. In fact, Gauss had even estimated where Ross would find the South Magnetic Pole.

Magnetic declination, or magnetic variation, is the angle on a horizontal plane between a magnetic pole (the point on the Earth where that pole is currently located) and its nearest geographic pole. This angle varies depending on where you are standing on the Earth's surface – and even that changes over time, because unlike the geographic poles, the magnetic poles are not fixed points.

The South Magnetic Pole displays the same characteristics as its northern counterpart. To record these angles at the stations chosen by the expedition leaders they had to conform to a certain convention: when the North Magnetic Pole was measured as being to the east of the geographic North Pole the angle was said to be positive, but when the North Magnetic Pole was measured as being to the west of the geographic North Pole, the angle was negative.

Another measurement taken in conjunction with the declination is the magnetic inclination or dip angle. The observer turns their attention to the vertical force magnetometer. This will reveal the angle between the horizontal plane and the Earth's magnetic field lines. As with the declination angle, measurements of the angle of dip will vary as to where on the Earth's surface the measurement is taken. The nearer the observer to a magnetic pole, be it north or south, the more the compass or magnetometer needle will tilt downwards; on a very accurate scale a reading can be taken and plotted to reveal the angle of inclination.

The needle of a magnetometer is of course a magnet in its own right and, like all magnets, when it is allowed to pivot freely about its centre point it swivels according to the lines of force that emanate from the two magnetic poles. In the northern hemisphere – contrary to what you might have expected from your earliest physics lessons – it is the north pole of the compass needle that is attracted downwards on approaching the North Magnetic Pole (and vice versa as you approach the South Magnetic Pole) because what we *call* the Earth's North Magnetic Pole is in fact the south pole of the vast magnet that forms the Earth's core.

As with the angle of declination there is a convention that governs the angle of inclination as being negative or positive. On approaching the North Magnetic Pole, the needle will have a positive angle of dip, and due to the opposite action of the needle in the south the angle is given in negative degrees.

The Ross Bank Observatory was built to an exacting standard and the instruments were set up with great care to ensure they would not suffer from any undue influences from the surrounding environment. Over a period of several years modifications took place to make doubly sure the temperature was kept as constant as possible, and by banking up the outside of the building with soil an effort was made to stop draughts from creeping in under the floor. Even vibration from any outside source could influence the readings. What was so staggering was that the results revealed that they could be influenced by even the lunar cycle and the position of the sun; this sensitivity came as a great surprise to the scientists who analysed the records.

By traversing the southern oceans, Ross was able to plot angles from hundreds of different points, not only from the fixed stations he had set up but also from his ships and the remote islands they visited. Once these records were tabulated a pattern emerged that showed points on the globe where nearly identical measurements were obtained. Joining up these points on a chart revealed a pattern of lines circumscribing the globe. These became known as Isoclinic Lines, somewhat similar to the lines of latitude we are familiar with.

It was even established that a series of positions where measurements were taken that had little or no angle of declination could be plotted and this line was ascribed as the Aclinic Line or magnetic equator.

The study of magnetism was still in its infancy, and the instruments that Ross used during this expedition were of a fairly basic yet delicate construction, but despite their frailty the results were extraordinarily accurate and provided the scientists both in Great Britain and across the world with a vast amount of data to work on. The analysis of this information would lead to a far greater accuracy in chart drawing, and as a consequence sailing the world's oceans became less hazardous. The Hobart observatory was perhaps the most important of all the ones that were set up, as it was almost diametrically opposite to one that had been set up and run in Toronto at the same time by the military party led by Lieutenant John Lefroy of the Royal Artillery. This enabled the two sets of results to be compared, and many of the correlated results proved to have similarities to one another.

When the two ships departed the following summer to explore the regions of the Antarctic where Ross was hopeful of locating the South Magnetic Pole, Lieutenant Kay would be left behind to run the observatory, assisted by two members of the ships' crews: Peter Scott, first mate from *Terror*, and Joseph Dayman, third mate from *Erebus*.

Rossbank Observatory, taken from a black-and-white scan of the painting by F.G. Simpkinson in about 1840.

The financing of all the observatories was carried out by the Admiralty, but after about seven years the cost of the Tasmanian one was transferred to the Tasmanian authorities. They regarded the observatory and its maintenance as an unwarranted expense and closed it down a couple of years later. For the seven years until that point, Kay was in charge of it, and when *Erebus* and *Terror* returned after that first summer in Antarctic waters, he was assisted by various other members of their crews.

During that first stay in Hobart in 1840 a romance blossomed between Alexander Smith, the first mate aboard *Erebus*, and Sarah Aubrey Read, a young local lady, but due to Smith's commitment to the expedition they had to wait for its conclusion before they could get married. On his return to England in 1844 Smith applied for and was granted a position on what was called the Australian Station. The newly promoted Lieutenant Alexander Smith, late of *Erebus*, took up his post in Hobart and was duly married; he settled down to a new appointment at the observatory, where he would become the senior scientific officer after Kay's resignation in 1847.

While the observatory was working there was a regime of taking readings every hour on the hour, for every hour of the day and night. This must have been a very tedious employment and eventually Kay resigned from the post, as he had become aware that his promotion within the naval service was thus jeopardised. He was eventually promoted to captain – but then was put on the retired list at half-pay. Not a very satisfactory end to his promising naval career.

As mentioned earlier, the French, under d'Urville, had been in the regions Ross was hoping to explore. The Americans, too, led by Wilkes. Once Ross had found out that the other two expeditions had been to the area he had earmarked, he set about looking further east, and decided that longitude 170°E would be his starting point. He states in his book that his orders before leaving England had given him leeway to attempt to reach the frozen continent anywhere to the south of the sector that lay nearest to Australia and New Zealand. Both the other enterprises had hoped to achieve a furthest south, but in the event neither of them reached the benchmark 74°15'S set by James Weddell back in 1823. In fact, neither d'Urville nor Wilkes even reached the 67th line of latitude.

Whilst stationed in Hobart both Ross and Crozier spent a considerable amount of time at the observatory overseeing the routine that they wanted established whilst they were away exploring.

Cunningham, meanwhile, spent many a happy hour eating and talking with an old friend, Sergeant Cameron of the 51st King's Own Light Infantry, stationed in Hobart as part of the military presence to help maintain law and order. This was required because between 1812, when the first convicts were brought to the island, and 1853, when the practice was stopped, over 74,000 prisoners were shipped over from England. These people were for the most part from the poorest level of British society and consisted of not only men and women but also children, such was the desire to rid the mother country of its criminal class once and for all.

McCormick spent the first week of his stay at Hobart paying his respects to Sir John Franklin and his wife, and he received an invitation to visit the officers' mess of the 51st King's Own where, like Cunningham, he could renew his acquaintance with several of the officers he had met prior to his departure from England. He also met several residents, among them Mr Anstey, the solicitor general, Mr Bedford, the chief medical officer at the hospital, and Dr Clark, the inspector general of the forces stationed at Hobart. For the leading townsfolk of Hobart, the expedition's stay there was probably the highlight of their social calendar, judging by the invitations received by the senior officers of the two ships.

Of course, what McCormick really wanted to do was to explore the surrounding country-side to add to his precious natural history collection. He didn't have to wait too long because the colonel of the 51st invited him and Hooker to take part in a kangaroo hunt. This was held in the same style as a fox hunt in England, following a pack of hounds on horseback, so it may not have been quite the sort of outing McCormick had been hoping for.

During the course of the various landings made whilst the expedition had been at sea McCormick had formed a firm friendship with Lieutenant Charles Phillips of *Terror*, so it was no surprise when they arranged to take a trip into the interior of Tasmania. Setting off from Hobart and travelling in the company of Judge Montague in his smart carriage and matching greys they prosecuted a ten-day journey taking them through many miles of varied countryside and stopping overnight at inns in the villages they passed through. They arrived back in Hobart on 21 September.

The journey took them from Hobart in the south all the way to the north of the island, where they visited Launceston, and back again to the capital. This must have been in the region of 200 miles. Most of the places they passed through can be seen on today's modern maps. It is remarkable that in the relatively short period of about 35 years since the first colony had been set up in 1804 at Sullivan's Cove on the west bank of the Derwent a road network had been established and so much of the eastern side of the island had been surveyed and settlements founded.

Friday 25 September saw the first anniversary of the expedition's departure from Chatham.

Another journey, this time starting from Hobart in a private yacht, allowed them to visit Port Arthur, a small bay on the Tasman peninsula, where they were shown round a penal colony and got an idea of how primitive the convicts' barrack rooms were. McCormick has a few comments to make about them:

> The prisoners were arranged in tiers along the sides of the room, each narrow crib being separated by a low board. A light is constantly kept burning, and an overseer on watch throughout the night. What lamentable specimens of poor humanity, crime indelibly stamped in the vile physiognomy of each!

Where the narrow isthmus of the Tasman peninsula joined the mainland was a place called Eagle Hawk Neck, and here the visitors saw about a dozen of what McCormick describes as the most ferocious dogs he had ever seen, tethered by chains, forming an impenetrable barrier

Van Diemen's Land (Tasmania) mapped by John Dower, 1837.

to anyone attempting to leave the penal colony to reach the mainland and possible freedom.

Coal had been discovered in Tasmania, and there was a convenient seam of it in the vicinity of the convicts' housing; about 60 of them were employed in extracting it. McCormick was extremely interested in anything to do with geology and spent some time examining the area.

He and Phillips arrived back in Hobart just in time to witness a funeral procession of ships' crews carrying the body of Edward Bradley, the captain of the hold from *Erebus*. To everyone's dismay of he had died as the result of an accident. It was a custom aboard naval ships to cleanse each hold using hot charcoal. It would appear that Bradley had been overcome by fumes and had collapsed into the hot embers causing severe burning and unconsciousness resulting in his demise. The coffin used for his burial

Sir John Franklin's statue in the marketplace in Spilsby, Lincolnshire.

was made of best English oak, according to Cunningham, and made a considerable impression on the local population who had turned out to pay their respects.

Another casualty before they departed from Hobart was one Mr Molloy, who the surgeon had deemed unsuitable for the strenuous tasks ahead of them. He was repatriated to England.

7 FIRST TASTE OF THE ICE

BREAKING THROUGH INTO THE ROSS SEA – THE RIGHT COURSE TO TAKE

The time was now drawing near when the ships would depart for the south, and on 12 October, after restocking *Erebus* and *Terror* with as much fresh produce as they could stow, they sailed, accompanied by Sir John Franklin and the river pilot, down the Derwent estuary. When the pilot and Sir John disembarked into the accompanying yacht, the rigging of both ships was manned by two cheering crews, and it was farewell for the time being to what had been a very restful stay.

The two ships were embarking on the first leg of their journey into unknown waters. The Auckland Isles would provide the first landfall, but these were still some 900 miles away to the south-east. Both ships had set their studding sails to take advantage of the favourable breeze.[16]

Now that the expedition was once more at sea, the depth, salinity and temperature readings were resumed. The lookouts were kept busy in the expectation of an imminent sighting of the island group, and on 19 November they realised they were approaching land. As night was falling, sail was shortened and the ships hove to, awaiting daylight. Early the next day the first signs of the islands came into view: the group consisted of the main island with many bays, coves and inlets, and a number of islets. The group had been discovered in 1806 by one of Messrs Enderby's sealing captains, Abraham Bristow.

The two ships rounded Enderby Island, off the northern extremity of the main island, and headed into one of the inlets of Auckland Island. As they edged nearer the land they encountered several whirlpools caused by conflicting currents and tides sweeping round the rocky shore. Squally weather threatened them with the possibility of having to withdraw out to sea, but Ross states that with the utmost vigilance by the officers and crew they were able to

---

16 Studding sails, or stunsails, set outside the normal square sails on extensions to the yards, increase the spread of canvas when sailing downwind, and thus increase the ship's speed.

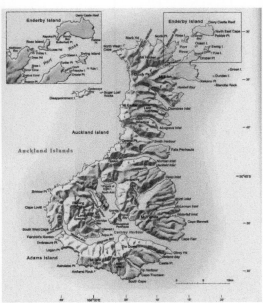

Above: Port Ross in the Auckland Islands. The painting is attributed to Charles Enderby, who led the first settlers there in about 1850.

Right: Auckland Islands, courtesy of the New Zealand Department of Conservation.

find a safe haven in a small cove; it had, however, taken nearly five hours of beating back and forth to gain this refuge.

Erebus and *Terror* were soon swinging to their anchors, sails furled and decks cleared. A stay of about three weeks would be necessary to erect a small portable observatory and for some exploration to take place. The surveyors amongst the officers also wanted to confirm their position and chart their harbour. The bay was known to them from information received from Messrs Enderby, and it proved to be an ideal sanctuary from the prevailing winds, unlike the one they had used at Kerguelen Island. As Ross and Crozier had made arrangements to meet here in the event of separation, Ross christened it Rendezvous Harbour. The bay turned out to be about 4 miles deep and terminated in a small inlet that they named Laurie Cove. Two other small features received names: Erebus Cove and Terror Cove.

Sixty-four years later another famous Antarctic expedition was to pass this way. In 1904 the National Antarctic Expedition, led by Robert Falcon Scott, was finally homeward bound, having been released after two years trapped in the ice of the Ross Sea. Their ship, *Discovery*, and two relief ships, *Morning* and *Terra Nova*, had also arranged a rendezvous in the harbour that Ross had named, but by the time of Scott's visit the cartographers had renamed it Ross Harbour. Sealers, however, gave it a more familiar name: Sarah's Bosom!

During *Discovery*'s stay the crews went ashore and did some exploring and leg-stretching of their own. This was the first time they had seen green plant life for nearly three years, and the contrast with the sameness of ice and snow must have been exhilarating. Like Ross and Crozier's men they took advantage of the opportunity to obtain fresh meat. Several seals were caught – but fishing produced results similar to their predecessors – not much success. They did manage to secure a couple of pigs, though, and one wonders if these were the descendants of those left behind by Ross's crews.

As *Erebus* and *Terror* dropped their anchors and prepared to send a party ashore, two notable features on the shore were unmistakeable signs of previous visitations to this spot. Curiosity soon prevailed and a boat was sent ashore from *Erebus* to investigate. It turned out that both the French expedition under d'Urville and the Americans led by Charles Wilkes had been here, and as evidence of their visits had painted signs: d'Urville had sailed from Hobart to this cove on 11 March 1840, and the American brig *Porpoise*, one of Wilkes's squadron, had been to the same cove on 7 March (but no year was stated on the sign).

Ross's expedition, following the pattern that they had set at nearly every other landing place, set up a small observatory and for the next three weeks logged readings of the variations in magnetism. In addition, the naturalists aboard both vessels were soon out in the wild, seeking out new plant and bird species, and crew members who were handy with a gun were sent in search of game for the table: albatrosses, seals, penguins and even a couple of wild pigs. These pigs had been probably been left on the island by passing ships to provide a source of food for any unfortunate mariner marooned there. Ross's expedition had, as mentioned earlier, been supplied with a selection of animals, seeds and plants to leave on islands to help sustain any future visitors, and here they left four sheep and two rams, more pigs, and some chickens and rabbits. The plant section included soft fruit such as gooseberries and currants, and a selection of vegetable seeds. A small patch of ground was turned over and the seeds planted. The vegetable patch was protected by a brushwood barricade to keep out browsing animals. Fishing was carried out using a seine net, but this operation had only limited success.

The remains of some sort of roughly built habitation were discovered, as were the sites of two graves, both marked by crude wooden crosses; one of these, that of a Frenchman, had a small inscription giving his name as Armand Francois. He had died on 14 May 1839. He was probably from a French sealing vessel, but would not have been one of d'Urville's men as he had died before their visit.

The weather during their stay was, as usual in these parts, very mixed. When it was at its worst hail seemed to predominate, judging by the descriptions in the diaries and Ross's book. The land supported a good covering of vegetation, mostly thickets, but some trees were noted as being of a useful size. There was an abundance of fresh water, and the two crews were soon replenishing their ships' tanks in preparation for their departure, which was achieved very early on the morning of 12 December 1840.

It only took 24 hours' sailing to get their first sighting of Campbell Island, but accessing a safe anchorage would prove to be more difficult than they at first realised; it took *Terror* nearly 12 hours of tacking backwards and forwards – and just as they thought the way in was assured she touched bottom on a mud bank. With the tide on the ebb it was going to be a struggle to get her away again, but fortunately there did not seem to be any rocks damaging her bottom. Many hours were spent pumping out the water tanks that had been so laboriously filled just a day or two before, and some stores were unloaded using the ship's boats. Finally, when the ship was lightened and the tide turned in their favour, *Terror* slipped easily away from danger, but by now it was well past midnight.

Once the excitement of refloating *Terror* had subsided and the crew had rested, the usual routine of going ashore and setting up the observatory could begin. Ross had found that the compasses were severely affected both here on Campbell Island and back on Auckland Island. All these islands being of volcanic origin, the iron in the rocks strongly influenced the results.

Hooker took the brief opportunity that the short stay allowed to go ashore collecting as many specimens as he could. He came to the conclusion that on Auckland Island and on Campbell Island the vegetation and insect life were very similar in the number of varieties found, but he noted some differences; plants abundant on Auckland had been replaced by other species on Campbell. Whilst carrying out his research he came across evidence of a previous occupation of the island. Almost hidden from view were two graves, one of them that of a woman who it seemed had drowned in the bay they were anchored in.

Campbell Island and its few satellite islets had been discovered in 1810 by Frederick Hasselborough while on a seal hunt, but he had drowned in what is now known as Perseverance Harbour, named after his ship.

The time the expedition was to spend at Campbell Island was very brief: just two days to erect the observatory, take some measurements from it, take a quick look around and collect some birds' eggs. By 9 a.m. the next day they were setting sail once more.

We have seen the expedition island-hopping all the way from Chatham Dockyard to Campbell Island; now they were poised to sail into a virtually unknown part of the globe and trust in the wind and God as to what they would find and whether they would return safely.

A short quote from Ross's book sets the scene as he saw it:

> The fifteen months which had elapsed since we took our departure from England had in no degree diminished our eagerness for the southern voyage: and now that we had at length the prospect before us of entering upon those labours from which we all hoped the most remarkable and important results of our voyage might be fairly anticipated, joy and satisfaction beamed in every face; and although I could not but look forward with much anxiety of mind to the issue of our exertions, yet this was greatly diminished by the assurance that we were in possession of the best of human means to accomplish our purposes.

Monday 21 December, midsummer day in the southern hemisphere – and a daytime temperature of just 40°F (4.4°C) was recorded. Even the sea temperature was a degree or two higher than that. A couple of days later the sea temperature had dropped several degrees and with it a northerly[17] drift of about 10 miles a day was detected. It was this current that was bringing about the changes they were experiencing. Several sightings of penguins led them to think they were approaching land, and due to the squally weather and restricted visibility Ross ordered the ships to be hove to so that Christmas Day could be celebrated without the fear of sailing head-on into an iceberg or running aground on an uncharted shoal or reef.

Ross and Crozier had decided before leaving Hobart that they would try and follow 170°E as they headed south. They knew that the French and Americans had already taken their previously preferred route and not really achieved much in the way of establishing the coastline of the southern continent. The fact that both of those expeditions had had problems with the pack ice meant that if this expedition headed in the same direction they would probably have the same problems.

Two days after Christmas they encountered such violent weather that the seas crashing onto *Terror's* decks did a considerable amount of damage to two of her boats, and she was battened down until the sea moderated. On the 28th they sighted the first of many of the large tabular icebergs that they were to meet over the forthcoming months. Snow showers made it uncomfortable to work the ship – and, worse, the seawater temperature had now dropped below freezing so any waves that washed aboard tended to freeze on the decks and rigging; then, as now, the ice on the rigging in particular needed to be removed as rapidly as possible, as its weight at height would unbalance the ship and create a serious risk of capsize. Whales were numerous and Ross comments that they were so tame that he could have run the ship alongside and killed them. In one of his reports when the expedition returned home, he publicised this fact and within only a few years the wholesale slaughter of the southern whale population was in full swing.

On New Year's Eve *Erebus* and *Terror* intersected the path of the famous Russian explorer Fabian Thaddeus von Bellingshausen's circumnavigation of the Antarctic 20 years earlier. Bellingshausen had sailed from Russia in 1819 with two ships, *Vostok* and *Mirny*, and like Cook before him had sighted South Georgia but had never really come close enough to the actual continental landmass to substantiate his claim of being the first to see the fabled icy continent. Then in January 1820 Edward Bransfield landed on the South Shetland Islands after which he claimed to have sighted land at what is now Trinity Peninsula, the northernmost point of the Antarctic mainland. The Americans under Wilkes, too, claimed to have seen continental land, but this was disputed, Even today the identity of the true discoverer of the Antarctic mainland is still in dispute.

New Year's Day saw the issue of more winter clothing and footwear to the crews of both ships, and they celebrated the day with an additional ration of food and by splicing the mainbrace. The sea was littered with pack ice and broken fragments from the now more numerous icebergs; this ice was encountered at a much lower latitude than they had expected, so hopefully this was not a portent of a bad ice year. Ross and Crozier and some of the other officers were, however, very experienced in sailing in these conditions, and the ships had been

---

17 Whereas winds are described in terms of the direction they have come *from*, ocean currents are described in the direction they are going *to*, so a northerly drift would be flowing northwards.

strengthened for just this eventuality, so at this stage no serious concerns were voiced in the narratives about the journey.

There would of course be quite a number of men to whom this ice experience would be their first, especially when icebergs were sighted. McCormick records that he had his first view of the snow petrel, *Procellaria nivea*, associated with the early indication that ice floes were nearby. This is a striking bird with an all-white plumage highlighted by its black eyes and black bill. McCormick was so keen to secure a sample of this bird that he took his gun up on deck with him and waited for one of them to fly to windward near the top of the mast, where it would hopefully finish up on the deck after he had shot it; after several attempts he secured a couple of samples.

It was at about this time that the expedition crossed the Antarctic Circle, and from now on a lookout was posted in the newly installed crow's nest. The officer of the watch would frequently climb up to assess the ice situation, and even the two captains were not averse to doing the same. An iceblink[18] was seen; this was their sign to prepare for the next stage of the expedition. As they approached the pack ice, they sailed along its fringes for a couple of days; Ross was waiting for a north wind before he gave the order to enter the ice. They didn't have to wait long before a shout from the crow's nest indicated that pools of open water connected by open leads to the south were visible. Caution would be necessary at this early stage; if the leads looked like closing up the ships would withdraw and wait for a more opportune moment.

Progress was spasmodic mostly due to the wind dropping when the floes tended to close up, making it difficult to make headway. In fact, the only incident worth recording during

'An Iceberg in Polar Seas', a painting by Keith Shackleton.

---

18 An atmospheric phenomenon: a bright white light, often reflected off low cloud, indicating the presence of an ice field out of direct sight.

this lull was a member of *Terror*'s crew who received an unexpected dunking when he slipped overboard whilst the cutter that had ferried Crozier across to *Erebus* was being hoisted back on board. The crewman was soon restored to the ship, very cold and very wet, but lived to tell the tale even though he couldn't swim. To the members of the two crews who had never before seen floating ice in such quantities it must have presented a daunting sight, especially when the ships were being buffeted by the pack. The noise below decks would have been truly awesome, and would have left crew members wondering if one of these collisions would prove terminal.

Of course, it wasn't just the ice that impressed the crews: whales moved sedately along the leads and into the open pools, and seals and penguins could be observed, seemingly uninterested in the approach of the ships. Icebergs provided additional interest, and when one was seen to have something embedded in it, Ross despatched one of his boats to bring back a sample. On examination the true significance of the find, rocks and soil, could mean only one thing: somewhere to the south lay land, the undiscovered continent they were looking for.

Now that the Antarctic Circle had been crossed, and given the fact that it was the middle of the southern summer, they could expect to have 24 hours of daylight every day. As the sun approached the horizon towards midnight it brought about some magical effects on the clouds and the pack ice, presenting a magnificent range of colours in such contrast to the whiteness of the pack as it extended towards the distant horizon.

Less than a week after the ships had entered the pack ice a strong breeze brought them into open water, and once the snow – which had been falling for several hours – let up, it was apparent that to the south the sea was clear of ice. They were through the pack in what was probably the quickest ever passage until the advent of ice-breakers over 100 years later. Ross set their course towards what he had been advised would be the South Magnetic Pole.

But after the interlude of drifting in the ice without much happening came a dramatic change in their fortunes. The two ships broke out into an area free of ice, and on 9 January 1841 they made an impressive 30 miles of southing. They appeared to have breached the Antarctic's defences and were now in clear water as far as the eye could see. Two days later, still sailing on a southerly course, at just before 4 a.m. the lookout reported land ahead. Even at this early hour there was a mad scramble topside for everyone to get their first glimpse of this unknown territory. There having been a false call earlier that land was visible, there was some scepticism that this might be a similar one, but as the early morning mist cleared even the most sceptical man became convinced of the reality of the situation.

Slowly but surely the level horizon that they had become so used to became broken up by the snow-covered tops of a range of mountains in the distance. Now began in earnest the discovery and naming of all the geographical features revealed to the expedition. This range of mountains, seen for the first time on 11 January 1841, they called the Admiralty Range.

The highest peak they could see at the time was named Mount Sabine, after Lieutenant-Colonel Edward Sabine, who had been with Ross during one of his earliest journeys with his uncle, John Ross. They had known one another ever since that expedition, which had taken place in 1818, and had been in regular contact ever since. Sabine was an expert in the study of

The hut at Cape Adare was built in 1899 for the Borchgrevink expedition. This was the first expedition hut ever built on the Antarctic mainland.

magnetism and pendulum experiments, and had attained one of the most senior positions in the Royal Society. Mount Sabine was estimated at just under 10,000 feet but when measured many years later it turned out to be over 12,000 feet, making it the fourth-highest in the Admiralty Range.

At this stage I am not going to repeat all the names bestowed by Ross and Crozier except one, and that is Cape Adare. It was here in 1899 that the very first expeditionary party ever spent a winter on the Antarctic mainland. It was led by a Norwegian, Carsten Borchgrevink; he took his ship, *Southern Cross*, down to Cape Adare with a multinational team and there built two huts which, following recent restoration, can still be visited. The expedition was funded by a Victorian magazine publisher, Sir George Newnes. Cape Adare was named after one of Ross's friends, Viscount Adare, member of Parliament for Glamorgan. It not only hosted the first Antarctic land expedition but its other claim to fame took place in 1895 when the same Carsten Borchgrevink had been a member of a sealing voyage that touched at the cape and some of the crew, including Borchgrevink, landed on the mainland. Although this was the first landing actually recorded, it is possible that others might have happened but had gone unnoticed and, more importantly, unrecorded.

Ross was ever hopeful of reaching the South Magnetic Pole, but as they ventured further south little by little, his magnetic readings showed that the sought-for spot would be in the icy wastes, hence inaccessible to him by ship. At this stage, however, he still had hopes of mounting a land search should the opportunity arise.

Disappointed as Ross must have been, he did not lose sight of the other most important aim of the expedition, notably the discovery of new land and the declaration of sovereignty over it. In this instance, however, he would have to be satisfied with his first landing taking place on an island, as the mainland coast in this vicinity was icebound, and the seas crashing against the ice foot precluded any chance of a landing.

Each ship sent a party ashore on the first island they reached; amongst the boats' complements were the two captains and several other officers, one of whom was McCormick. The island was named, appropriately, Possession Island. The ceremony was kept as short and simple as possible; it consisted of planting a union flag on a staff, reading a short dedication, recording the date as 12 January 1841 and toasting the health of Her Majesty the Queen, whose name, Victoria Land, still defines the vast territory that Ross claimed for the British Empire. Apart from the men who had come over in the two boats the ceremony was witnessed by the thousands of penguins whose colony the explorers had entered.

Lieutenant Bird had been left in charge of *Erebus* and, having been under strict instructions to raise a signal flag should he believe that sea conditions were deteriorating to the point where a recall would be necessary, he did this. Those ashore, on seeing the signal, hurriedly concluded the ceremony, scrambling back into their boats for a rather turbulent row back to their ships. Soon after they had been picked up by their respective ships the weather deteriorated to such an extent that the island they had secured for their country was lost to view. Their exodus had been accomplished none too soon.

For the next two days the weather kept the continent shrouded in secrecy, almost as if its revelation on the 12th had been an embarrassment that it now wished to keep secret. The murky weather withdrew, however, on the 15th to once more reveal in its stunning raw beauty the full splendour of the coastline. Several of the officers with artistic skills were seen sketching the magnificent scenes revealed as the ships continued to sail southwards, hoping to find another landing place.

Between the mighty peaks, tantalising glimpses could be obtained of huge glaciers making their way towards the sea, and from time to time came the mighty explosive sounds of large portions of them breaking away and tumbling into the sea, creating huge waves that surged outwards into what a few minutes before had been

Possession Island. In January 1841 the Ross expedition landed here and claimed the whole segment of Antarctica for Great Britain, naming it Victoria Land after the Queen.

a placid, flat, glimmering surface, mirroring the magnificent backdrop of the mountain range.

The expedition, now experiencing daylight for the full 24 hours, had achieved their furthest latitude south thus far, at nearly 72°S. Ross, ever mindful of his commitments to the scientific policy of the venture, needed to secure for the ships a suitable anchorage for the next term day, on the 20th of the month. On 15 and 16 January the efforts to locate a suitable station were frustrated by a stiff wind that forced the ships back northwards about 25 miles, leaving them an estimated 90 miles from the coast. Refraction brought new land into view but played tricks with them by the land seeming to recede from sight before returning once more to tantalise them with its mystic presence. It was on 17 January that an island they eventually christened Coulman Island after Ross's future father-in-law, Thomas Coulman, appeared in the form of a mirage, and as the ships approached the image floating in the sky, the island itself finally became reality. But as there was never going to be a chance now of securing another landing, this magnetic experiment was not achieved. There would be other term days.

Proceeding further south, the two ships reached a new record of 74°23'S on 23 January, breaking the record set in 1823 by James Weddell, a sealing captain working for the Enderby Brothers. He had crossed the Antarctic Circle on the other side of the continent and in a particularly ice-free year had pushed his little sealing ship *Jane*, accompanied by a consort, *Brisbane*, into what we now call the Weddell Sea. They had reached 74°15'S before turning back. Weddell, in deference to King George IV, had named the sea after him, and in about 1900 its name was changed to commemorate Weddell.

Four days later the two captains were taken in their respective boats towards another island to try and effect a landing. Ross transferred to *Terror*'s whaleboat and with Crozier managed to leap from the boat to the rocky shore. This was not without risk, but several other men succeeded in reaching the land with the help of a rope thrown back by Ross to the boat. There was one casualty who finished up getting a serious ducking; the unlucky fellow turned out to be Hooker. Luckily for him the men still in the boat soon hauled him out, but he was miserably cold until the boat returned to the ship.

It was the tradition set up many years previously of naming geographical features and Ross could not resist calling this latest discovery after his dear friend Sir John Franklin. They had now sailed to a position just short of the 76th S and by Ross's estimate were about 200 miles from the South magnetic Pole. The dip of the compass needle had reached its most acute angle giving a reading of 80° 33'.

Following the unfortunate incident involving Joseph Hooker or perhaps because of it, Captain Ross issued an order that neither ship should be without its surgeon until further notice. Robert McCormick, the man this would affect most, because he was surgeon on the *Erebus*, was quick to air his thoughts privately on the restriction to Ross, but notwithstanding his remonstrations the order stood. McCormick's diary, that later became the basis of his book, notes the disappointment and frustration that this restraining order had on him. He was, of course, one of the most enthusiastic of the officers to take advantage of any opportunity of going ashore and exploring.

8 AMAZING DISCOVERIES AND WONDERS TO BEHOLD

GEOGRAPHY AND EXPLORATION AT THEIR VERY BEST

On 27 January 1841, with the ships proceeding in a southerly direction, higher land was taking shape ahead. Imagine their utter surprise when, as they closed with this new discovery, they realised how the clear air of the region could be so deceptive of distances and heights. The image that grew before them became a reality; a fully formed conical mountain many thousands of feet high and discharging what at first sight was thought to be snow blowing off its summit but which then turned orange by emitting flame mixed with smoke, revealing itself to the astonished observers as a live volcano.

A twin mountain set behind the first but without signs of volcanic activity brought their day to a magnificent climax. Eventually it became clear (erroneously) that neither of the new mountains were part of an island as had at first been thought, but were part of the mainland.[19] Despite a search, however, no way could be found to gain a foothold on this huge yet elusive land.

Ross described the scene in Volume I of his book:

> With a favourable breeze, and very clear weather, we stood to the southward, close to some land which had been in sight since the preceding noon, and which we then called "High Island"; it proved to be a mountain twelve thousand four hundred feet in elevation above the level of the sea, emitting flame and smoke

---

19 The reverse is actually true: Mounts Erebus and Terror and two smaller volcanoes are in fact on what is now called Ross Island, which is joined to the mainland by an ice bridge, giving the island the erroneous effect of being part of the mainland.

in great profusion; at first the smoke appeared like snow drift, but as we drew nearer, its true character became manifest.

The discovery of an active volcano in so high a southern latitude cannot but be esteemed a circumstance of high geological importance and interest, and contribute to throw some further light on the physical construction of our globe. I named it "Mount Erebus," and an extinct volcano to the eastward, little inferior in height, being by measurement ten thousand nine hundred feet high was called "Mount Terror".

Having studied the two volcanoes and the area around them from the ships – a landing was out of the question – they turned their attention to sailing east-south-east, taking advantage of a north-westerly breeze. Their attention was soon drawn to what appeared at first sight to be a massive wall of frozen cliffs. This geographical phenomenon had no known equivalent anywhere in the world at that time, and as they progressed along it speculation was rife as to what would have caused it. The height was estimated as being from 150 to over 200 feet, so it was impossible to see across the top of it from even the highest point on the mainmast. The numerous ice blocks floating close to the foot of the icy cliff made a landing here too dangerous to contemplate. Just a few miles out, where the ships were holding their station, the seabed was found to be over 400 fathoms, so it appeared to Ross that this massive wall must be afloat and therefore consisted of ice alone. They moved closer to the wall for a more detailed inspection but the wind changed, forcing them to move further out to sea for their own safety.

By following the ice wall, they found they were still making a track taking them further and further south, and on the last day of January measured their latitude at 77°6'S. They had now traversed the face of this enormous ice feature for over 100 miles, and still it extended out of sight. It is difficult to imagine what the impact this mammoth ice wall must have had on the crews of both ships, along with all the other natural wonders they had so dramatically come across in the relatively short few weeks since leaving Hobart.

They had set sail from Campbell Island on 17 December 1840, and two weeks later had encountered the fringes of the pack ice. It had taken them just a few days to

The two expedition ships with the Ross ice shelf in the background, painted by J.E. Davis, the second master aboard HMS Terror.

break through that, and within another day or so the officer of the watch had called out 'Land-ho!'

When Scott sailed south in 1910, starting out from New Zealand, his first call was to have been Campbell Island – but on arriving there on the evening of 2 December, too late to land, he decided to keep going rather than wait for daylight, which would have lost him some precious time. The ship he was using for this, his second expedition, was *Terra Nova*, and under sail and steam if required she could cover an impressive 180–200 miles a day, at least twice the distance Ross and Crozier could have normally hoped for under sail. Scott then reached the pack ice in just seven days' sailing from Campbell Island, compared to thirteen days for *Erebus* and *Terror*. Now, to illustrate how pack ice conditions can affect an expedition we have only to see how quickly Ross with sail power alone broke through the barrier. He took five days, yet Scott with the ability to manoeuvre using his engine and also to drive against the consolidated pack to break through, took twenty-two – over four times as long.

Scott followed the 177°E line of longitude, which was nearly the mid-point of the Ross Sea. Ross, however, with virtually no knowledge of what was ahead of him, followed 170°E longitude, which brought him out into the sea – later to be called the Ross Sea – very close to Cape Adare. From the sea the enormous front of the ice barrier displayed a flat, even top, so now Ross and his Arctic veterans, used to the irregular-shaped icebergs that calved from the glaciers in Greenland, could understand why the icebergs they had recently seen had a tabular profile.

Snow showers and fog kept the two crews alert, and every quarter of an hour they would fire several muskets to check that they had not become separated. The cannon they carried could also be used should musket fire fail. At night-time a blue light was often displayed at the masthead as another means of communication.

After the fog cleared they found they were still in front of the barrier and had now travelled a total of 250 miles along its face since leaving Cape Crozier near Mount Erebus. The furthest south they reached was 78°S.

Ross was now acutely aware that the sea was starting to freeze over and he was anxious to establish the extent of the ice barrier before retreating from the imminent danger of being confined for the winter. The temperature was dropping every day, and the loose ice at the foot of the barrier was starting to coalesce into a single solid sheet. The date was now 11 February and they had been in the Ross Sea for nearly five weeks. These weeks had been effectively one long day due to the 24 hours of daylight. But Ross, knowing he would

Dr Alexander Mackay, Prof Edgeworth David and Douglas Mawson, the first men to reach the South Magnetic Pole, during the Nimrod expedition led by Ernest Shackleton.

in all probability return the next season, wanted to maximise his exploration this year, thus allowing time next year to extend his knowledge of the vast area they had so far only touched upon.

So the decision was made to set off back along the barrier for one last attempt at the magnetic pole, to which Ross had attached so much importance. Although he did not want to get frozen in, as the winter storms could prove fatal to his ships, there seems to have been a thought at the back of his mind that should a suitable harbour be found he had sufficient stores to anchor the ships in a safe haven and stay for the winter. This might give him and a selected team the opportunity of repeating his exploit when trapped in the ice during his uncle's expedition to Prince Regent Inlet a decade earlier: you will remember that he and several colleagues had sledged to the North Magnetic Pole.

By 17 February they were once more abreast of Mount Erebus which was excelling itself with a magnificent display of unbridled power; the flames and fumes discharged were rising even higher than on their earlier visit. During Shackleton's 1908 expedition the first successful attempt to climb it was made, but even then its height was not accurately measured. Ross had estimated it at 12,400 feet and that turned out to be a very good approximation; the peak is actually just 48 feet higher. The volcano is still active today but not to quite the same degree it appears to have been in Ross's time.

It was during this visit to the environs of Mount Erebus that the bay was discovered that would become the centre of most of the activity associated with the modern-day exploration of the Antarctic continent: McMurdo Bay, now known as McMurdo Sound. The supplies for the USA and New Zealand bases are taken there, and in the case of the USA these supplies are then flown inland to the Scott Amundsen Base at the South Pole.

McMurdo Sound, named after Lieutenant Archibald McMurdo of HMS Terror, *is now the site of the New Zealand and United States of America Antarctic bases.*

A recent photograph of Mount Herschel, named after the famous scientist Sir John Herschel.

The list of place names left behind on the earliest maps of the newly discovered coast of Victoria Land are testimony to the dedication of the officers that accompanied Ross. He also recognised thus many notable personages who had been instrumental in promoting the enterprise that he had the privilege of leading, and many of the capes, bays and other prominent features carry their names to this day. The main geographical features can be divided into four categories: mountains, capes, islands and bays; 180 years later most of those that were named still exist, a reflection on the accuracy of the surveying that led to those first charts being drawn up.

The prominent peaks of the Admiralty Range were soon christened. Ross had many important and influential friends back in Britain and as the new peaks came into view, he set about bestowing names on them. The Earl of Minto, Sir William Parker, Lord Dalmeny, Sir Edward Trowbridge and Sir Charles Adam were prominent members of the Admiralty. Sir David Brewster and Sir John Herschel were leading scientists of the day. The Royal Society, the Royal Geographical Society and the British Association were represented by the likes of their presidents, secretaries and chairmen, notably Sir John Lubbock, Sir Roderick Murchison, the Marquess of Northampton, Professor John Phillips and, as mentioned earlier, Sir Edward Sabine. Academics and politicians would also be honoured by their names appearing on the map as the ships progressed further and further south.

Capes and bays were predominantly attributed to the officers on the expedition. Lieutenant Bird, one of Ross's closest advisers on the trip and probably the one he had sailed with the most, gave his name to Cape Bird, the northernmost tip of Ross Island. Another prominent cape on Ross Island was named after Ross's second in command, Captain Francis Crozier. It featured dramatically in Cherry-Garrard's book *The Worst Journey in the World*, in which he recalled the story of untold agony and suffering as he, with Edward Wilson and Birdie Bowers of Scott's second expedition, spent some five weeks trekking to this cape to bring back some unhatched emperor penguin eggs, an enterprise intended to prove or disprove a theory that the embryos would reveal a secret connection to dinosaurs. Only Cherry-Garrard would live to find the answer; his two companions perished with Scott on the return journey from the South Pole.

Ross's expedition paved the way for most of the Golden Age explorers to find the shortest route to the Pole over 60 years later. Of Ross's two other lieutenants, John Sibbald had a cape named after him and James Wood's name was added to a bay. Joseph Hooker can be remembered by a cape along the coast of Victoria Land, and his superior, Robert McCormick, saw his name appended to the cape at the extreme end of the Adare peninsula; this had originally thought to be an island in its own right but this misapprehension was corrected by later explorers when they realised it formed part of the peninsula. Cape Hallett, after Thomas Hallett the purser, is located at the foot of Mount Sabine. It became the site of an International Geophysical Year base staffed by a New Zealand scientific party in 1957. Ross's three mates, Alexander Smith, Henry Oakley and Joseph Dayman, contributed their names to an inlet, a cape at the entrance to Smith Inlet and a further cape at the entrance to Yule Bay; Henry Yule was the second master aboard HMS *Erebus*.

Terror's officers' names, too adorned the charts brought home, and most are retained to this day. We have already mentioned Crozier and his first lieutenant, McMurdo. Charles Phillips has a cape named after him along the coast of Victoria Land, and Joseph Kay – he who stayed behind in Hobart to maintain the observatory there – can see his name attributed to a group of three small islets in Wood Bay (subsequently found to be just one island but retaining his name). Cape Cotter was named after the master of *Terror*, Pownall P. Cotter. Later explorers could not locate this cape but designated his name to the seacliffs of Cape Hallett. Robertson Bay and the Lyall Islands were named in recognition of the services provided by the surgeon, John Robertson, and his assistant, David Lyall. George Moubray had his name attached to a cape that still bears his name today; it can be found along the coast of Victoria Land near Cape Hallett.

By the time the expedition reached Antarctica only two of *Terror*'s original three mates were still aboard, Peter Scott having remained in Hobart to assist with running the observatory, but even so he was not left out, having Cape Scott named after him; of the other two mates, Thomas Moore transferred his name to Cape Moore which, together with Cape Oakley, formed the entrance to Smith Inlet. John Davis, the gifted artist of the expedition and the second master of *Terror*, had his name placed on the map to mark what Ross thought was a cape – but this proved to be an error and his name was given to an ice piedmont[20] that juts out from Victoria Land into the Ross Sea.

From the point of view of this book we now have a clear picture of how generous Ross was in distributing along the length and breadth of the newly discovered land the names both of his officers and of well-connected people back home.

---

20 A flattish area, covered in ice, lying at the foot of a mountain or a range.

9 TURNING NORTH

RETREAT FROM ANTARCTICA

Ross and Crozier carried out some lengthy discussions as to their next move, and the decision made was to call a halt to this season's exploration and return to warmer waters and safety. Already the new ice had reached a thickness of many inches and it was with great difficulty that the ships could be forced through it to reach the more open water several miles away: they had to resort to putting a couple of boats over the side and from these use ice saws to clear a path. With this method some progress was made, and by the next morning the ships were once more on their way, their men taking with them the memory of a spectacular series of visions that would have been difficult for any of them to have imagined just seven short weeks earlier.

Thursday 18 February saw the sun dip below the horizon for the first time in nearly two months. The Moon was at its fullest and the ice was starting its winter cycle when the sea's surface was taking on an oily look and the first vestiges of pancake ice were forming. It was time to sail north and seek out warmer climes.

The two ships sailed back along the coastline they had followed as they had entered the Ross Sea, and now, with a fair breeze to chase them, they logged a speed of 8 knots, in the space of four days covering over 400 miles. As they progressed further along this northerly track the sun set earlier every day so that as they reached latitude 70°S it dipped below the horizon as early as 9 p.m. During the whole of this retreat they could see numerous icebergs, some of them grounded but others drifting north, and it was these that they had to be wary of so, as the evening gloom deepened the ships would be hove to and lookouts posted to make sure they would be safe for the night. Despite the fact that there was now some urgency to withdraw from this region Ross could not refrain from searching the coastline, looking for any opportunity of making the landing that had eluded them since their brief stop at Possession Island.

Finally, on 26 February Ross and Crozier abandoned their search for a landing place and the ships' prows were turned to the north-west. They still had to find a way through the collar of sea ice that was a permanent feature of the Ross Sea. All they could hope for now was that it would release them as easily as it had let them enter this magical domain.

The crews had had a very hard time because of the wet conditions they were working in. This together with the damp quarters that was their lot made it exceedingly difficult for them to get warm and even to dry their clothes. The lower temperature brought an additional burden for them to bear. Any topside work usually had to be carried out in freezing weather that turned their clothes into something resembling boards.

On reaching the ice, evasive action had to be taken because the recent cold snap had consolidated the floes and was going to prove very difficult to penetrate. Now that the nights were upon them, they were at least treated to some magnificent displays of the Aurora Australis, and there was an abundance of whales which seemed to like being close to the pack ice.

The sighting of land on 4 March and the chance to investigate it at closer quarters was, as always, a tempting prospect which was duly carried out. Ross suspected it would probably be a small group of islands named in 1839 after John Balleny, a sealing captain, another of the commanders that Enderby employed to search for new sealing grounds and carry out exploration at the same time. During Balleny's voyage he not only charted the islands that Ross had now come across but it is believed he probably saw the distant mainland coast. Today the islands retain his name, and the coast he saw is called Sabrina Land after the consort that was keeping his ship, *Eliza Scott*, company. Balleny had spent about four days venturing as close to the coast as he could get to achieve a landing, but in the end he had to make do with Captain Freeman from *Sabrina* jumping into the icy sea up to his waist and scooping up a handful of stones to bring back as evidence of their having made a landfall.

D'Urville and Wilkes, too, had passed along this section of the ocean and both make references to sighting land. When Ross wrote his book about the expedition he went to great lengths to give Biscoe's[21] and Balleny's names priority when it came to who actually saw and visited this area first. Balleny had returned to England shortly before Ross and Crozier set sail, and had kindly given them a copy of his log.

Before Ross and Crozier saw these islands, they had faced some very rough weather and both ships needed a respite to carry out some urgent repairs. *Erebus* had crashed into some large floes and this had ripped away her dolphin striker, the main support for her bowsprit. *Terror* had suffered similar damage, resulting in the loss of her bobstay and bowsprit shrouds. To carry out these repairs men had to be lowered over the bows in slings to remove and replace the damaged parts. As the ships pitched in the swell these men, very exposed, were frequently near-submerged in the freezing water.

Once the repairs had been concluded they directed their course to the north-east, crossing to the north of the Antarctic Circle for the first time in over 60 days. They were now looking

---

21 John Biscoe had also sailed these waters between 1830 and 1833 working for Samuel Enderby, a whaling company which combined exploring with the whaling.

A recent photograph of Balleny Islands, seen by the expedition as they headed towards Tasmania and safety at the end of the first summer of exploring to the farthest south ever known to be achieved.

out for some land that had been marked on a chart given to Ross by Charles Wilkes before the expedition left Hobart. As they neared the land's supposed location, and with darkness becoming a major factor during their search, they were constantly vigilant for fear of being driven onto a lee shore.

However, having carried out a detailed search of the location on Wilkes's chart it became apparent that a mistake must have been made because no sign of land could be found there. It was this sort of inaccuracy that frustrated Ross to the extent that once back in England he took up the issue with Wilkes in an extensive correspondence, backing up his assertions with the numerous soundings he had taken with a 600-fathom line, which had revealed no bottom.

On 7 March they were driven into an embayment in the pack ice from which they had great difficulty in extracting themselves. From the masthead they could count over 80 icebergs of considerable size together with innumerable smaller ones, and an easterly swell was driving them ever closer to this dangerous area. The wind that could have assisted them to clear the danger had fallen away and the ships were now in a situation that could threaten their very survival. As they drifted closer, the sound of the surf crashing against the ice came to their ears and the narrative in Ross's book reads like an extract from some biblical volume, where he unashamedly calls on the Good Lord to come to their aid.

Erebus and *Terror* *battling with the storm and ice, seeking a way out of the Ross Sea as they headed north back to Tasmania. Painted by John Wilson Carmichael.*

> We called upon the Lord, and he heard our voices out of His temple, and our cry came before Him. A gentle air of wind filled our sails; hope again revived, and the greatest activity prevailed to make the best use of the feeble breeze.

By 21 March it would appear that apart from deep sea soundings and the taking of the temperatures at varying levels in the ocean most of the exploratory work for this season was complete.

Thursday 1 April saw them plunging through the ever-turbulent waters around Antarctica on their way back to Tasmania for a well-earned rest. It must have been almost impossible for the three scribes, Ross, McCormick and Cunningham, to convey in simple words what they and the other members of the ships' crews would have felt on seeing and experiencing what they had been so privileged to have been through.

At long last, after nearly six months had elapsed, they entered the Derwent estuary, taking on the pilot the next morning to guide them into the safe waters from whence they had started half a year earlier. Sir John Franklin was soon welcomed aboard, and he was rewarded with three cheers from both crews mustered for the occasion.

The crew were given some freedom from the restrictions that life on board ship for the previous six months had imposed upon them, and it would appear that they took full advantage of the opportunity offered. As usual, every sailor going ashore after time spent at sea would be given some money, to be booked against their accounts and paid out in coinage in the currency of the relevant country; a ship calling at many foreign ports would therefore need to have available a comprehensive assortment of coinage to suit the countries being visited. In Tasmania, though, of course, the men could enjoy spending good old British pounds, shillings and pence. Finally released from their confinement, the sailors made straight for the alehouses, resulting in quite a few of them ending up in the cells of the local police station to cool their heels after what turned into a drink-inspired near-riot through the streets of Hobart.

The officers, meanwhile, were wined and dined in military messes and at Government House. To return this hospitality Ross and Crozier arranged for their ships to be moored alongside one another and dressed overall. A gangway was constructed to the shore and *Erebus*'s deck was turned into the ballroom while the adjacent *Terror* became the dining area, with food and drinks served by crew members dressed for the occasion. The success of this dignified yet enjoyable party became the talk of Hobart society for many months; the local paper reported that over 300 visitors had attended the ball.

No sooner were the formalities of paying respects to friends and dignitaries over than McCormick, now released from the restrictions about leaving the ship following the Hooker incident when he slipped into the water getting ashore on Franklin Island, took his leave and recommenced his personal exploration of the island. He had arranged with his friend Gregson to be included in a shooting party at this gentleman's property, and stayed on for dinner.

On several occasions he stayed with the Gregsons overnight as well, but a few days before the date set for the ships to leave for Sydney he was woken early in the morning by a noise near the open window. Looking towards it he discerned the outline of a man attempting to climb into his room from the veranda that ran along that side of the bungalow. The man needed to force the window open a little more and taking his opportunity to detain the intruder McCormick slipped out of bed and made his move – but the man must have seen the movement for the next moment he was fleeing across the lawn. McCormick squeezed through the opening and, dressed only in his nightshirt, set off in pursuit, armed with a piece of iron from a carriage crosspiece that had been propped against the wall outside. When he challenged the would-be burglar as if it was a gun he held, the intruder took to his heels and was well out of reach before he could be apprehended.

At about this time in Tasmania and Australia there were a number of escaped convicts, known as bushrangers, living in the bush to evade capture. Their livelihood came from robbing travellers, burgling houses and even raiding banks, so there were many similarities to the Wild West outlaws that plagued America during the middle to end of the 19th century. This threat to Australian society lasted for many years and only declined with the advent of better policing and the telegraph, enabling the authorities to exchange information more quickly and act on it. Probably the most notorious of the bushrangers was Ned Kelly; his capture and execution in 1888 virtually brought to an end the era of the bushranger.

After the successful evening on the two ships it was business as usual for the crews and their officers. All the trappings of the night-time revelries were taken down, and *Terror* was once more anchored a short distance away from *Erebus*.

As the time drew near to resume the expedition, the ships received a thorough overhaul. Ross comments that both vessels had come through their recent ordeal with very little damage.

All their stores had been moved into a warehouse provided by Franklin as a temporary store, allowing the ships to ride higher in the water and reveal more of their hulls for inspection. Some copper sheathing needed replacing, and the caulking was checked and replaced where it could be accessed. The extra layers of timber that had been secured to the original planks inside and out when the ships had been prepared in Chatham Dockyard precluded a complete appraisal of any damage. Nevertheless, the fact that no serious leaks had occurred was a good indication that the hulls had withstood the onslaught of the ice and should be more than adequate to engage with the polar seas once more.

As the stores were reloaded an inventory was drawn up and shortfalls were made good. There was of course a fresh supply of water, and some livestock to keep the crews in fresh food for a period. And of course there were the stocks of canned goods.

What was not known at the time was the potential for this method of food storage to poison the people consuming the content of the cans. This only came to light over a century later, following some extensive research carried out by an anthropologist, Dr Owen Beattie, and his journalist colleague, John Geiger, between 1981 and 1986. Their best-seller, *Frozen in Time*, tells the story of their investigations.

They had secured permission to carry out autopsies on the bodies of three members of Sir John Franklin's lost expedition; the men in question had died on Beechey Island in the far north of Canada, and their gravestones show that they had been interred whilst the expedition had been camping on this island for its first winter, 1845/1846.

In 1984 the first body was exhumed. Pickaxes were used to break through the frozen gravel and sand covering the coffin. Once the coffin lid, made of mahogany, had been removed, the slow and delicate operation, employing warm water to release the body, could begin. The sailor's headstone revealed him to be John Torrington, just 20 years old. The visual inspection and autopsy, carried out with great care, revealed that he had been extremely emaciated, weighing only about 6 stone (~38 kg), when he died. Samples of his internal organs were removed and stored in sealed containers for later examination, as were hair and nail clippings.

When the expedition returned to Beechey Island in 1986 they exhumed the two men buried adjacent to Torrington, employing the same procedure. It was expected that scurvy would have played a major role in the men's demise, but the researchers were looking for another, more significant, reason. After all the tests had been completed, and additional factors had come to light from other human remains found on King William Island (where the remainder of the expedition had finally come to grief), scurvy was found to have definitely been a contributory cause to the demise of the expedition members, but Dr Beattie's findings would bring a whole new slant to the cause of the deaths. He detected a level of lead above normal in the bodies, and this evidence was corroborated by an examination of the hundreds of empty meat tins that had been discarded in heaps. The tins had survived the ravages of time well enough to reveal that when they had been sealed the solder, which contained a large proportion of lead, had seeped into the food chamber, and this could well have contaminated the contents.

Lead introduced into the human body, even in relatively small quantities, is a toxic chemical that affects the brain, and the larger the amount absorbed the quicker the deadly poison brings about its devastating results. In addition to the lead detected in the hair and fingernails, symptoms of tuberculosis and pneumonia were revealed in the lungs. The conclusion reached was that the debilitating effects of scurvy had probably started to attack the bodies, encouraging the lead to start its lethal work. The signs of lead poisoning are loss of appetite leading to lethargy, weakness and despair. Those three dead men were all skeletal in appearance, giving credence to the autopsy reports.

This seemed like pretty conclusive evidence of lead poisoning, and publication of the autopsy results caused a considerable amount of speculation as to whether this was in fact the reason why the 129 men had lost their lives. To support the case for lead poisoning another hypothesis was put forward some years after Beattie had completed his report. This directed attention to the ship's plumbing system. In Victorian times lead was used extensively in water pipes and tanks. Both *Erebus* and *Terror* had lead pipes and lead-lined drinking water tanks. In addition, their ovens had been fitted with a device for melting ice to obtain the ship's water supply while they were in the polar regions, and this device contained lead.

Before Sir John Franklin took the two ships to the Arctic in search of the North-west Passage, they had of course been employed in the Antarctic expedition that this book is focusing on. So you might well ask: Why had this problem not become apparent in the Antarctic? The major difference between the Ross expedition and Franklin's was the time the expeditions spent in their respective spheres of operation. Ross never seems to have had a case of scurvy, and if lead poisoning was to have played a part in any health issues that his crews experienced, then maybe the fact that no more than five months was ever spent away from fresh food and a clean water supply could well explain why lead poisoning was not apparent in his crews.

Compare this to Franklin's expedition. By the time of the first deaths they had been at sea for about a year, and it was known that scurvy could gain a hold in that time, especially as the men had been incarcerated aboard the ship for the majority of that period. History is littered with examples of scurvy devastating ships' crews. Many men that did not have the additional hazard of lead poisoning to cope with fell victim to scurvy alone.

During the second stay at Hobart Alexander Smith, the first mate of *Erebus*, had been reunited with his lady love, Sarah Aubrey Read. She was the second daughter of Captain George Read and his first wife, who were comfortably well-off Hobart residents. Smith's romance was not the only dallying that went on, however, and the ships' commanders, both bachelors, were (in the case of one) being pursued, and (the other) actively pursuing. Neither of these potential romances, however, came to anything. Ross was already spoken for by his fiancée back in England, and Crozier was chasing a forlorn hope trying to get the attention of Sophie Cracroft, a niece of Sir John Franklin. Her comments on Crozier were none too complimentary, and the relationship never developed. James Clark Ross, reputed to be the most handsome captain in the Royal Navy, would marry when he returned to England in 1843, but his sojourn at Hobart gave the ladies of the Franklin household a few flutters every

No	Sailor's name	Rank	Deserted or discharged	Departed ship date	Reason for leaving ship
1	Richard Evans	A B	Deserted	16/Sept/39	Discharged at Woolwich
2	Peter Wallace	A B	Deserted	19/Oct/40	Run at Hobarton[22]
3	James Harris	A B	Discharged	23/Sept/43	Completed voyage. Very Good
4	William Beautyman	A B	Deserted	19/Oct/40	Run at Hobarton
5	Samuel John	A B	Discharged	20/Sept/39	Hospitalised before sailing
6	Thomas lee	A B	Discharged	23/Sept/43	Completed voyage. Very Good
7	Thomas Chatworthy	Purser's Steward	Discharged	10/July/39	Discharged to HMS *Gorgon*
8	*Fred* Collins	A B	Deserted	8/Nov/40	Run at Hobarton
9	James Grimes	A B	Discharged	23/Sept/43	Completed voyage. Very good
10	James Wailing	A B	Discharged	23/Sept/43	Completed voyage. Very good
11	George Knight	Blacksmith	Discharged	23/Sept/43	Completed voyage. Very good
12	Isaac D Munday	Gunroom Steward	Discharged	23/Sept/43	Completed voyage. Very good
13	Tilden Taylor	Young gent's Steward	Deserted	9/Feb/40	Run at St Helena
14	Alec Craig	A B	Discharged	23/Sept/43	Completed voyage. Very good
15	William Abernethy	A B	Discharged	23/Sept/43	Completed voyage. Very good
16	Joseph Busbridge	Cook	Discharged	23/Sept/43	Completed voyage. Very good
17	Chas Gregory	AB	Deserted	27/Mar/40	Hospitalised in S Africa
18	Edward Mitchell	A B	Discharged	23/Sept/43	Completed voyage. Very good
19	James Cleat	Quarter Master	Promoted	3/July/41	Completed voyage. Very good
20	William Tyler	A B	Discharged	22/Oct/40	Hospitalised in Hobarton

22 Hobart.

time he relaxed when away from his duties as the ever-efficient captain of *Erebus*. There were probably other liaisons amongst the members of the two crews as they prepared to depart once more on their voyage of discovery, but when it comes to divulging any further details history has her lips sealed.

On the other side of the coin there had been a number of crew members who had deserted or been stood down for medical reasons whilst the ships were at Hobart. During their first visit, in 1840, at least four men had absconded, and in 1841 the same thing happened. A couple of men were recaptured and returned to their ships. One man died, and two more were sent home or to hospital, too ill to continue. Several exchanges of crew members took place to fill the vacancies. In Ross's account of the expedition there is no mention of recruiting new crew members at any of the places where they revictualled the ships, but the muster lists tell the story in full.

The accompanying chart sets out in a more readable form the salient information found in the extract from *Terror*'s muster roll. It can be seen that of the twenty crew members listed in the chart four deserted, three were hospitalised at various points, one had been discharged before the voyage had even started, and one was transferred to HMS *Gorgon*, again before the expedition left Chatham. The remaining eleven completed the voyage, and some even gained promotion. The extract from the muster roll is only a portion of its two-page spread: other information detailed where each sailor hailed from, and his previous ship. A comment of 'Very good' would inform any future commander that the sailor in question came with a recommendation from his current commander.

10 AUSTRALIA AND NEW ZEALAND

ANOTHER FATALITY

The first week of July 1841 saw a raised level of activity aboard the two ships. Everything was being done to get them out to sea once more; the next stop would be Sydney. Another routine of setting up an observatory, taking measurements and yet more social engagements would be accomplished before they could sail away to New Zealand for more scientific work. The ships finally set out from Hobart on 7 July, accompanied by squally showers which moderated to a fine breeze.

Cunningham had spent many social hours with his counterparts ashore in Hobart, and was in a relaxed mood as the ships slipped along, achieving 7 knots with their studding sails set. The seven days it took to reach Sydney seem to have passed off without any major incident, and they were soon entering the entrance to famous Botany Bay. McCormick's first impressions of the approach to the harbour can be summed up in a few words:

> Barren looking cliffs of horizontal sandstone interspersed with low sand hills
> and sandy beaches, a forbidding aspect.

The entrance to the harbour was marked by a lighthouse 300 feet up on a headland, and the harbour itself was found to be a natural inlet with plenty of depth of water, making it a perfect destination. The ships berthed at the government jetty, and a round of socialising began for the officers. The governor of the colony was Sir George Gipps, and in 1840 it was under his governance that the first democratic elections were carried out to determine the way the colony should be run. As with the mother country, it was personal wealth that determined the right to a vote, and some businessmen could have as many as four votes each. Voting was of course for males only, and then only those who could prove possession of personal wealth of at least £1,000; it would be many years before the vote was open to men of all social classes, and even longer for the emancipation of women voters.

The colony had been established in the late 1700s with the arrival of about a dozen ships from England, carrying about 1,000 people. This number included a military detachment to maintain law and order and defend the settlers against any hostilities from the displaced indigenous population, and to control the large penal colony that was going to be set up to accommodate the many criminals that had been sent out with the colonists. These convicts, men and women, would be the backbone of the labour force and would serve at least seven years' indenture before being considered for parole or possible repatriation back to England.

The ships' two commanders soon set about organising the erection of yet another observatory and managed to meet the deadline of 21 July, the next term day.

Hooker took the opportunity of visiting the house and grounds of one of the colony's senior residents, Alexander MacLeay, a former colonial secretary. He had established a botanical garden of some importance with plants obtained from the various countries he had visited during his term in government office, and Hooker was suitably impressed with the care and attention to detail that had been taken in the layout and variety of plants on show. Sydney proved to be one of the wettest places the expedition visited; only four of the 21 days they were stationed there provided a break from the rain. In one 24-hour period the rain gauge measured nearly 9 inches. Despite this abundance of rain, the colony also experienced periods of drought which on several occasions during its 60-year history thus far had brought famine and near-disaster. Such was life for the first settlers of this new colony. In addition, about this time the United Kingdom government stopped sending out convicts, the result of which was that the convict slave labour force gradually became one that had to be remunerated, causing even more financial hardship to the colonists already struggling with the high cost of living in lean times.

Ross did manage at least one outing, when the governor invited him to visit Parramatta, about 15 miles upriver, where an observatory had been established by Sir Thomas Brisbane, a wealthy Scottish-born retired army general and an earlier governor. He had had the wooden building constructed and equipped in about 1820 at his own expense for observations of the then little-known southern sky.

Brisbane, having fought at the Battle of Waterloo, had been recommended for the governorship of the colony by none other than the Duke of Wellington; and James Dunlop, one of the assistants Brisbane had taken out to Australia with him, still ran the observatory. Dunlop was only too pleased to escort his distinguished visitors around the building and show them some of the results. Having travelled up the river by boat to Parramatta, the governor and Ross returned to Sydney by carriage. Ross was not, however, impressed with the condition of the track, which had suffered as a result of the recent rain.

It was getting near to the time of the expedition's departure and there was just time for an experiment to take place involving firing rockets from the observatory at Parramatta and from the observatory just set up at Sydney. By carefully observing the timings of these firings, Ross could work out to a very fine degree the precise latitude of the new Sydney observatory. This

Obelisk and old foundation stones to commemorate the site of the old Parramatta observatory that Ross saw when he visited Sydney in 1842.

would be logged in the maritime tables, to be used as a navigational reference point.

Whilst stationed at Sydney, Cunningham noted at least two ships entering port with immigrants from the United Kingdom. It is difficult for us to imagine how they would get work or where their families would be housed and fed in a colony that had so little infrastructure to cope with such influxes. Hooker had become acutely aware of the great disparity between the well-off and the working classes, how poverty-stricken the latter were, and the hovels that most of them lived in.

The day of departure finally arrived and early in the afternoon of 5 August 1841 the wind picked up sufficiently for the two ships to raise a good spread of sails and ease down the channel to the open sea. Possibly as a result of the desertions that had taken place in Tasmania, there had not been much shore leave given to the two crews.

Erebus now had on board a naval commander, Thomas Sulivan,[23] who had arrived at Sydney just in time to be taken on to New Zealand, where he was to take command of HMS *Favourite* following the death of her previous commander. This leg of their journey would be over 1,000 miles, to the Bay of Islands at the northern end of New Zealand's North Island.

Once again it was *Terror* that held back their progress by having to shorten sail following a more turbulent wind building up. Both ships were heavily laden with their three years' supplies, and *Terror* was finding it difficult to cope with a rising sea and not much freeboard to play with. Despite this handicap they made over 150 miles a day when the wind moderated.

Every ship in the Royal Navy carried spare booms and spars, not to mention sheets and sails and other important items, but after several spars were broken it was very fortunate that in New Zealand they would be able to cut their own timber to make any replacements that would be required before setting off towards Antarctica.

On the nights of 8 and 9 August the men on watch were requested to keep a lookout for shooting stars. None were recorded on the 8th, but on the 9th as many as 15 were seen. One in particular was noted to have a tail: a reward indeed for the observers, both ships' crews having seen the same display.

Water samples were continually being taken at various depths, and graphs and charts were drawn to record the results for later analysis. These tests were now much more successful

---

23 The spelling used by Ross in his book.

Erebus and Terror *in the Bay of Islands in 1842. Painted by John Wilson Carmichael. The original is held by the National Maritime Museum.*

since a set of replacement thermometers had been obtained in Sydney; the new thermometers did not suffer from the breakages that the original ones had been susceptible to. As ever, one of the other tests carried out on the oceans they passed through was to detect any appreciable currents, which were plotted on charts to help later seafarers.

The first sighting of any territory that could be identified as part of New Zealand occurred on 15 August, when a group of rocky reefs came into view. They had been found by a Dutch explorer as early as the middle of the 17th century, and named the Three Kings; today they are a wildlife sanctuary. The same explorer had gone on to discover the North Island of New Zealand.

Erebus, in company with *Terror*, closed with the mainland towards the evening of the 17th, but they were prevented from running into the anchorage by a temperamental wind and darkness coming on. The next morning, although they crossed a sandbar with very little clearance under their keels, they safely dropped anchor in the Bay of Islands. They were welcomed by Captain Aulick from an American corvette, *Yorktown*, at anchor, and just preparing to sail for the Sandwich Islands (now the Hawaiian Islands), so the meeting was short but very amicable. Next, Ross and Crozier sought out the company of a Mr Fitzgerald, who was temporarily stationed nearby. He was shortly to take up the vacant post of chief magistrate and would eventually move to his new residence in Auckland, which was to be the capital of New Zealand for the next 20-odd years.

As with most of the other ports that the ships had called into since leaving England, another series of observations needed to be made, so a suitable construction site had to be found. Ross and Crozier soon located one, and after the landowner's permission had been secured it was now a smooth and practiced operation to take the building ashore and piece it together. The deeds to the land were held by a Church of England missionary society, and from their Mr Williams a little of the history of the area was learnt. New Zealand had been discovered as early as the 17th century by the Dutch exploring further afield from their trading centres in the East Indies, but in 1772 two French ships put into the bay to allow their scurvy-ridden crews time to recuperate. The fate of some 26 of their number and their leader, Captain Marc Joseph Marion de Fresne, was sealed when they were attacked by a formidable force of Māori.

There are at least two versions as to why the massacre took place. The version told to Ross and Crozier at the time of their visit alluded to the French sailors transgressing a Māori taboo placed on them for fishing in a sacred place; on ignoring this warning they were all slaughtered, and their bodies were taken back to the Māori settlement, cooked and devoured. Other information came to light at a later date, indicating that it was not so much the taboo but more the fact that the Māori objected to intrusion onto their land, and they saw this as an opportunity to obtain a quantity of the white man's firearms with which to defend themselves from settlers. This tale convinced the new arrivals that they should be on their guard at all times, so it would have been a busy period for Cunningham and his platoon.

In 1840 the British government signed the Treaty of Waitangi with the chieftains of the Māori tribes in the North Island. In essence the treaty gave the British sovereignty over New Zealand to the exclusion of any other colonial power, such as France or the Netherlands. In addition, any settlers from England could legally buy land from the Māori chiefs. This was intended to stop the indiscriminate land grabs that were taking place and put an obligation on the tribes to respect all legal transactions. Unfortunately, however, the scheme was only a partial success and it soon became apparent to the Māori people that unscrupulous settlers were taking more than they were entitled to. Resentment built up to the point where reprisals started taking place, and deaths on both sides occurred. To defend themselves against the superior weaponry of the colonists the Māori set about raiding homesteads and stealing any guns and ammunition they could find.

The resentment over the problem continued for over 100 years, and it was not until 1970 that a detailed study of the events that had taken place revealed that the primary cause of the conflicts was the differing ways in which the treaty had been interpreted. Since then there has been a very serious attempt by recent governments of New Zealand to rectify some of the errors and give compensation for the wrongs committed nearly 200 years earlier.

Apart from the magnetic observatory and its measurements the other reason for the expedition to visit the Bay of Islands was, as mentioned earlier, to obtain some suitable timber for a spare set of spars. But before any trees could be felled, they had to be paid for, and the local Māori chief insisted on the deal being settled with two rifles and ammunition in exchange for the timber. Taking into consideration the general unrest that prevailed at the time this was a high price to pay, but needs must and the deal was struck.

On their return to the anchorage in the Bay of Islands following the building of the observatory, Captain Aulick, the American commander, informed them that he had an outbreak of smallpox on board his vessel and he was seeking medical assistance. Unfortunately, neither of the exploring ships had any medical remedy they could offer, nor was there any possibility of procuring help locally; apparently in England some research had been successfully carried out into an inoculation that could prevent people catching this most contagious of diseases, but it was not universally available.

It transpired that Aulick had been the commander of one of the exploring vessels that had accompanied Wilkes down to the Antarctic. So Ross took the opportunity of imparting to Aulick some information regarding the charts he had received from Wilkes. You may remember that Wilkes had left the charts of his discoveries in Hobart for Ross's use; Ross now felt it was only right to pass his own, contradictory, results directly to Wilkes rather than Wilkes seeing them only later, when Ross published his own findings.

As mentioned above, Ross had brought with him from Sydney Commander Sulivan, who was to take command of HMS *Favourite* when she arrived from a tour in the Pacific Ocean. The expedition did not have long to wait, and as they lay at anchor *Favourite* arrived, under the command of Lieutenant Dunlop. The lieutenant needed medical attention, and arrangements were put in place to repatriate him back to England, so Ross took the opportunity of sending back his data and reports at the same time. Hooker and McCormick, also availing themselves of this opportunity, duly boxed up their samples for forwarding to the various museums and botanical centres that would carry out further research into the new discoveries. Among the letters that were to be sent home were personal ones to William Hooker (Joseph's father), and Charles Darwin, with whom Joseph had been in frequent touch. Joseph explained to his father that he had been informed by Ross that his collection en route to England from Tasmania had been lost at sea.

Whilst ashore Hooker made a point of searching out one William Colenso, who was known to his father; although Colenso worked principally for the British and Foreign Bible Society, he was knowledgeable about the local flora and natural history of the area and could guide Hooker to places of interest. The two of them explored extensively in the time available, and due to Colenso's local knowledge Hooker was able to see far more of the place than he otherwise might. They visited some spectacular waterfalls, called Keri Keri by the Māori: the water fell in a single drop of nearly 80 feet into a large pool surrounded by trees. Another sight included some gigantic kauri trees; their trunks could measure about 30 feet in circumference and would grow to over 100 feet before the branches started sprouting. They were reputed to live for 2,000 years, but the majority soon succumbed to the woodman's axe. Now the remainder have to be protected to avoid the complete destruction of the species.

The settlement of Kororāreka in the Bay of Islands was at the time of Ross's visit probably the largest and most important point of entry into the North Island of New Zealand due to its good natural harbour, timber, fresh water, and the willingness of the local tribes to trade with the visiting sealing and whaling vessels. As a result of the early trading centre that had sprung up it had also attracted the earliest settlers. The new governor, however, could see that Auckland was in a better geographical position for the capital, and over the next few years Kororāreka gradually diminished in importance.

On 25 September there was a tragic incident when George Barker, one of the marines stationed aboard *Erebus*, was drowned. The skiff he was sailing in whilst crossing the bay to regain his ship capsized and, unable to swim, Barker succumbed to the elements before anyone could reach him. His fellow marine managed to hold onto the upturned boat long enough to be rescued. Efforts to recover Barker's body failed. This day was the second anniversary of the expedition's departure from England, and the very next day a local man suffered the same fate whilst attempting to swim ashore. It was believed he was probably drunk at the time.

Friday 21 October 1841 was another of the term days designated to synchronise the observatory readings with others across the world and especially the ones set up by this expedition. In the event all went to plan and the two commanding officers were well pleased with their effort, but it could have been a very different story. Adjacent to the wooden observatory there were a couple of tents for the use of the men working in the building. Due to some carelessness one of the tents caught fire, which destroyed both it and its contents. Had the wind been in the opposite direction who knows what else would have been consumed in the blaze; the loss of the precious recording instruments would have seriously curtailed the expedition's scientific programme. But in the end only some personal possessions were lost, and fortunately there was no loss of life nor any damage to the observatory.

A French corvette, *Héroine*, had anchored in the bay near the two British ships, and her captain, Carrier l'Évêque, paid the usual courtesy visit to the two commanders. During the conversation it transpired that his mission was to check on the health and welfare of a small colony of French settlers in the area. He found that although they had been allowed to establish themselves, they had at once been put under the jurisdiction of the local British magistrate and not allowed to build any form of defensive structure nor bring ashore any weaponry that could be used for an offensive purpose. This action by the British authorities was a direct result of the treaty that had brought the whole of New Zealand under the protection of the British crown.

L'Évêque was naturally disappointed, but he could see that the settlers were prospering and that they had accepted their situation without complaint. He then, on hearing of Ross's route down to the Chatham Islands, very kindly gave him a copy of the chart of the islands that he had made just recently. They had first been seen, and named, by a Lieutenant Broughton in 1791 in *Chatham*, accompanying HMS *Investigator*, captained by the famous navigator George Vancouver, but in the half-century since then, no Royal Naval ship had visited the islands, so l'Évêque's gracious offer of his up-to-date chart was gratefully accepted.

Their stay at the Bay of Islands lasted nearly ten weeks, from mid-August until 23 November 1841. During this period the surgeons and their assistants were very busy exploring and collecting samples of the natural history of the surrounding district. Ross had initially put an embargo on any of the crew members venturing very far from the two ships, but by the end of October, when no serious incidents had occurred, it is probable that Ross had eased the restrictions, because on 1 November he, with Crozier, Sulivan and Bird, set off in the ship's cutter to explore the River Kerikeri. They had a strong pull against a stiff headwind, but eventually landed some distance below the missionary station, owned by an English couple called Taylor. It was not possible to proceed further by boat and Mr Kemp the schoolmaster provided them with a guide to take them to the upper waterfalls and then to the missionary station. Ross knew from talking to McCormick and Hooker what lay ahead, so they unloaded the boat and back-packed their supplies and equipment the rest of the way. They reached their destination late in the afternoon having seen the magnificent waterfalls on the way. They were welcomed by Mr & Mrs Taylor.

The Taylors had obviously spent many hours crafting a very English-looking garden out of the fertile countryside. Ross was very impressed by the sight, which reminded him of home, and he spent some time wandering at will amongst the flower borders and lawns surrounded by numerous shrubs. But even as he enjoyed the relaxing atmosphere he was still exploring, and the surveying instruments he had brought were soon in action to establish the exact location and elevation of the site.

During the next few days the Taylors acted as guides and hosts to the party. Among the sights taken in was a large lake where some fishing was carried out; its depths were plumbed and its size was measured. Then Puki Nui, the highest mountain in the area, had of course to be climbed and its height determined. The explorers were shown a large crater with hot springs, and they noted the temperatures of the surrounding terrain. Most of the travelling was on foot, and although horses were available Ross deemed it wiser for humans to carry the delicate instruments rather than subject them to the jolting of a packhorse.

They were given the assistance of a local guide by the missionary's schoolmaster, Mr Kemp, and were led up some steep and slippery paths to the waterfalls that Hooker had visited. Past the falls, a recently constructed track led to Waimati, a Māori village.

Their stay lasted three days, and when the weather took a turn for the worse they set off back to their boat and then downriver to the ships.

In 1845, four years after Ross's visit, the trouble that had been brewing between the settlers and the Māori came to a head. The root cause of the grievances by the Māori was the wording of the 1840 Waitangi Treaty, which had been variously interpreted and unscrupulously administered. Following an appeal from the governor for help, Britain sent out a force of 600 soldiers under the command of Colonel Despard. Their objective was to attack a stronghold of the Māori under the leadership of one of their chiefs, Heke. He had a formidable reputation as a fearless leader of his people, and was determined to sweep the settlers from his country.

The British force needed cannon to breach the defences, and the track that Ross had walked along in 1841 provided the only feasible way of transporting the heavy guns near enough to blast away at the palisade around the village. The first series of assaults failed to break through, but eventually the British, with their superior advantage of firepower and greater numbers, were able to drive home their attack. The end was not in sight, however, as the Māori regrouped.

The next phase was peace talks, which failed, then the fight moved to a different Māori stronghold. No conclusive victory was ever achieved, and both sides suffered substantial casualties. The stalemate that followed festered, and the truce that ensued was never a satisfactory one.

A day or two before the ships sailed on the next leg of their expedition, Ross and his group experienced a disturbance. An appeal for assistance had come from Kororāreka, just across the water from the ships' anchorage.

The purchase of one of the islands by a settler family called Robertson seems to have been the trigger for the trouble there. Mr Robertson had recently drowned, and his widow and her children had continued to reside at the dwelling. They were set upon and killed by a member of the local tribe who wished to regain the ownership of the land. The story that was played out with such tragic consequences revolved around the Treaty of Waitangi and its interpretation by one of the local Māori; he had believed that on the death of the purchaser, Mr Robertson, the land would revert to its original owner. When this failed to come about he must have taken the law into his own hands with such tragic consequences. The house and outbuildings were consumed by fire, and the sight of this terrified the inhabitants of Kororāreka, who naturally thought they would be the next victims. The main perpetrator of the crime fled into the hills but was eventually captured, taken to Auckland, tried and hanged.

During the ten-week sojourn at the Bay of Islands some of the crew had been employed in fishing. Most of the time they used a seine net, which would be set across one of the small inlets; the following day it would be hauled in and the catch sorted, then the net reset. The species caught were varied; Ross indicates that some of the fish resembled those of the waters surrounding the United Kingdom, such as plaice, sole and mackerel. One variety, though, referred to as yellow tail or cavallo, measured 3 feet 9 inches, and although on the coarse side provided good eating. Sharks of various kinds were caught, but there is no mention of them turning up on the menu.

This variation would have helped to provide a balanced diet, and was a good reason why scurvy did not break out amongst the crew of either of ship. Another source of nutrition came in the form of wild pigs. These had initially been a domestic variety that, having become feral, had succeeded in breeding. During the explorations of the 18th and 19th centuries domestic animals were released in new lands on purpose. Chickens, goats and even cattle, in addition to pigs, were the commonest animals taken aboard exploring ships to drop off at remote islands and provide a larder for shipwrecked crews or any vessel calling and desperate for food.

Sometimes this practice was successful, but time and again it destroyed the fragile environment into which the animals had been liberated. The local flora and sometimes the fauna were not used to the newcomers' partiality to them, and would soon succumb to their ravages, to the detriment of the whole ecosystem. Old-established food chains would be threatened, and long-established colonies of seabirds in particular would be wiped out. Rats, although not deliberately set free, were responsible for the destruction of seabird colonies, and cats could also carry out the same depredation to the birds, especially ground-nesting ones. Hooker, on his visit to St Helena in 1839, was extremely concerned that introduced varieties of plants were outgrowing the local plants on the island, and when he succeeded to the presidency of Kew Gardens on the death of his father he sent botanists to that island to study the effects of the imported species on its natural plant stocks. He knew that by then many of the endemic varieties were being threatened to the point of extinction, and being exclusive to that location would be lost forever.

Cunningham reported in his log on 14 November that the captain was not well, and he continued to be ill for at least a week; meanwhile the time of departure was drawing close. The mention of the captain probably refers to Crozier, and this must have been quite worrying to Ross; at this late stage of the journey he would find it extremely difficult to replace his old and trusted friend. No further mention is made of the sickness, however, after Cunningham's entry on 21 November, and Ross does not refer to it, so the illness must have cleared up. There might have been a lingering feeling of disharmony in the officer's mess at about this time; it was noted by a junior officer aboard *Terror* that the commander was 'out of temper' and the senior lieutenant was not getting on with his fellow officers. This was all probably due to a relatively slack period at anchor in the Bay of Islands, and once they resumed their voyage the problems, whatever they were, apparently faded into the background.

The unfortunate incident involving the murder of the settler family and the destruction of their homestead set the departure date back a couple of days. Last letters had been written some while earlier, and despatched to Sydney aboard *Favourite*. She had been sent there for substantial repairs to her hull, which had been leaking badly, and the facilities for this work were not yet available in New Zealand. But now she was back on station, and on the day of *Erebus* and *Terror*'s departure she too left the Bay of Islands and headed to Auckland, to make the governor aware of the tragedy that had so recently taken place.

11 SOUTH AGAIN, TO THE GREAT ICE BARRIER

FAREWELL TO NEW ZEALAND, AND DETENTION IN THE ICE

The two commanders, knowing that they had successfully broken through the pack ice in the second week of January 1841, would have been hoping to repeat that exercise on this, their second foray into the Ross Sea. As well as seeking out the South Magnetic Pole, Ross was keen to carry on along the barrier's edge from the point where they had retreated at the end of their first visit. Their departure from New Zealand in the last week of November would give them ample time to explore the Chatham Islands before embarking on the much more difficult project of penetrating the pack ice. Then by mid-December the Antarctic summer would be at its height and Ross and Crozier would have felt supremely confident that, with 24 hours of daylight to help them on their way, they would have a second successful season in the ice.

A fresh breeze accompanied them as they bade farewell to New Zealand on 23 November 1841 and headed out to sea. The wind increased in strength and sent them scudding south-easterly across the ocean under short sail. The very next day land was sighted, but this was probably part of the New Zealand coast because it was not until 30 November that the Chatham Island group could be seen. Although a landing had been anticipated, a belt of fog and a rising sea precluded the attempt, so they skirted the coast and proceeded on their way. Although water samples were taken and a few depths were recorded, no use could be made of the chart so generously given them by the captain of the corvette in the Bay of Islands.

On the same day that they came close to making their landing the crew of *Terror* were summoned on deck to witness the punishment of one of their crewmates. He had been caught stealing from a fellow crew member, and he received a total of 46 lashes for his trouble. This was the first incident of its sort recorded in any of the published records, but it was followed a couple of days later by a member of *Erebus* jumping overboard to evade punishment for a misdemeanour he had carried out. But he allowed himself to be rescued and was summarily dealt with.

On Royal Naval ships, stealing from another crew member always carried a stiff punishment but this could only be carried out on the orders of the commanding officer. The official naval list had 36 punishable offences, including swearing at or striking an officer, sleeping on watch, neglecting personal hygiene, desertion, wilful damage to naval property; and of a very serious nature, murder, buggery and treacherous acts in time of war.

Desertions were usually spontaneous decisions taken when an opportunity arose, and could be attributable to several causes such as dissatisfaction with conditions aboard, the desire to seek a fortune in a new country, or frustration at being ordered to carry out meaningless tasks on the ship. Of a more serious nature and endemic to the way naval discipline was enforced, an officer with a disposition to cruelty towards his charges could meet with open defiance by a sailor, resulting in the man being subjected to corporal punishment. Then at the first opportunity desertion would be the only option open to the miscreant. As a testament to the good organisation of the expedition, generally speaking it was free of corporal punishment, which was only used as a last resort.

One of the important functions of the expedition was chart-making. This entailed keeping a daily record of the distances travelled, strength of currents encountered, accuracy of sightings of land, and searching for and checking on the geographical features discovered by other mariners. History is littered with reports of islands and land masses where it has ultimately been proved that no land exists. A sharp lookout could detect signs indicating land in the vicinity, such as the type of birds that preferred to stay close to land, or the presence of masses of seaweed floating on the surface (mid-ocean gyres excepted). It was known, too, that cloud formations of the right type could indicate the proximity of terra firma. So, it was no surprise when Ross altered course to seek out the Nimrod Islands. They had first been reported by Captain Eilbeck in 1828 aboard his ship, *Nimrod*. These islands were looked for by a number of expeditions right up to the 1930s. Ross, Biscoe and even Shackleton's own Nimrod expedition looked for them, but to no avail. Signs of land would be reported, but each time it turned out to be cloud formations hugging the horizon. The islands have now been dismissed as phantoms.

Saturday 4 December was the finest day so far since their departure from New Zealand, and the good weather continued for several days. The ships were surrounded by a number of whales, and even penguins were seen from time to time – but then on the 9th a change took place in the weather. The sea that had been so gentle soon became erratic, and the gale that was building started to whip off the tops of the waves. The air was getting distinctly colder despite it being the beginning of the southern summer. Sleet and hail made for a very unpleasant watch for the next two days. The weather calmed down for a while, but the two commanders were acutely aware that the next week or so would change their dispositions for quite some time to come. On the Sunday after divine service had been conducted, the crews were issued with warmer clothing and waterproof boots.

The 20th-century RRS James Clark Ross,
*after resupplying the British Antarctic Survey
Research Station Rothera on Adelaide Island.*

Fog now hampered their progress, and at this stage neither vessel wanted to lose contact with her sister ship, they rang bells and fired muskets at intervals. As the fog thinned a lookout called down that there were icebergs ahead, and the sea temperature was recorded as having dropped to 33°F (~1°C). It was imperative to keep well away from the bergs because there were signs that they were breaking up; a trail of bergy bits and growlers floating behind the bergs indicated their gradual demise. The height of the largest of the three was estimated as 130 feet, and it had deep caverns cut into it by the sea pounding against its sheer walls. The deep blue of the ice could be clearly seen from the decks.

Ross had chosen to attempt a penetration of the pack ice down the longitude line 146°E. This, he calculated, should bring them out into the sea he had discovered at about the point where they had turned back the previous season, but at this stage he had of course no idea how successful he would be. He knew the great ice barrier had to terminate at some point, and it was there that he was hoping to discover more new land. When on 18 December there were signs of an ice blink ahead, the moment was approaching when the hazardous task of battling with the ice was about to begin.

Initially the track they were able to follow led them in a southerly direction, but progress was steadily reduced as the pack intensified. To avoid the worst areas a more westerly course was steered. A few whales were observed in the pools of open water, and men could see some seals basking in the sunshine on the ice. Overhead the diminutive snow petrel was seen for the first time on this visit. A patchy yellow stain on the ice was thought to be of volcanic origin, but the eminent German biologist Ehrenberg later pronounced the samples he had received as being a microscopic life form never before seen.[24]

They were making steady progress through ice that was extending much further north than on their previous encounter, and by 20 December Ross reported that they were over 100 miles into the pack and still advancing, albeit now in a south-westerly direction. Several interchanges to each other's ships were made by the two commanders . On one trip Crozier and his men were very nearly tipped out of their boat as a whale surfaced from immediately beneath them. Luckily the whale sounded swiftly, and the danger was avoided.

This Christmas Day, their third since leaving England, was celebrated in the usual naval fashion. A bullock had been slaughtered a few days before and provided the centrepiece of the repast, so they all ate a hearty meal. The officers as usual dined separately, and the crew on

---

24 A possible answer to that conundrum is that in 2017 yellow stains on Antarctic ice were detected by NASA satellites; it turned out these had been made by the droppings of huge colonies of Adélie penguins

watch had to wait to be relieved before they could sit down to enjoy theirs. The ice surrounding them needed to be observed continuously for the safety of the ships and all aboard them. This precaution was emphasised the next day when *Terror* received a severe knock that had to be investigated. It was feared that some structural damage might have been done to her bows but upon inspection it appeared they had got off very lightly.

By the end of the year their progress had been restricted considerably, and they were still short of crossing the Antarctic Circle. In addition they had now drifted at least 6 degrees to the west of their original longitude of 146°E. The pack was a chaotic jumble of brash and growlers, with hardly a level area to be seen. No further progress was made between Christmas Day and New Year's Day but a convivial atmosphere for the New Year celebrations helped to relieve the cloud of boredom settling over the men.

The previous year it had taken them just five days, from 4 to 9 January, to get through about 200 miles of ice – but this year the effort was becoming much more protracted. Ross estimated they had already travelled 250 miles with no sign of release, and as 1842 began they had been surrounded for two weeks. He was still hopeful, however, that a break-out would occur very soon. To alleviate the boredom improvised games were organised out on the ice, and the men could be seen gambolling around like small children out for a picnic.

During the first week of January more ground was lost than won as the two ships, still held fast by the ice, drifted gently back northwards, and even a short period of favourable winds failed to regain them the lost mileage. During this static period, they were able to capture and kill several large penguins and seals. Referred to as 'large penguins', judging by the weight of each – they were about 75 lbs (34 kg) – they were probably emperors. They were submerged in a pickling solution and taken back to England as the first of their type to receive that dubious honour.

By January the men had resorted to using the boats to tow the ships through any small leads they could find, until the wind veered round to the north-east, and now they observed a distinct darkening of the sky ahead. Was this 'water sky', indicating clear seas ahead? On the 13th, they gained 20 miles to the south – but once again the ice closed their lead and they were left tacking around a pool just large enough for the ships to keep moving. Despite yet another hold-up, the dark sky persisted to the south of them, holding out the hope of their eventual release.

Then two days later the swell, which until then had been barely noticeable, increased dramatically, causing the ice to strike the hulls, and the 8-inch hawsers tying the ships to a large ice floe snapped like carrots. Eventually a gale helped subdue the ice, to the relief of all aboard, but it was still imperative that they stayed secured to the largest floe they could find. They even managed to raise a small amount of sail, and with the two ships tied to opposite sides of the floe they made some headway. But then fog descended, and when the hawsers broke again the ships had to depend on their bells to ensure they stayed in contact. Separation now would have put both ships in jeopardy.

Another gale struck them on the 19th, and sail was immediately reduced to reefed mainsail and storm staysails. As the ice broke up under the onslaught of the gale, solid chunks of it hurled against the hulls with such enormous force that the masts quivered in their mountings. Both ships suffered a considerable amount of damage to their rudders – in fact, a signal was received from *Terror* to indicate that her rudder had been completely wrenched away from its stern post – and Ross was forced into backing and filling the sails; allowing the sails to fill then releasing them and filling them again meant that a degree of control could be maintained, enabling the steersmen to help save them from the worst of the impacts from the ice.

The situation they now found themselves in was probably the most dangerous since the expedition began. They had to stay alive and afloat; anything more than that was now out of their hands and in Ross's words 'in the hands of Him who alone can preserve us and bring us to safety through this extreme danger'. Some of the ice blocks weighed many tons, and the ships' timbers were beginning to spring from the massive forces exerted on their sides. The larger pieces of ice, too heavy to be lifted out of the water, had an added danger built into them; they were mini-icebergs in their own right, and like all bergs were far larger below the surface than above. This meant that if the wind drove the ships too near them the bottom of the ships' hulls, their most vulnerable area, could at any moment be rent open. Even in the fading light of day the crews could look over the sides and see the loom of the submerged blue ice appearing to beckon them to destruction.

No less than 28 hours, it was estimated, the fury lasted. The seas reached such a height that when both ships were plunged into troughs either side of a wave only the mastheads could be seen from each other's decks. Without the reinforcement built into both ships at Chatham, neither would have pulled through. Worse, at the comparatively northerly latitude they were being held at by the ice, darkness was another factor in their dire situation; they could get separated or worse still collide with each other. Neither option held any appeal for them. It was only when the barometer began to climb from 28.4 inches (~962 mb) that any relief from their nightmare could be envisioned.

Dawn came none too soon for the weary crews, who could then inspect the damage they knew had occurred. Both ships had suffered a lot of superficial damage, the worst of which was to the rudders. Ross made the crossing to *Terror* as soon as the seas subsided and viewed her rudder with dismay. Although they carried a spare it was the destruction of the mountings that caused his anguish: the sternpost had been completely destroyed, and most of the fittings that had held it to the stern of the ship had been wrenched away. They would need several calm days at least to be able to reconstruct the unit, and the way things had been recently that did not seem likely to happen.

Fortunately, however, the seas started to moderate and the wind shifted, enabling them to manoeuvre the ships deeper into the pack ice. This gave them sufficient protection to start the repairs that would be so essential to the steering of their ships. As luck would have it, they found a large floe to which they attached a series of hawsers, enabling them to stabilise the vessels so that work could commence. The first priority was, however, to feed the crews and then let them get some well-earned rest. The continuous thumping and banging of the ice blocks against the hulls had precluded any sleep for well in excess of a day and night while the men had fought their battle against the ferocity of the churning ice pack.

Every Royal Naval ship had on board as a matter of necessity at least one competent carpenter, and it was now that he would be essential. Another worker essential to the maintenance of the ships was a skilled blacksmith; he would be able to repair or replace the metal brackets, braces and pintails that had been twisted and snapped by the ice at the height of the storm.

The expedition was detained for several days, repairing and replacing the rudders. Whilst the ships were secured to the ice floe they were drifting to the south-west. This, as it turned out, eventually brought them into a band of ice that was the loosest they had encountered for many days, so with the rudders exchanged and repaired they could resume their efforts to force a passage towards open water.

The sun was conspicuous by its absence for most of the time they were struggling to survive, so they were unsure of their position; they estimated that they were safely past the Antarctic Circle, but it was not until 28 January that they could verify this. Still trapped and at the mercy of the ice, after six weeks of frustration Ross estimated they had probably covered about 800 miles since entering the ice the week before Christmas. He contrasted this with the previous season's progress, and bemoaned the fact that when James Cook had sailed these waters in 1774 he had been only about 30 miles further north than they were now, yet had never entered any pack ice.

Another calamity beset them on 30 January when smoke came billowing out of Terror's hold. The crew were immediately set to work ferrying water down below, and after a frantic half-hour the air once more was clear enough to ascertain what had happened. The Sylvester heating apparatus had been lit to dry out the cabins and crew's quarters, and some stores placed too close to it had dried out to the point when they had combusted. This gave the impression that the fire was far more serious than, fortunately, it turned out. Once the fire was under control, there only remained the job of clearing up the mess left by all the water that they had used.

The ships' boats were put into the water the next day, and the men were once again employed in the thankless task of trying to tow Erebus and Terror through the maze of small leads that presented themselves. Each time the ship changed direction the oarsmen would be pulled up short as the hull dragged along the side of a piece of pack ice that had floated into their path. Their efforts finally paid off, however, as by night-time the ships lay in a polynya, an ice-free area. So much time had been lost by now that every effort was made to take advantage of it.

To undertake such a hazardous voyage in two sailing vessels with no other means of propulsion had never been tackled before in these seas, and would never again be attempted. The next time a ship explored the Ross Sea would be 50 years later, and this ship would have an auxiliary steam engine. Such was the daring shown by the commanders of Erebus and Terror and their crews.

They were still not completely free from the ice; there were many large bergs to negotiate, and the sea had some fairly dense patches of pack ice on it. Snow and hail frequently hampered any men working on the decks of the ships, and at the latitude they were at even the 24 hours of daylight they had become accustomed to were coming to an end. Yet to accomplish any sort of results this year, they must push on to the south.

Then on the 5th fog added to their misery, slowing any progress they hoped to make. It wasn't until 8 February that they actually managed to turn directly south; most of the previous week or so had seen them heading in a more westerly direction than they had wanted and as a result they had now tracked as far west as longitude 173°W. More bad weather hampered them on 14 and 15 February, and the pack ice that lay before them forced the helmsman to continue steering west. On the 15th they crossed the 180° line. The air temperature was close to freezing every day, and any spray that came on board froze rapidly to the rigging and decks, making them extremely slippery and dangerous.

Just when they were beginning to despair of making a decent mileage towards their objective the seas around them slowly became free of the pack ice and a fair breeze enabled them to set a good spread of sails; at 6 knots they were back to being exploring ships with an objective in sight. The thermometer recorded the lowest temperature so far at only 19°F (−7°C). The ice on the rigging and decks had to be rapidly removed with axes to allow the ship to be worked; and, as mentioned earlier, accumulations of ice above a ship's centre of buoyancy can easily capsize and sink her.

Setting as much sail as possible they drove the ships southwards at a good rate; hopes were much higher now than they had been for the last two or three weeks that some practical work could still be achieved this season. They crossed 77°S on 19 February, and could see an ice blink far ahead, indicating yet more ice. A depth check revealed green mud at 250 fathoms (~460 metres), a good sign that the sea was getting shallower.

The air temperature continued to drop, and a southerly gale brought more water over the decks where it froze and again had to be chipped off. It was now so cold on deck that when one wave crashing over *Terror*'s bows had in it a small fish, it was instantly frozen to the deck. Dr Richardson, the surgeon on *Terror* tried to make a drawing of it, but the ice encasing it prevented him from seeing much detail.

At the latitude they had now reached they were able to enjoy and make the most of 24 hours of daylight once more, and from the masthead at about midnight on Tuesday 22 February 1842 the great ice barrier was first glimpsed. They approached to within an estimated 6 miles of the wall that had defeated them the previous season. Their ambition had been to put men ashore on solid land to make a claim on behalf of Great Britain and Queen Victoria. With the wind now blowing towards the ice cliffs their approach to it, as a lee shore, was understandably very tentative. The ships were still managing to keep company with one another, and after some consultation between the two commanders they turned eastwards along the front of the barrier in the hope of finding some chink in its armour that would allow them a sighting of the land that it so obviously concealed. Even at the safe distance they maintained, they could see great chunks of ice tumbling into the sea as the front of the barrier continued its cycle of decay and replenishment.

After checking their latitude they discovered with a certain sense of achievement that they were now 6 miles further south than the point they had reached in 1841. The hope they had held of going even further south, however, looked forlorn, as the face of the barrier now turned slightly towards the north-east. Notwithstanding this disappointment, the barrier was declining in height, and their hopes were buoyed that a sighting could be made across its vastness. As they progressed steadily along this previously unseen part of the barrier, its height gradually became less until it was nearer 100 feet than the 150–200 it had maintained up to now. Lookouts were sent aloft to gain a first glance of this hidden world, but their hopes of seeing new land were to be frustrated, as the sloping icy surface that came into view rose gently to the south with no sign of solid rock or even a broken surface that could indicate the presence of land underneath the snowy mantle.

Ross was acutely aware that any misinformation on his charts would be immediately pounced upon by later explorers as proof of his claims being void, so he marked the chart with the cautious wording 'appearance of land'.

New sea ice was already forming, and this early warning was heeded by the expedition. Ross, still harbouring hopes of locating the elusive South Magnetic Pole, now had to pin his ambition of doing this on a third visit to this inhospitably icy realm the following year. They planned to spend the forthcoming winter in the Falkland Islands, and to that end now reluctantly turned northwards.

On the 25th *Erebus* made a long run courtesy of a favourable breeze, which took her well ahead of *Terror*. So *Erebus* hove to, enabling *Terror* to make up the leeway, and taking the opportunity to send down a weighted line to check the depth of the sea. This, however, proved to be greater than the 450-fathom line employed.

Following the edge of the pack ice, the two ships ventured into several embayments and spent several hours extricating themselves. The danger with this type of exploration was that the wind and ice could suddenly turn against them and trap them for the winter. Getting clear of the newly forming ice was a matter of some urgency, carried out successfully as they tacked, once again slipping through the trap. During a really pleasant sunny afternoon on 27 February, Crozier was rowed over to *Erebus* for some discussions as to their plans for the attempt soon to be made to breach the outer pack ice. The health of the crews was also on the agenda, and both commanders could report that not a single man had been invalided up to this point in the expedition.

Resuming their northward passage, they were confronted by a chain of icebergs creating what looked like an impenetrable barrier across their course. Cunningham's diary notes that *Terror* went considerably too close to one of the bergs, and all hands were called; by manipulating the sails they were able to slip past the end of the berg by the narrowest of margins. At the speed they were travelling – an estimated 5 knots – a collision with an iceberg would have proved disastrous.

12 IMPENDING DISASTER

SKILL, SEAMANSHIP AND THE ALMIGHTY'S HAND

The ships carrying the expedition steadily northwards now experienced slightly warmer temperatures but on the downside the midnight suns of summer were rapidly turning into a defined period of darkness. Although bergs were few and far between, the constant snow showers made it exceedingly difficult for the lookouts to see more than a mile or so ahead, so as darkness descended the ships shortened sail; then by keeping a constant watch and listening for the telltale sound of water breaking against ice they continued to force their way towards the distant Falkland Islands. Friday 4 March 1842 saw the barometer drop to one of the lowest points yet recorded on the expedition, 28.162 inches (~969 mb), heralding the approach of a mighty storm. They were saved on this occasion by the wind unexpectedly backing from north-east to north-west. The effect this had on the rising seas was as dramatic as it was welcome: the waves dropped and the ships could proceed. Interestingly, even though the barometric pressure stayed low right through the next two days the weather remained reasonably fair.

The Antarctic Circle was crossed during this period and it meant that they had spent a total of 64 days to the south of it. Every degree of latitude they travelled took them about 60 nautical miles further north and by crossing of the 60th parallel on 9 March they had covered over 300 miles in just three days. Ross intended to sail eastwards along this line of latitude to carry out some magnetic observations as part of their ongoing research; this would also be a more direct route to their next port of call, in the Falkland Islands.

Despite frequent snow showers the two ships fairly skipped along with a good spread of canvas for the best part of three days. Caution was only instigated by the arrival of small bergy bits, warning of the possibility of icebergs in the vicinity. The officer of the watch ordered an immediate reduction of sail. Hands were sent aloft to close-reef the topsails. No sooner had this been achieved than a large berg was seen dead ahead, looming through the murk of the night and the incessant snowfall. All hands were immediately summoned, some of the crew members very scantily clad: this was an emergency of the highest magnitude and it was imperative that they should report to the officer of the watch for further orders. Immediate action was required to avoid a collision with this massive berg, which seemed to be growing with every passing second. The ship's wheel was spun to take *Erebus* onto the port tack. But no sooner had the ship started to go about than she was confronted by a further, and much greater, danger looming out of the darkness: *Terror*, which had been running parallel to *Erebus*, had also been forced to take avoiding action. and was now headed straight for her. The collision could not be avoided, and there was virtually no time to minimise the impact. As *Terror* forged forward her prow crashed into the bowsprit of her sister ship, ripping it away along with *Erebus*'s foretopmast and other spars and rigging. The two ships were now locked together amidst a tangle of broken spars and severed rigging. Worse, they still had enough momentum to carry them closer and closer to the iceberg, which threatened to overwhelm them and cast them all into the sea.

The waves then threw the ships apart and together several times; as one of the ships rose on a wave she would come crashing back down on the other, causing ever-increasing damage to the timbers of the two. Their crews were helpless to take any action that would bring about their salvation, and as the seconds that seemed like eternity ticked past the ships were getting closer to the iceberg. Somehow the ships detached themselves from one another, but by this time the lower yardarms of *Erebus* were colliding with the walls of the iceberg as she wallowed, unable to steer or make headway.

As the sails had been close-reefed just before the collision the only way to regain steerage was to send men aloft to release the reefs and trust that the sails would fill sufficiently to release them from this terrible situation. Mercifully, at least some of the waves breaking against the berg were acting as a buffer between the ship and the icy cliff that towered above her, but even so more and more of the rigging was getting damaged as she gradually reacted to the pull of the filling sails. Above the howls of the wind and crash of the waves the men aloft were finding it almost impossible to hear the commands shouted up to them.

It was by supreme seamanship that total disaster was averted. The sails were backed, and the ship oh so slowly drew herself backwards along the face of the berg – only to find that instead of open water she was faced with a second berg close alongside the first. Ross now had mere seconds to bring about their salvation as he realised that there was the slimmest of chances that they could squeeze through the gap between the two bergs. Providence must surely have been looking down on them; *Erebus* slipped through the space with barely a ship's width on either side. Once through, they found shelter under the lee of the bergs, giving them time to take stock of the dramatic episode they had just endured.

While *Erebus* was extricating herself from her perilous position, *Terror*'s crew had been in turmoil too. Her men scrambled aloft to carry out the most dangerous of tasks: the severity of the collision had shaken the masts and spars to which they were clinging, and only providence came to their rescue. How none of them were thrown into the churning sea no one will ever

Erebus *and* Terror *escaping from the clutches of the two icebergs. Painting by J. E. Davis, the second master of* Terror. *The original is held at the National Maritime Museum in Greenwich.*

know. An estimate of *Terror*'s speed prior to her hitting *Erebus* was as high as 7 knots, and *Terror* had also suffered damage right across her bows, losing an anchor and her cathead, jib and flying jib boom. After the initial separation and with the seas now playing a big part in the chaos, *Erebus* at one point rose high on a wave and crashed down onto *Terror* amidships, doing considerable damage to her woodwork and nearly staving her side in.

In the three-quarters of an hour it took *Erebus* to back away from the scene of the near-disaster, *Terror* had been able to get under way, and she was in fact the first of the two to find the passage between the bergs. That miraculous gap brought home to the expedition members how close they had come to annihilation. At this point, however, neither commander knew the fate of his opposite number; for several hours both ship's companies were left wondering whether they were the sole survivors.

Of all the incidents throughout the four years of the expedition this one – the collision of the two ships and their expected demise – generated the longest entry in Cunningham's journals, which he so religiously maintained throughout the expedition. His account of the event, written on Sunday 13 March 1842 is, unsurprisingly, by far the most dramatic, and I have reproduced it here with the kind permission of Captain Richard Campbell RN (Rtd), who transcribed and edited the original version held by the Public Record Office in Belfast for the Hakluyt Society in April 2009 (spellings and punctuation are, however, per Cunningham's original).

> Such a one as I hope I may never spend again. 0 30 AM, had just turned in and was dozing off to sleep, when All Hands was call.d with the dismal cry of large bergs close ahead. The people jumped out of thier Hammocks and made thier way on deck naked as they were, but before they all got up the two ships run foul of one another. When I got on deck a sight presented itself which made

the Stoutest heart quail and I believe every man resigned himself to eternity without hope of except in his maker [*sic*]. It is requisite to say that it was pitch dark with nearly a gale of wind and both Ships going before it under double reefed Topsails at the rate of 7 Knots an hour and Steering very wildly. The *Erebus* was on our Starboard beam something under a ¼ of a mile. At Midnight She observed a large berg on her Starboard bow and also ahead with apparently clear water on her port bows. We observed a large berg on our Port bow and also ahead with apparently open water on our Starboard bow. The consequence was She bore down We bore up and both Ships came in collision with a Violent crash: us to leeward with a tremendous berg so close on our lee beam that you could throw a biscuit on it: with a fearfull Sea foaming against it.

The *Erebus* took us on our Starboard bow carrieing away our Cat head and best bower Anchor, Our jib and flying jibboom. At the Same time carrying away her own Anchor Cathead and everything before her Knightheads. Bowsprit short off to the Gammoning. They then recoiled from one another for a moment (which was one of awfull Suspense to the poor half naked beings that crowded these decks). She took us again then on our main beam with a most terrible crash taking away her own foretop mast close to the Cap, and nearly Staving our side in, breaking our rubbing pieces right up and tearing the iron Sheathing into ribbons. They hung together a few moments Keeping us in awfull suspense and driving us nearly on the berg. She then disengaged herself in doing of which she carried away her Main Top Galt Mast and our Top Mt Studg Sails booms and Yard ram Irons. Also, our Qr boat & Davids spike plank, Stern Davids &Spanker boom and leaving us both nearly wrecks: fortunately for us the sea raging against the berg caused a heavy drawback which Kept us from it and we got clear through a passage between two fearfull looking barrier bergs each Miles long. For ½ hour our feelings was indiscribable we were aware that we were comparatively Safe: but we could see nor hear nothing of the poor "*Erebus*", and in fact we could see no means how she could be safed. At length a Blue Light announced that She was above water and not a great way from us which made every heart bound again with joy. Immediately afterwards two horizontal lights told us She [was] wearing which both Kept doing until Daylight. At which time we both presented a very Shattered appearance. She looking much worse than us. The *Erebus* then signalled they were all well onboard and making no water. Which signal we repeated relative to ourselves. I must here say that it was a most wonderful interposition of Divine providence that we were not all Sent into the presence of Our Maker with all our Sins on our Shoulders without one moments preparation. Not even an accident occurred for all of which I hope we will be all thankfull during the remainder of our lives and that may tend to reform us in a consumation devoutly to be prayd for.

On looking at the ice every man felt astonished to think how we came through it for the passage would have been a most difficult one by daylight much less in the dark and by accident or Gods good will. There was Six large bergs all close together with apparently only the one opening amongst them.

How *Erebus* was Saved I Know not yet. Hands employed all day repairing damages. The day middling fine: Night very dirty.

Ross wrote that it was not till daylight that the signal flags they had hoisted to indicate they were all safe were seen by the crew of *Terror*, but from Cunningham's account it would appear that *Erebus*'s blue lights were seen by *Terror*, so they at least knew that *Erebus* had come through the ordeal.

The shelter of the two huge icebergs gave the crews a chance to clear away the debris and make good some of the damaged rigging, so the ships could once again be steered conventionally. One rather unusual type of damage was caused by the bower anchor of *Erebus*: it had been displaced and was now deeply embedded in the ship's hull. Checks were made internally to see if it had penetrated right through and might be causing a leak, but no untoward damage was reported and about a week later the anchor broke away after the ship had been struck by an extra-large wave.

Even when the two ships left the lee of the iceberg that had so very nearly terminated the expedition their two crews were hard at work restoring the rigging and sails to some semblance of order. The carpenters on *Erebus* reshaped a small mast into a jury bowsprit, and this was followed by joinery work to the upper timbers of the bow that had borne the brunt of *Terror*'s first impact. One of the more intricate jobs was to manufacture a new cathead, which, providing as it did the main support for raising and lowering the anchor, was made from a curved section of seasoned timber.

Icebergs, both great and not so great, were still proving an obstacle to navigation, especially in the dark, but a lesson had been learnt and more diligence was applied to the observations. The crew aboard *Erebus* worked so well that by the next day more sails could be hoisted, and, with *Terror* setting the pace, the voyage of over 2,000 miles to the Falklands could begin in earnest.

Most of the time they made steady progress, but the sky was constantly obscured by dense cloud and from time to time they were struck by squally showers. The heavy seas that swept the decks made life very unpleasant, as the water penetrated below deck, making everything wet, then musty. The patent heating system was in operation all day long in an effort to counteract the dampness.

After a dismal week the only good thing to report was the steady progress they were making; the log showed they were covering up to 160 miles a day. The westerlies had worked their magic and the ships, despite the terrible trouble they had been in just a few short days earlier, were responding very well. Then on the 18th, just as the men were congratulating themselves on the progress they had made, the weather once more intervened and for a day and a half they had to endure another violent storm. This must have been the storm that dislodged the anchor embedded in *Erebus*'s bow. Then on the night of 20 March the sky cleared long enough to reveal the Moon: the gale force winds they had endured over the preceding two days had cleared the air and allowed the heavens to be seen.

As the storm abated, the reefs that had been so hurriedly put in were shaken out again, and the journey was resumed. Staying on 60°S latitude, or as near to it as the wind allowed, was bringing them ever closer to Cape Horn, and on 1 April 1842 they were closing with the first of the outlying rocky islets, the Diego Ramirez Rocks, that presaged the cape. By early evening the rocks were about 20 miles away.

These islets had been discovered by the Spanish in 1619 and were for 150 years the most southerly known piece of land on the globe, until the South Sandwich Islands were located in 1775 by James Cook. Chile, now controlling Diego Ramirez, has had a naval weather station on the largest of the group since 1957. They are also an important nesting site for a number of different species of birds including albatross and rockhopper penguins.

Ross now gave the order to heave to, as he wanted to take a sighting of Cape Horn when daylight broke. But the seas around Cape Horn were about to live up to their formidable reputation as some of the stormiest in the world: the barometer plunged and the sky blackened. Men were immediately send aloft to fetch in as much sail as possible, leaving just enough to keep the ship head to wind. The men were still aloft when the first blast hit them, and it caught the quartermaster, James Angeley, off balance, hurling him overboard. Immediately a lifebuoy was thrown out towards him. The ship was of course heading rapidly away from the man, and it would take some time to put her about to rescue him. Angeley was observed to have grabbed the lifebuoy, and the crew started preparing a boat to effect a rescue. But as the seas were rising at an alarming rate the command was given to hold back on launching it, for fear that the boat and its crew would be pitched into the water. As the unfortunate sailor was holding onto the lifebuoy it would not be long before *Erebus* could return to retrieve him. However the first run had to be aborted due to a shift in the wind, and going about for the second time they were making good progress towards him when it was perceived that the lifebuoy was abandoned; there was no sign of Angeley. The conjecture was that he might have sustained a severe knock to his head as he had gone overboard and had then passed out from shock and cold.

They had now lost four men since leaving home, three to drowning and the one overcome by fumes in the tank during their stay in Hobart. James Angeley had been a popular crew member ever since they had set sail from Chatham, and his loss brought a deep sense of grief to the officers and men alike.

Sadness prevailed in the two ships as they plunged on past Cape Horn, which was soon far astern and its position updated on the charts. A strong current was detected, which bore the ships 30 miles to the north-east, and after resetting their position they were now just two days away from Beauchene Island, the southernmost sentinel of the Falklands archipelago. There are several hundred similar rocky outposts scattered about the two principal islands, East and West Falkland which, like nearly all islands of volcanic origin, rise up from great depths.

Just before they sighted Beauchene Island, they sighted the first sail since leaving New Zealand that did not belong to their partner. Signals were hoisted, but the stranger did not stop and the pair continued on their lonely way. You might like to imagine the thoughts flying through the mind of the captain of this unknown vessel on sighting two British men of war converging on his ship: the reputation of the Royal Navy was known throughout the world for looking after the mercantile interests of British traders, and woe betide any vessel failing to stop when challenged. In this instance, however, interception and arrest would have been far from the thoughts of the two commanders.

Because they were tracking along the line of the 60th degree of latitude the presence of ice was still a very strong possibility and a constant watch had to be maintained. Ross was also constantly taking recordings of air and water temperatures and noting any variations in the dip of the compass needle, not to mention carrying out salinity tests and soundings for ocean depths. All of these took place on a daily basis, and he ensured that the officer of the watch noted down any physical phenomena that could be observed. One such was the occurrence of the southern lights, Aurora Australis. Although at the same latitude on the way down to the Antarctic they had experienced some magnificent displays, Ross noted there was now a paucity of them and he was at a loss as to why this was the case.

During the voyages carried out by the two ships it had become a regular practice to cast over the side sealed bottles, each of them containing a message clearly stating the date, the location's co-ordinates and who had put the message into the bottle. Ross had come up with the interesting procedure of putting several bottles over the side simultaneously, each one partially filled with a different quantity of sand. This, it was hoped, would allow the heavier ones to submerge to lower depths and possibly get carried away by undetected currents to finish up in a range of locations.

One of these bottles was recovered 9,000 miles away in Australia, three and a half years after it had been cast adrift. The local newspaper, *The Port Phillip Herald*, carried an article on the finding of the bottle near Cape Liptrap in Victoria in September 1845. The article was reproduced in *The Scotsman* in August 1846, where it came to the attention of Ross. A number of questions need to be asked as to the route taken by the bottle, such as: did it travel in a reasonably straight line, and was it one of the bottles without sand or had it been loaded with sand? – there is no mention of sand by the discoverer. Allowing for some drift the distance travelled would have been considerably longer than the direct line, but the fact is that it found its way eastwards across 9,000 miles of tempestuous ocean in three and a half years at an average drift of 8 or 9 miles a day. What a shame, though, that of all the bottles thrown over the sides of *Erebus* and *Terror* during their four years at sea this was the only record of one found.

By now 24 days had elapsed since that terrible night involving the life-and-death encounter with the two great icebergs, and in that time the men had carried out all the repairs needed to enable the ships to continue their voyage. The sighting of Beauchene Island meant that they now had just one day's sailing left until they could drop anchor in Berkeley Sound in East Falkland. The prospect of spending a winter there did not exactly excite the men but after the stresses and terrors they had endured, any port in a storm would be a welcome relief.

The final run into East Falkland was accomplished safely even though fog had drifted in. They negotiated Berkeley Sound with the help of a chart supplied before they left Chatham, which had been drawn up by Fitzroy of HMS *Beagle*. Between 1831 and 1836 he had circumnavigated the globe, and this voyage would of course have worldwide implications because the young naturalist on board was Charles Darwin, later to write *On the Origins of Species* and shatter the scientific world. The Falklands was one of the places *Beagle* called in at, and while Darwin was botanising Fitzroy was charting the coastlines.

At the far end of Berkeley Sound, *Erebus* and *Terror* located the narrow entrance to Port Louis. Due to the fog they arrived unseen by the folk of its little community. They had arrived on 6 April 1842, having been away from civilisation for a total of 137 days.

Despite the lateness of the day, the purser, Thomas Hallett, was rowed ashore to announce their arrival, collect mail from England and if possible buy some fresh meat and vegetables. On his return he brought two lots of news. The mail had not arrived; but on a brighter note he was able to inform several of the officers that their promotions had come through. Commander Crozier was now a full captain, and Alexander Smith, the first mate on *Erebus*, could now be addressed as Lieutenant. There was also good news for Lieutenant Bird, who became a commander and was transferred to *Terror*, and George Mowbray, the clerk in charge on *Terror*, now became her purser. There were more changes to the crew lists; McMurdo had been ailing for some time with an internal complaint and the surgeons recommended that he be repatriated to England at the earliest opportunity. His place was taken by Lieutenant John Sibbald from *Erebus*.

The community of Port Louis consisted of less than 20 people, and the arrival of the two ships would soon exhaust any spare beef, so shooting parties were organised to set out onto the moorland to capture some of the plentiful wild cattle. The locals were short of other provisions as well, due to the lateness of a supply ship due to bring flour and other basic groceries from Buenos Aires; Ross was able to help to a limited extent by sharing some of the ships' rations with the residents.

Before the cattle hunt could begin, the expeditioners needed to find a couple of local men experienced in the art of the chase; they knew there would be great risk to life and limb as the cattle were unpredictable and extremely dangerous. Dogs would be used to track them down, and then the technique would be similar to that of hunting caribou, musk oxen and even bears in the Arctic. The delay, however, was of no immediate consequence as the tidal flats further up the inlet were a haven for ducks and geese, which did not present the dangers that the cattle were likely to impose on the hunters.

Another project that had to be attended to was the erection of the wooden buildings used for magnetic and astronomical observations. This would be their first outing since the ships had left the Bay of Islands in November 1841, and the observatory needed to be completed before 21 April 1842, the next term day. It was put up on a slight rise in the otherwise rather flat terrain, close to a fort built in 1764 by settlers of French descent.

The Falklands, having changed hands a number of times since their discovery, had suffered a very chequered history until Britain claimed sovereignty over them in 1833. Until then,

French, Spanish and Argentine settlers had wrested a livelihood from its bleak peat bogs, with their very limited use for growing crops such as potatoes, and rearing hardy livestock. Fishing was always a staple source of food and a limited way to make a living. So in 1842, when Ross and his two ships entered Port Louis, not a lot of infrastructure existed, and with the settlers living in homesteads constructed of sod walls with reeds thatching the roofs and peat fires for cooking and heating, the settlement must have appeared very reminiscent of a remote Highland village, especially with the hills forming a dramatic backdrop to the settlement.

13 WILD CATTLE HUNT AND THE THIRD WINTER AWAY

A LIVELY INTERLUDE THOUSANDS OF MILES FROM HOME

The round-up and cull of the wild cattle was held up for a few days, waiting for expert help. It transpired that there was a technique that would enable the hunters to procure a good supply of beef while reducing the risk of serious injury, and the experienced hunters were sailors from a Royal Naval ship due to arrive shortly: HMS *Arrow*, commanded by Lieutenant Robinson. She anchored in the sound at the end of April.

A small group of officers and men from *Erebus* and *Terror* were to take part and, accompanied by the men from *Arrow*, set off in a boat up the sound. They took with them tents, sleeping mats and blankets, and provisions to last them until their return. Sharing the boat was a motley collection of dogs, so essential to the success of the hunt. Although guns were not to be used in the chase they were taken along as an emergency form of defence.

Hooker, one of the officers taking part in the foray, wrote a very detailed account about the days they were away from the ships. The start of the expedition involved manhandling the boats and the stores across a short portage to another stretch of water, the shortest route to the place where the hunt would begin. It turned out to be somewhat inauspicious; the weather was depressing and the wind drove sleet into their faces as they refloated the boat and pulled up the sound to the place where they were to get their first glimpse of the quarry. Meanwhile, the dogs had to be kept quiet of course, not an easy task.

The settlers carried out their hunts in a similar way to the gauchos of South America – that is, from horseback and with the aid of lassos in what Hooker described as 'a sickening display of revenge against an innocent animal unable to defend itself'. But these sailors' method involved stalking; a quiet approach to the herd downwind of it, to reduce the chances of being detected. Most of the herds contained from 10 to 30 animals, consisting of cows, calves, young bulls and nearly always the alpha bull. He was the one most feared, hence the guns. An angry or antagonised bull would rapidly cover the intervening ground, giving little chance of an escape, and serious injuries or worse would occur to any member of the hunting party unlucky enough to get in his way. Hooker described the lead bull as 'generally black, have [sic] a noble carriage and one possessed of indomitable courage and untameable ferocity'.

The bulls sometimes roamed independently of a herd, and woe betide the traveller who crossed his path, especially if there was nowhere to hide or shelter. In fact, *Erebus*'s gunner, Thomas Abernethy, was caught in the open, and was unbelievably lucky to escape with his life.

On this hunt, once the distance to the herd had been closed and no cover remained, the dogs were released. They apparently knew instinctively what was expected of them: they set the herd in motion and the chase began in earnest. Several dogs pursued one of the cows, and like a pack of wolves the others picked out a weaker or slower animal and set off after it. The dogs were followed by men who were fleet of foot and unburdened by equipment other than a knife.

Hooker described the scene of the first kill as he attempted to catch up, hampered as he was by his gun, an ammunition box, and his weatherproof jacket and waterproof boots.

> Yoke, a noble dog, held her by the throat; 'Laporte', his scarcely less powerful comrade, had seized the middle of the tail; and anchored her, in spite of kicks and struggles, which caused him to twist round and round as if on a pivot; whilst little 'Bully' a smaller more mastiff-like dog, had fixed his teeth into the poor brutes tongue, and all were mingling snarls and stifled barks with her pitiful moans. It was a most cruel sight; but happily, her suffering did not last long. The runner, scarcely less fleet than the hounds, was already up with his knife, and quick as lightning hamstrung both hind legs: she fell with a deep agonised low to the ground: he sprang to her shoulder like a savage, and before she could turn her head to butt, plunged the steel into her neck; when she rolled over, a dying creature.

The dogs were once more sent off after the fleeing herd and the process was repeated until several animals had been killed. The carcasses were butchered on the spot into portions that men could haul back to their campsite. By the time dusk was descending it was essential that everybody set off back to the boat; darkness was now closing in and they still had to locate the two men they had left to look after it. Their supper would of course be a suitably chosen piece of beef cooked in the hot ashes of the camp fire. By wrapping the chunks of meat into pieces of the cow's hide and casting these parcels into the embers for the best part of an hour, a hearty meal could be produced; the skins not only kept all the juices inside but also kept the meat clean and free from ash. The light of the fires cast ghostly shadows and silhouettes onto the tent walls as the men moved quietly around the camp eating their beef supper.

Hooker reflected on the day's hunt in an almost remorseful manner. He and his tent companion that first night spent an hour or more discussing the events of the day as they lay in their sleeping robes, and neither man could put together an argument in favour of such barbarity as they had witnessed that day. Memories flooded back of the time when they had carried out the first such exercise on the island of Kerguelen and taken the life of a sea leopard. Quoting from the essay he supplied to Ross, Hooker stated:

> It was not without remorse that the first sea-leopard was lanced on the ice; whose bravery before death, and mild supplicating eyes when writhing under the spear, seemed to ask if passive courage deserved such a fate, if it were meet that any other motive than stern necessity should tempt a generous foe to witness a gallant endurance of wrongs, which the sufferer can neither avert nor requite.

Despite Hooker' misgivings as to rights and wrongs of this form of hunting he would soon be off again, this time to seek out and kill a cow that had been adopted by a herd of wild horses. Having located the horses the five men and their dog approached in the same way as before but failed to reckon with the bravery of the herd, which rallied round the lonesome cow and prevented the dog from setting its teeth into the intended victim. It was only when a shot was fired over the animals' heads that the horses relinquished their defensive stance and left the cow to defend herself. The end was now in sight and she fell to a fusillade of shots from the marksmen. Then, not content with the demise of the cow, they turned their attention to the fleeing horses and succeeded in bringing down several of those as well.

Having received tutelage from the crew of *Arrow*, whose commander, his ship away from England for nearly five years, was keen to return there, the trainees soon became adept at procuring enough of the wild cattle to fill the bottomless larders of the two ships.

Their commanders were now anxious to assess the damage their ships had sustained in the battle with the icebergs, and to that end had been supervising the construction of a small pier to remove the ships' stores and spars, anchors and cannon, so that the ships could be beached and careened. The *Erebus* was the first to be inspected, and as she lay on first one side and then the other the carpenters from both ships set to and repaired the timbers, recaulked the seams and recoppered the hull. *Terror* also received some remedial work to her hull, but was found to be not so badly damaged as *Erebus*.

While they were carrying out the work another Royal Navy ship

Wild cattle hunt, painted by Richard Trevor Wilson.

Astrolobe and Zélée *stranded in the Torres Strait, painted by Louis le Breton.*

made her way up Berkeley Sound and dropped anchor. Ross sent one of his officers to offer assistance in piloting the new arrival through the narrow channel to the inner part where *Erebus* and *Terror* lay. It transpired that the ship was HMS *Carysfort,* and her commander, Lord George Paulet, had brought the new bowsprit for *Erebus* that Ross had requested when *Arrow* had departed for Rio on her way home. Also on board was a great assortment of stores to replace those consumed by the two ships' complements since New Zealand.

With the arrival of *Carysfort* bringing with her some new faces, there began a series of exchange visits and a considerable amount of socialising. This could not last long, however, because she was on her way to Hawaii, where there had been some problems between the local population and British subjects living on the islands. She took her departure on 7 July, leaving the explorers to look forward to a long winter and another journey to the far south.

After building the observatory, the men not involved in servicing the ships' hulls were set to work on building a wall to surround the small cemetery. The idea would appear to be based on the assumption that idle hands get into mischief. On a number of occasions the men had been allowed shore leave only to finish up so drunk that even the act of getting them back aboard ship required a lot of organising. Ross stipulated that the wall should be constructed from grass turves, and the sizes of the wall given by his own hand in his book about the expedition are as follows; the thickness was to be 7 feet, and as many high.

It transpired that one of the very early sealer/explorers, Matthew Brisbane, had been murdered by some gauchos during a conflict while the islands were not under the control of any particular country. Brisbane had made his name in conjunction with James Weddell in the early part of the 19th century, exploring and at the same time carrying out sealing operations in the highest latitudes of the southern hemisphere that had ever been attained. It was Weddell and Brisbane's record that Ross and Crozier had broken when they ventured into what is now known as the Ross Sea in 1841.

Brisbane had visited the Falklands a number of times, and on 26 August 1823 he had met an untimely end there at the hands of the gauchos. His body had never been properly buried, and Ross was determined that his remains should be put to rest with the honour and dignity they deserved. A wooden headboard was made and an inscription written on it giving the date of his death, his achievement of furthest south, and the fact that he was reburied under the auspices of the crews of *Erebus* and *Terror* in 1842.

None of the two crews had ever experienced a winter in the Falklands but by the end of May they has been given a stiff warning of what it might be like. While they were working outside, refitting the two ships as they lay hauled up above the high water line, the wind started to drive sleet and snow showers across the open countryside, making their occupation a very unpleasant one. Others were out hunting wildfowl on the marshy areas of the bay, and a team of officers and men were out on the moorland hunting for more cattle to build up their larder for the winter. All would return to the shelter of the ships thoroughly cold and wet, and thankful to seek shelter from the bitterly cold wind and driving rain, and get the chance to change into dry clothing.

The weather seemed to relent as June approached the halfway mark, but of course the days were now down to their shortest of the year and it was essential to complete the refitting of both ships and put back on board all the stores and equipment that had been removed several weeks earlier.

Friday 1 July turned out to be Cunningham's birthday, but apart from mentioning this fact in his diary the day is recorded as passing without any special conviviality. The snow had resumed and now it was compounded by a sharp frost, but even this did not put a stop to the outside activity. Hunting continued, and the stockpile of slaughtered cattle had to be butchered, and the joints manhandled back down to the two ships, now back in the water and lying at anchor.

The lieutenant-governor of the islands, Lieutenant Richard Clement Moody, a military engineering officer, sent a request to Ross: he wanted to know whether Port William would be a better anchorage than Port Louis. This would require soundings to be taken at Port William, and a chart made to determine its suitability or otherwise. Ross was only too happy to comply with the request, and on 25 July *Erebus*'s pinnace set off on the mission. The journey wasn't a long one, as Port William, a little to the south of Berkeley Sound, could be reached from the open sea far more readily than Port Louis.

Ross submitted his report, with a clear chart indicating all the benefits that he found: access from the sea was much easier, and the harbour was in two parts; the outer portion would give adequate anchorage for ships seeking a safe haven or just taking on water and supplies, leaving the inner part free for any vessels needing a longer stay or urgent repairs. Ross's appraisal indicated that from Port William ships could be sent to sea without having to negotiate the length of Berkeley Sound (in an easterly wind, ships had to tack along the sound for several miles to reach open water). In fact, Captain Fitzroy of *Beagle* had already carried out soundings around Port William, and these being satisfactory Ross had no hesitation in recommending the transfer to Port William as soon as possible.

Ross's findings were implemented in 1845, and the move to establish Port William as the administrative centre began; today it is Port Stanley, the capital of the Falkland Islands as a whole.

Moody stayed on in the Falklands for a further three years before returning to England. In 1858; he was them promoted to colonel and took the post of lieutenant-governor of British Columbia, one of the developing regions of Canada.

Ross had taken Crozier with him to Port William, and after they had completed the survey they carried out several experiments using rockets. Launching two at a time, they fired them towards *Erebus* and *Terror*'s anchorage, and two answering rockets were launched from *Erebus*. This happened on two occasions over two consecutive days and was probably a similar experiment to the one they had carried out in Sydney.

The colony at this point in time was still in its very early years and Ross estimated that there were less than 50 inhabitants, with an additional 20 or so involved in the administration and security of the islands. It would be another five or six years before some semblance of organisation became the norm and a routine established whereby supplies from the United Kingdom, but mostly from Argentina, could be relied on to maintain the foothold that was so obviously precarious when the explorers were there in 1842.

By the beginning of September, the time had come for the two ships to resume their explorations, and for everybody on board this moment had not come soon enough. It had been a long southern winter and boredom was rife despite the officers' every effort to keep up morale.

Thursday 8 September 1842 saw the two ships close-hauled to the strengthening wind as they left from the protection of the land on a course for Tierra del Fuego, heading directly for Cape Horn. Ross described the rock that gives its name to one of the most feared landmarks in the world as looking like a sleeping lion.

Cape Horn, the sleeping lion described by Ross in his book.

Replica of a Yahgan canoe used by the natives who visited the ships as they lay at anchor in the cove chosen for the magnetic observatory.

On 19 September they closed with the cape, about a mile and a half away. Even from this relatively safe distance they could see the waves breaking violently against the rocky shoreline. Ross describes the coastline as wild yet beautiful with many islands and high peaks along it. From a description they had seen in *Beagle's* logbook a few years earlier, they were on the lookout for a small harbour from which they hoped to continue with the magnetic observations so important to the research they were carrying out. Finally they discerned the entrance to the cove they were seeking, and sent in a boat to reconnoitre a suitable anchorage. The next morning, when Ross and Crozier set out to see for themselves where to land and set up the observatory, much to their surprise they were hailed by three natives in a bark canoe, paddling out to meet them. Apart from what turned out to be an otter skin acting as a shawl, none of the men wore any garments despite the near-freezing temperatures.

Much effort was needed to bring in the two ships and anchor them, due to the narrowness of the cove and the lack of a favourable breeze. This protracted labour meant that, much to Ross's chagrin, the observatory would not be unloaded and ready in time for the next term date. He had, however, had the forethought to arrange a second date a week later when John Sibbald, who was still on the Falklands, could take a second set of measurements to coincide with the ones to be taken at Tierra del Fuego. Additional time was needed to dig a firm foundation for the building; after several days the work was complete and the observations were successfully carried out.

McCormick likened St Martin's Island, where the observatory was located, to the west coast of Scotland. The indentations of the coastline forming narrow arms of the sea were, he felt, reminiscent of the Scottish lochs he knew so well. The sight of fully-grown trees was indeed a strange one to men who so recently had only beheld icebergs or at best the low-growing scrub on the tundra of the Falklands. The trees here resembled for the most part the sturdy beech commonly seen on the chalk soils at home, and although there was a dearth of any substantial undergrowth there was ground cover in the form of mosses and a few fern-like plants, which excited Hooker.

Ross made notes about the local natives. He was disappointed by their appearance and lack of basic creature comforts; in comparison with other primitive people he had encountered during his extensive travels he put the Fuegians far below. They possessed little in the way of clothing, and their weaponry, upon which they depended, was equally basic. It consisted of three types of spear of different lengths, and a small bow and arrow. Despite their access to proper trees the quality of their weapons was far inferior to that of even the Inuit, who crafted their hunting equipment and tools out of nothing more than whale and caribou bones and the odd piece of driftwood.

The prospect of sending out parties to gain further knowledge of their surroundings was considered, but it proved almost impossible because of the sudden gusts of wind, 'williwaws', which, sweeping down off the higher land, would have been more than capable of overturning the ship's boats. So during the course of their stay they carried out a simple set of observations regarding the rise and fall of the tides, with an average determined by a simple mathematical calculation. To leave a record of this data a rock face near to water level was chosen, and a groove chiselled across its face to indicate the mean, like one they had made at Port Louis.

HMS Beagle *as used in the HMS* Beagle *Project, painted by John Chancellor.*

An interesting experiment they tried was uprooting a large quantity of young trees and shrubs to take back with them to the Falklands, in order to supplement their native specimens, so very meagre and stunted. Ross hoped these saplings would survive and thrive in a climate not so very different from their original environment.

Then they departed the most forlorn of berths they had ever experienced during their four years at sea.

14 RETURN TO THE ANTARCTIC

ONCE MORE UNTO THE BREACH, THEN HOMEWARD BOUND

On 7 November they set sail back to the Falklands, and Sibbald met them at the entrance to Berkeley Sound with despatches and their long-awaited mail from England.

Their final stay here was short; once the beef and other necessities had been loaded they set off, hoping to explore the Antarctica peninsula and possibly attempt the route that Weddell had successfully pioneered into the frozen sea that now bears his name. Although the peninsula had never really been explored it had already been given two different names; Graham Land was the one familiar to Ross, but the Americans called it Palmer Land. At one stage it was also referred to as the Trinity peninsula. Today it is divided into several sections, and Graham Land, the farthest north, extends down to 69°S, where Palmer Land takes over. The very tip is now Trinity Peninsula. Meanwhile Argentina refers to the area as Tierra de San Martin, and Chile has named it after one of its national heroes, O'Higgins.

Just as the two ships were about to leave Port Louis a salute to wish them well on their journey literally backfired; the two men firing the gun received serious injuries, one to his hand and the other to his arm and both hands. The ships were immediately hove to while the surgeons carried out first aid.

Resuming its departure, the expedition directed its course once more to the frozen continent that had been the centre of its attention for the last three years. Three days after leaving Port Louis the ships were rapidly closing in on the first of the South Shetland group, but poor visibility restricted the horizon and although they knew they were approaching Clarence Island – the presence of seabirds indicated that land was not too far distant – they saw no sign of it. One week into the voyage and with Christmas Day just one day away, they saw the first of the floating fields of ice and their accompanying sentinels, the icebergs. Providing the weather cleared these would not present any danger, but ever-present in their minds was the catastrophe that had so nearly overwhelmed them the last time they had ventured into this icy realm. Sailing with much-reduced canvas due to the stiff westerly, they celebrated Christmas lunch, feasting on Falkland Islands home-grown beef courtesy of the governor who had had two bullocks fattened up for the occasion.

Wednesday 28 December 1842 was spent probing the edge of the pack ice but not venturing too far into it, as the position would be much exposed should they get beset. As evening was approaching, land was sighted for the first time since leaving the Falklands. Using charts from the d'Urville expedition, Ross estimated that they must be close to the northernmost point of land, which the French admiral had named Terre Joinville. No landing was contemplated, however, due to the most unfavourable conditions, and Ross was not able to establish an accurate position. They turned southwards, along a series of high ice cliffs resembling those of the Ross Sea two long years ago, then they spent the 30th manoeuvring amongst icebergs, when again land was seen. It took the form of high sea cliffs surmounted by snow, and Ross started to name some of its prominent features after naval officers of his acquaintance. A small conical islet became Paulet Island, and in the first decade of the next century it was to feature in two of the early expeditions that explored this remote region: Ernest Shackleton and the Finnish-Swedish geographer Otto Nordenskjöld would become closely associated with this small outcrop of rock.

On New Year's Day the crew members of the two ships received a complete outfit of warm clothing, and good wishes were exchanged between the ships, the officers of *Erebus* rowing across to visit their counterparts on *Terror*. Soon afterwards, as they coasted along in the light breeze, they saw ahead one of the highest peaks yet observed, and estimated it at over 7,000 feet; they named it after the first lord of the Admiralty, Lord Haddington. Today it is listed as rising to 5,350 feet above sea level and can be located on the island named after James Clark Ross.

A sudden turn in the weather catching them unprepared resulted in an enforced stay in the ice that had closed around them. They anchored to a large floe during their stay, and the sailors went onto the ice to catch a few penguins. Two types were caught, and as the larger of the two species scaled in at over 60 lbs (~27 kg) it can be assumed that these were emperor penguins. The following afternoon the sea ice relaxed enough to give the ships room to manoeuvre, and eventually both sailed free once more.

On 5 January they made a historic landing on an island they christened Cockburn after Sir George Cockburn, a senior admiral. With due ceremony the two captains took possession of it in the name of the Queen. Hooker and the other naturalists were then allowed some time to search out any interesting life forms and carry out a quick geological survey. In the time available a total of 19 species were located, mostly mosses and lichens. Of these, Hooker stated that seven were to be found nowhere else in the world. The distributions of the lower orders of plants would become a speciality of Joseph Hooker, and once this expedition had been completed he travelled extensively to various parts of the world, to amass one of the most comprehensive collections, housed at Kew Gardens.

After the ceremony the party returned to their ships, but the tide sweeping in from the open sea defied their efforts to leave the inlet. Despite sending out their boats to tug them clear their best efforts were thwarted, but as luck would have it the water was clear of any

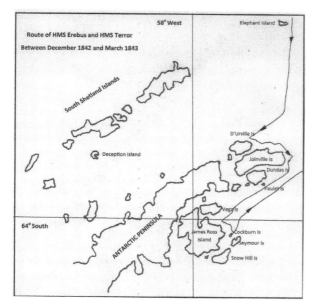

Erebus *and* Terror *set out from the Falkland Islands on 17 February 1842 for a final voyage to Antarctica; it would lead to a landing on Cockburn Island and the exploration of the northern end of the Antarctic peninsula.*

Cockburn Island, named after Sir George Cockburn, the senior lord of the Admiralty.

major obstructions such as ice or rocky outcrops, and as the tide swept out again later that day they rode out on it without incident. Admiralty Inlet was the name they gave to the place where they had been for the past 24 hours. Nordenskjöld's expedition in 1902 explored it further and found it to be a passage between what is now known as James Ross Island and Seymour and Snow Islands, so the name has been corrected to Admiralty Sound.

Frustrated at the lack of progress the expedition was making penetrating more to south, Ross decided to try further to the south-east. but first of all, they had to extricate themselves from the pack ice barring them from the open sea, and in the process the ships became separated: *Terror* was swept out of sight, driven away as the floe holding her broke up. The next day early in the morning the two ships were reunited and both having been released they could make good their escape. For nearly two weeks they continued to probe the ice but with the fear of getting beset, caution prevailed.

They had now spent three precious weeks zig-zagging, and had arrived almost back at the point where they had first seen Cockburn Island; on the last day of January 1843 Paulet Island had just hove into view once again. The season for sailing in these latitudes was now coming to a close, and Ross was about to make one last attempt at achieving something significant: he had always held out the hope that where James Weddell had penetrated so far to the south there might still be a chance for them to emulate that feat. They set their target now at reaching 40°W, the line where Weddell's chart indicated that he had found an ice-free way into the sea named after him. In 1823 he had achieved a furthest south of 74°15'S.

When the expedition first reached 40°W they will still only at 65°13'S – but, as Ross wrote in his book, 'under what different circumstances'. There was no passage to be seen, and the conclusion they reached that Weddell must, fortunately for him, have been in just the right place at just the right time. Years later others were to try, and all of them had a similar experience to that of Ross. Weddell's opportunity had clearly been a one-off. There is actually a passage that is navigable most years, but it is much further to the east, along what is now known as the Caird Coast of Coats Land. But to Ross and Crozier this was unknown territory.

They did succeed, however, in recording that they had crossed the Line of No Variation on 22 February.[25] Other sections of this long and winding line were identified by the expedition on several occasions in different parts of the southern hemisphere; the charting of this line, as well as that of the Magnetic Equator, was part of the magnetic studies they were tasked with.

By early March the two ships, sailing further east, did eventually reach their furthest south for that season, achieving 71°30'S. Thus far the weather had been very kind to them as they pushed into the open pack, but on the night of 6 March a high sea brought spray onto the decks and rigging, making it extremely dangerous both to work the ships and for them to stay in contact with each other. This late in the season there were quite a few hours of darkness each day, and the position was becoming very serious indeed. Encased in the pack ice were a number of icebergs and the memories of the previous venture south must have been at the forefront of their minds. Salvation came with the dawn, and as the wind dropped the seas fell away.

Despite the significant cloud cover a remarkable observation was made: the crews could clearly see what appeared to be a beam of light high in the sky. It was visible for more than a week and then seemed to skim the surface of the sun. They surmised that it must be a comet, and not, as first thought, a display of the Aurora Australis.

---

25 It is now known as the agonic line, and it writhes up and down the globe; at the time of writing part of it runs north–south through the UK. For an animation of its movement through the centuries from 1500 to 2000, see https://www.wikiwand.com/en/Magnetic_declination .

The sun setting across the icy wastes of the Antarctic Sea.

They were right; what they had witnessed had been seen in many places across the world at around the same time; it was called the Great Comet. Back in 1705 Edmund Halley had calculated that the comet that would be named after him had a cycle of about 75 years – but this new comet, according to one scientist's calculation, was not expected to return for at least 600 years. The expedition was extremely lucky to be in the southern hemisphere at the time, as in the northern half of the world cloud cover severely restricted viewing. All told, however, it was visible in various parts of the world between its first sighting in early 1843 until the middle of April.

On 10 March the ships, now clear of the entrapping ice, put on a full spread of canvas and struck out for the north, crossing the Antarctic Circle the next day. An anomaly that Ross was keen to find the answer to was the correct location of a small island that had reputedly been discovered by the French explorer Jean-Baptiste Charles Bouvet in 1739, but as his co-ordinates were inaccurate several attempts to find it, including Ross's, failed. Having criss-crossed the location he had been given, yet with no positive sighting, the expedition resumed its course for Cape Town, nearly 600 miles away.

Bouvet Island has had a chequered history regarding its location. Several sealing captains recorded sighting it, but no known landing was made on it until 1927, when a Norwegian expedition successfully achieved it. The Norwegians were eventually given jurisdiction over the island, and as it lies outside the Antarctic Circle it is not subject to the treaty that governs all lands that fall within it. Since about 1971 it has been set aside as a nature reserve.

The expedition arrived in Simon's Town on 4 April. Ross claimed that there were no crew members on the sick list. This was true to a point – but it was here that James Cleat, a gunner aboard *Terror*, had to be discharged to the naval hospital. According to Cunningham's diary Cleat had been found prostrate in his bunk, having attempted suicide. It was only by luck that he was discovered in time and rushed to the hospital, where his life was saved. This was a sobering occasion for the expedition, as he was a popular man. But by his own admission he had tried before to end his life, and he blamed drink and the devil for his actions. Later he returned to England and can be traced through the census records; he lived with his first wife, Barbara, and their five children.

For nearly three weeks the crew were allowed shore leave, and the officers took full advantage of the hospitality liberally offered to them by the residents and other senior military personnel on the station. Loading the ships for what was to be the beginning of the end of the expedition proceeded with all haste, and as the end of April approached all was ready for them to set sail.

Two weeks later they let slip the mooring ropes at James Town in St Helena. The purpose of this short visit was to collect the men who had been looking after the observatory erected on their outward voyage three years before. An even briefer stay took place at Ascension Island, where they called to take a set of magnetic readings. With these completed the two ships turned their prows towards their next destination, Rio de Janeiro, where they arrived on 7 June.

Thomas Jones, one of *Terror*'s able seamen, was taken ill as the ships crossed the Atlantic towards Rio de Janeiro, and as they made port on 18 June he slipped peacefully to his death. This was the first recorded death from natural causes during the expedition, and the first aboard *Terror*. It was recorded only in Cunningham's diaries.

McCormick made the most of the short stay in Rio, visiting various parts of the town, which he thought had improved significantly since his visit aboard *Beagle* back in 1832. He was impressed by the firework displays that took place to mark St John's week, on each day the church bells chimed in celebration and the atmosphere was generally one of joyfulness. Having visited a shop that made wreaths and other displays from colourful feathers, he seems to have been encouraged to purchase a grey parrot and a green one, which it must be assumed took their places in his cabin.

The ships' officers exchanged visits with an American naval squadron anchored nearby and after bidding farewell to the British ambassador, Mr Hamilton, they prepared for their final departure and set out on the morning of 25 June, bound for home.

On the journey from Rio back across the Atlantic the newly promoted Lieutenant Alexander Smith was taken seriously ill as they headed north, and his sickness puzzled the medics – but just as suddenly as he had fallen ill, he made a rapid recovery, just before they docked at Woolwich.

The passage up the Atlantic did not present any problems and even the doldrums were transited with ease. After all the adverse conditions they had endured in the preceding four years it was almost an anticlimax to sail towards their last destination.

One more disturbing incident, however, awaited them when they finally dropped anchor and lay waiting for the customs officers and for the wages clerks to pay off the crew: tragedy struck. Able Seaman William Pennant, who had been aboard HMS *Terror* for the four years of the expedition, lost his life in a freak accident. He fell overboard and before a rescue could be mounted he had drowned, casting a gloomy and sombre mood on both ships' crews.

This brought the total deaths since the expedition had set out in September 1839 to six, a remarkably small number given the era, and the route. Sickness and injury had resulted in

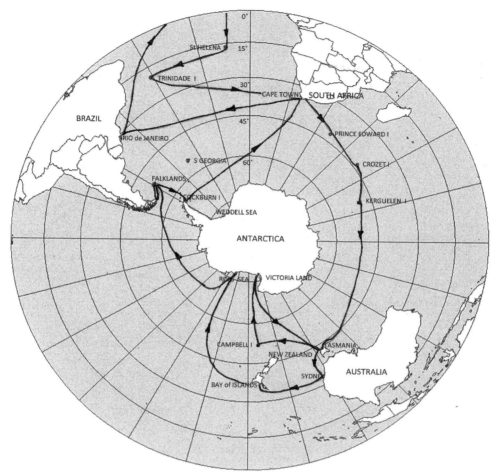

Chart of the 1839 to 1843 Ross expedition.

other crew members and officers being discharged along the way, and of course desertions had played a part in the composition of the two ships' assemblies; but not one case of scurvy had erupted, and for this full credit must be given to the commanders of *Erebus* and *Terror*, Captain James Clark Ross and Captain Francis Crozier.

Promotions followed the return of the two ships, the chief of these being the knighting of the expedition leader, who now became Captain Sir James Clark Ross.

PART TWO

THE SAILORS' STORIES

The story of the Antarctic expedition led by Captain James Clark Ross from Chatham in 1839 has lain largely undisturbed since it was completed in September 1843. Yes, authors have dusted it off from time to time whilst putting together a history of exploration in the southern hemisphere when the brave men who ventured into those turbulent waters were seeking out the unknown continent, but it would seem that the greatness of this expedition has been largely forgotten. Reminders of its presence can of course be found in the numerous landmarks named after the expedition members – but that form of nomenclature applies all over the world, and I wonder how many of today's visitors to Antarctica realise how so many of its geographical features came to be named. I will elaborate on some of those places as we meet the people concerned, and in some cases repeat or refer to information found in Part One.

My purpose in composing this extension to the story of the expedition is to turn over the pages of that almost forgotten and extremely hazardous journey, and look deeper into the various sources to see if I can elicit some details never seen before. The routes the expedition took and the itinerary carried out had been planned months before they set out, and to a great extent it was completed to everyone's satisfaction; so successful indeed was the voyage that Ross was given a knighthood; his opposite number on board HMS *Terror*, Crozier, received promotion to a full captain; and other officers, both junior and senior, progressed up the ranks of the navy – surprisingly, though, not as much as one might have thought: McCormick for example, ruefully observed that neither of the surgeons nor their assistants received any recognition despite maintaining two healthy crews for the complete voyage. Looking back from our 21st-century viewpoint that was an extraordinary achievement, and an extraordinary omission.

James Clark Ross's two-volume story of the expedition of 1839 to 1843

Held in various archives are sources of information and documents containing interesting facts relating to the officers and crew who took part in the expedition. To follow the subsequent careers of the men who sailed with Crozier and Ross has required the searching out of this information. It is mostly held by organisations that exist to act as repositories for naval historical records, but before I delved into their archives I was able to access a more immediate source of information about the sailors.

Naval regulations obliged the commander of each ship to maintain a record of the personnel who served on her, no matter how short the service. This record was, and still is, called the Muster List, or Roll, and from it all sorts of interesting facts emerge: the names and the dates of each sailor's entry and discharge; their age at entry and the posts they hold; whether or not they complete a voyage, and if not the reason for them leaving. The wages earned can also be gleaned from these records.

It is worth comparing the muster lists of the two ships that took part in this voyage of exploration and discovery, so let us have a look at them.

The very first thing that catches the eye is that *Erebus* is referred to as Her Majesty's Ship, whereas the HMS prefixing *Terror* stands for Her Majesty's Sloop. This is because a ship commanded by a captain can be called a ship, but as Francis Crozier was only a commander *Terror* was classified as a sloop.

HMS *Erebus* was the flagship of the expedition under the direct command of Captain James Clark Ross. On her departure from Chatham Royal Naval Dockyard on 19 September she and her consort were towed down the Medway estuary by steam-powered tugs to moorings at Gillingham where the pay clerks came aboard and gave out the three months' advanced pay to the crew present. This would have been double pay because they were aboard an exploring or discovery ship.

With this formality over, the two ships were towed further out of the estuary to Sheerness where a pilot and customs officers came aboard to make last minute checks. At this point there would have been an opportunity to take on any other heavy stores and ordinance and then passage would have been cleared to proceed on the voyage that would see them absent for four years.

The Medway estuary at Chatham was quite shallow in places and the river meandered several times on its way to the open sea. Sailing ships could find the tide and wind against them and it became routine to be towed into and out of the dock basin. The draught of heavily laden ships also added to the problems they experienced reaching the open sea, hence the reason they took on the heavier stores, which could include cannons and ordnance, as the estuary deepened.

There too a pilot would come aboard, together with customs officers to make last-minute checks, then passage would have been cleared for the ships to proceed on the voyage that would see them absent for the next four years.

Captain James Clark Ross's brief was to explore as far south as possible to try and locate the South Magnetic Pole, all the while making extensive magnetic and oceanographic observations wherever they sailed. On *Erebus* he was assisted by his three lieutenants, James Wood, Edward Bird and John Sibbald. They were supported by 11 junior officers, 41 crewmen and 7 marines. Part One of this book gives a good idea of the routes they took, the ports and islands they called at, and the work they undertook during their four years at sea.

Sailing alongside *Erebus* was her consort, HMS *Terror*, commanded by Francis Crozier, assisted by his lieutenants, Joseph Kay, Archibald McMurdo and Charles Phillips. The petty

The gatehouse of Chatham Royal Dockyard. From 1722 all sailors using the port would have passed through this entrance.

officers numbered 11 and she had a crew of 42 sailors and a contingent of 7 marines, led by Sergeant William Cunningham.

For my sources I have principally used Ross's two-volume book; in addition, Sergeant William Cunningham kept a diary of events throughout the four years of the expedition, and Ross's great-great-grandson, M.J. Ross, compiled a volume entitled *Ross in the Antarctic*. The only other published book I have been able to find about the expedition was written by Robert McCormick, *Erebus*'s surgeon.

Cunningham's diary reveals more about the lower-deck activities than do the other publications. His entries describe the sailing conditions, the places the ships visited, the dates of arrival and departure along the route, and the exchanges of personnel and the people who visited the ship. He also described the enjoyable reunions he had with contemporaries that he came across in the various ports they called at. Many of the following details about him and the voyage have been gleaned from information given to me by Captain Richard Campbell RN (Rtd), who produced an academic transcript of the diaries together with copious footnotes and cross-references, and I submit my sincere thanks to him for his generous assistance. Joseph Hooker also kept diaries, but to my knowledge these have never been transcribed into a book and remain as handwritten documents held in the archives at Greenwich.

Both ships, having been fitted out at Chatham, had carried out their initial recruitment at the dockside. The officers, including most of the warrant and junior officers, would have been personally selected by the two captains, to ensure they took with them only the most experienced men, ones that they could rely on. It is not apparent whether an official recruitment officer had been set aside for the whole expedition and whether the men were apportioned according to experience and position applied for, but on looking at the handwritten muster lists it was noticeable that although the styles of writing were very similar there were sufficient differences to lead me to believe that each ship's company was responsible for looking after its own interests.

What became very clear as the expedition proceeded was that there was a significant turnover of personnel driven by illness, desertion, promotion and even death. It was not really surprising that so many men fell by the wayside; four years of sailing in the least-explored regions of the world with very limited shore leave – and that in strange countries – must have seemed a hardship most difficult to bear. Even the new colony of Tasmania, which was the most like England in its traditions and way of life, was still struggling to establish itself, and held little to entice sailors. Its inhabitants were for the most part convicts or at best poor people hoping to make a better life for themselves in this extremity of the British Empire. Also, in the town of Hobarton, as Hobart was called in those days, there was a distinct divide between those that had and those that had not. The upper echelon of this diverse society was led by the governor, the famous Arctic explorer Sir John Franklin who, accompanied by his second wife, Lady Jane, provided the entertainment for the senior men aboard the two sailing ships. Whilst the officers were thus well catered for, the crew were left to their own devices, which meant they usually ended up in a grog shop, to be hauled back on board by a party of marines to sleep off the inevitable hangover.

Most of the sailors would, unlike the officers, have had to make their own social life and it is unrecorded, but there is the one well-documented liaison that took place: between Alexander Smith, the first mate on *Erebus*, and Sarah Read. He subsequently returned to Tasmania, married her and helped run the observatory that had been set up during the expedition. One must assume from the number of deserters whilst the ships spent their two winters in Hobart that other crew members likewise formed relationships, but there is no evidence of this.

Throughout the course of the voyage 9 men from *Erebus* were listed as runners, and 16 men from *Terror* also decided that for better or worse they could find a better life on land. These all had to be replaced, and volunteers stepped forward: *Erebus* took on another 20 crew members throughout her four years at sea and *Terror* acquired 25 to top up her numbers. At other times there were other losses to make good, as men were hospitalised, transferred to other ships, dismissed as unsuitable or, in six cases, died in service. But Hobart, where the greatest number deserted, was of course the source of most of the new volunteers.

It is essential to understand that all the men involved in the expedition were volunteers; there were no pressed men. There were, however, a number of men who were listed as 'first entry' in that they had not sailed with the Royal Navy before this voyage. But they would probably have gained experience in the merchant marine or the whaling or fishing industries. Setting out from England, HMS *Erebus* had on board 11 first entries, and the subsequent intakes took that total up by another 16 men; 5 of those original 11 completed the voyage, as did 11 of the others who had signed on during the course of the expedition. *Terror* had a much greater number of first entries than *Erebus* right from the start; she had on board 32 first entries out of a total of 48 men who enlisted at Chatham, and of these men 20 lasted till the ship came home. She took on 18 more during her time away from England, the majority of them first timers; they may have been seeking passage back to Blighty and getting paid for the experience, but there is no way of knowing this.

All told there were 6 deaths and a total of 21 dismissals for one reason or another between the ships' two crews from the time they left England in 1839 until their return four years later. The reasons for dismissal were various, but included quite a few for disciplinary purposes or for not coming up to the very high standards required. A few sailors requested release from service, and on those lines a couple of them were given transfers to other vessels, but of the remainder hospitalisation was the predominant reason for leaving: 12 crew members required hospital treatment or repatriation to England as a result of medical problems.

The six deaths were caused by accidents rather than illness, and I note them again here. Edward Bradley, the captain of the hold on *Erebus*, was suffocated by fumes whilst carrying out a thorough cleaning procedure with the heated charcoal used to scorch the walls of the hold during the first winter's stop at Hobart. Then the boatswain, John Roberts, also from *Erebus*, fell overboard and drowned; this occurred ten days after they had sailed from Kerguelen, bound for Tasmania. Drowning was the cause of the next death as well; it came about when one of *Erebus*'s boats foundered on bringing two of the ship's marines back from a fishing trip in the harbour at the Bay of Islands in New Zealand. The unlucky man, who couldn't swim, was George Barker, a most popular individual who was missed greatly by his comrades. The fourth member of *Erebus* to lose his life was James Angeley; when manning the rigging in rough weather south of Cape Horn in April 1842, he lost his footing, and by the time the ship had been turned around to rescue him he had disappeared.

In the case of *Terror*, her luck held out until the expedition was making its way home. Her stop at Rio de Janeiro was, however, marred by the death of Thomas Jones, an able seaman who had not been well for about five weeks. He passed away on 19 June 1843, just three months from being paid off at Woolwich. The last, and probably the most poignant, death took place within the harbour at Woolwich on the day before payday: 22 September 1843 saw Able Seaman William Pennant fall into the harbour and drown. From the sources available to me I can find no further explanation of his death.

A mammoth undertaking such as this expedition could only give the best results when manned and led by the most experienced personnel available, and in this respect the Admiralty went to great lengths to achieve a successful outcome. Their choice of leader was a key starting point, and of the senior naval captains at the time none stood close to James Clark Ross. He was now 38 years old, and his expeditionary experience was second to none. He had started his naval career at the age of 12, not uncommon in those days. His uncle, John Ross, had already established himself as a naval officer of some repute. This was to benefit young James considerably; John Ross saw to it that his nephew spent the early part of his formative years in the navy under his wing, and James started to progress up the promotion ladder. For six years he followed his uncle from ship to ship, and at the end of this time he was a midshipman.

When he was 26, on his return from Captain William Parry's attempt in *Fury* and *Hecla* to find a way through the northern reaches of Hudson Bay, his next promotion was awaiting him; he had become a lieutenant. He was then invited to accompany Parry on the Prince Regent Inlet expedition in 1824 as second lieutenant aboard *Fury*. This was Parry's third and final attempt to discover the North-west Passage, forcing a path through the intricate labyrinth of channels between the many islands in the northern reaches of Canada.

As mentioned in Chapter 1, between 1836 and 1837 Captain George Back, commanding HMS *Terror*, had tried to achieve what all the others had attempted, but ice foiled his attempt and it was only by luck and extremely good seamanship that his expedition was able to sail back across the Atlantic. They finished up by beaching *Terror* on an Irish shore, and it would not be for another eight years that Britain would try again, with the Franklin expedition.

After Parry returned to Britain from Prince Regent Inlet the Admiralty turned to him once more, to establish if it was possible to reach what was believed by many to be an ice-free polar sea. Parry was still the leading authority on working ships through ice-packed seas, and in 1827 *Hecla* set sail for Spitsbergen. She did not have a consort on this voyage, as the plan was not for her to enter the ice pack but to just act as a depot ship. Lieutenant Ross, having gained Parry's respect, was his second in command. The expedition, however, turned into an abject failure with little or nothing of any consequence to show for it except the obvious fact that all the crew had gained valuable experience of ice travel with sledges. The idea of taking dog teams does not seem to have been considered; instead they took reindeer to haul the sledges onto which had been strapped two rowing boats that they intended to use for any open water. The expedition returned to Britain the same year, knowing that although they had reached the furthest north by a few miles when they had been forced to retreat, they had still been 500 miles from the North Pole.

Admiral Sir William Parry; James Clark Ross accompanied Parry on all his Arctic expeditions.

James's uncle had not been idle since the Croker Mountains débâcle; he had raised sufficient capital to start an independent expedition to find the fabled passage across northern Canada. With one of the smallest expedition forces – just 25 men – to ever attempt the search, he appointed his nephew James as second in command, and they bade farewell to England in 1829 on what turned out to be the longest quest ever. Four and a half years they were still absent, and many had given up hope of ever seeing them alive again.

On their return to England in 1833, the two Rosses, hailed as heroes, were overwhelmed by offers of banquets, receptions and all manner of social engagements. John was knighted and James became a commander. They would never sail together again, however, and a split appears to have arisen between them over the actual position that James held on the expedition; had he been second in command, or did he have further responsibilities that had not been declared? Whatever the situation between the two, it became public knowledge that neither man would concede to the other as to their professional relationship during the voyage.

Following James's return to England from his gruelling expedition in the Arctic, he was appointed to serve for a year on HMS *Victory* at Portsmouth, and was promoted to post captain. The next year, 1835, he was offered a totally new position; to carry out a magnetic survey of the whole of Great Britain. He accepted the challenge and began work immediately. This was interrupted in 1836 when he volunteered to lead an attempt on HMS *Cove* to rescue stranded whalers in the Davis Sea. This brings his story up to the beginning of 1837, when the Antarctic expedition went before the Admiralty, the Royal Society, the Royal Geographical Society and finally the government for approval and the allocation of sufficient funds to execute the plan.

Captain Francis Rawdon Moira Crozier, RN FRS FRAS, became the commanding officer of an expedition only on the death of Sir John Franklin in the fateful Arctic exploit that cost all the officers and crews of *Erebus* and *Terror* their lives some time after 1847. Crozier had always had the misfortune of being a subordinate in any expedition. He had benefited from a good all-round education, albeit cut short upon his entry into the Royal Navy at the age of 14. His enrolment took place in Cork. In 1814 he found himself on the way to Cape Horn aboard HMS *Briton* as a midshipman, which led to a voyage across the Pacific, searching for an American raider attacking merchant ships around the East Indies. His ship visited Pitcairn Island by chance, and here he learnt of the fate of the mutineers who had set Captain Bligh adrift in an open boat with 18 of the ship's crew.

Back in England in 1817, he took and passed his mate's certificate, then sailed to Hudson Bay with William Parry and James Clark Ross; as a result of this venture he would form a lifelong friendship with Ross. The North-west Passage would first feature in Crozier's career as he set out once more with Parry and Ross aboard HMS *Hecla* and HMS *Fury* to Prince Regent Inlet. A further visit to the Arctic via Spitsbergen, again aboard *Hecla*, was the 1827 attempt to reach the North Pole.

By now he had become a lieutenant. It was this sustained period of British involvement in polar exploration that despite the economies of peacetime saw some of the Royal Navy's best men progress up the promotion ladder, but the good times were coming to an end and Francis

Crozier found himself on half-pay with little prospect of furthering his career. Interspersed with periods on half-pay he had several short-lived commissions, one of which found him once more patrolling the Bay of Biscay, this time aboard HMS *Stag*, but it was a relatively short deployment.

Ross's invitation for him to join HMS *Cove* in the 1836 venture to rescue the trapped whalers revived Crozier's passion for sailing in the wastes of the Arctic seas. This invitation came at a timely moment, because he could renew his friendship with James Clark Ross, and it led to Ross's offer to him to command *Terror* as she set sail to the Antarctic.

Crozier's life ended tragically during the attempt to reach the Great Fish river, or Back river as it was also known, in northern Canada in about 1848 or soon after. His death occurred during the final stages of the doomed retreat by the men of the Franklin expedition. Inuit oral history told the story of a party of about 40 *kabloonas* (white men) dragging a boat and heading south towards the mainland. Their leader was described as being quite a large man who they remembered meeting when he had accompanied Parry into Hudson Bay over 20 years earlier.

Due to Crozier's friendly relations with the Inuit on that occasion they had given him a name of their own, Aklooka, and this was how they referred to him when the American explorer Charles Hall interviewed a party of Inuit as he tried in 1869 to establish the cause of the Franklin disaster. Hall travelled along the coast of King William Island in the wake of the doomed men some 20 years after they had all died.

We may never know the whole truth about the tragedy that unfolded so many years ago and in a land so far from our shores, but what adds credence to the Inuit story is the 2014 discovery of the wreck of *Erebus* and, two years later, *Terror* near the sites where for over 150 years the Inuit have indicated they had last seen them.

In the cases of Ross and Crozier we have seen how lads of just 12 or 14 could progress up through the ranks to become captains of exploring ships in the most prestigious navy in the world at that time. It took Crozier 28 years from first entry to post captain, but the country had just been through one of its most traumatic periods in history. The French Revolution and the rise and fall of Napoleon Bonaparte had created unrest across the world, but it is in such periods of strife that the armed services of any country produce their leaders, and due to the arduous nature of hostilities it is to the younger generation that those in high office turn to for help.

With the peace settlement there followed a period of stability and a unique opportunity to utilise the surplus ships and their commanders to carry out all the expeditions that manifested themselves at this time. Much of the Earth's surface lay unknown to the civilised world and humans, the inquisitive beasts that we are, started on these voyages of discovery. Had it not been for this set of circumstances then no doubt the result would eventually have been achieved, but not in so short a timescale. The window of opportunity was open, and it was seized with both hands by the Royal Navy and its captains.

The 1839 voyage began in earnest when the two ships left Margate Roads on 30 September and, after several days becalmed, set sail down the English Channel. The breeze rapidly became storm force winds, and just three days into the voyage the two ships were separated. It was not too critical at this stage of the journey, but it would not be until Madeira, their first pre-arranged meeting point, that they were reunited. This gale would be the first test of the new crews, especially those listed as first entries. Each crew had experienced sailors, of course, who could show the new recruits how to work aloft and handle the sails. Men such as Samuel Barber, captain of the maintop aboard *Erebus*, and Andrew Johnson, captain of the foretop on *Terror*, would be crucial in the training carried out as the expedition progressed.

Both ships had virtually identical rigs, each with three masts: square-rigged foremast and mainmast and a gaff-rigged mizzenmast. Captains of the main and foremasts were appointed for each watch, and it was their responsibility to lead their team of four or five hands to set, trim or furl the sails during manoeuvres or as required for the efficient operation of the ship. With so many comparatively raw recruits amongst the two crews, the early storm must have been an extremely stressful time for all, and it is a testament to the skills of those senior crew members that not only did the two ships weather that storm – and many more – but also that throughout the entire four years of the expedition only two men were drowned whilst handling the sails.

The original design of the two ships had been bomb vessels, armed with mortars to fire shells at a land-based enemy during a seaborne assault. The hulls had been strengthened to withstand the huge recoil generated by the mortars. The removal of those guns from within the hulls resulted in a cavernous hold in which could be stored sufficient provisions for at least two and possibly three years. Further modifications were required for polar exploration, and in the dockyards at Chatham an enormous amount of strengthening work took place to ensure that both ships' hulls could withstand battering from the ice-infested waters of Antarctica.

On board *Erebus*, Ross had at least one lieutenant, **Edward Bird**, who had sailed with him on several polar expeditions already. Born in 1798, he had started his naval service at the age of 14, and his presence on the *Fury* and *Hecla* expeditions between 1820 and 1826 had given him the training he would need for his future role with Ross. Other ships he sailed in were all heavily armed warships, and between 1831 and 1834 he had passed his exams for lieutenant.

He even found a posting aboard one of the navy's newest steam-powered ships, HMS *Medea*, under Captain Horatio Austin, who would come to prominence during the search for Sir John Franklin.

When the Ross expedition reached the Falkland Islands in 1843 Bird found that he had been promoted to commander. This led to further rises up the ladder, and in 1848 at the age of 50 he was put in charge of HMS *Investigator*, one of two ships searching for the missing Franklin party. (The other ship was HMS *Enterprise*, whose captain was Ross.) Bird achieved the rank of admiral in 1863, taking retirement in

St Martin's church in Little Waltham, the burial place of Admiral Edward Bird.

1875. He passed away in 1881 and was buried in the village church yard of Little Waltham in Essex. He had lived in the village for many years.

His name is perpetuated in various landmarks in Antarctica such as Mount Bird and the appropriately named Cape Bird, the northern tip of Ross Island, where a colony of nearly 100,000 Adélie penguins can be found. At the time of writing it is not only used by the penguins as a breeding site but also has a hut for scientists studying the colony.

In HMS *Investigator*'s short life she took part in two voyages to the Arctic. When her keel was laid down her intended use had been as a commercial vessel, but she was bought by the navy to carry out a rescue voyage for Franklin and his men. After she had drawn a blank sailing in from Lancaster Sound, there was a school of thought amongst the Admiralty hierarchy that Franklin might have foundered further to the west, and that an approach from the Bering Sea would produce the results they hoped for. Now captained by Robert McClure, *Investigator* reached Mercy Bay on the northern coast of Banks Island, and there she spent three years entombed in the ice, never to sail again. The crew were finally rescued and could claim to be the first to pass through the North-west Passage although they were in fact taken some distance over the ice by a rescue party before sailing back to England in a different ship. *Investigator*'s sunken remains were discovered in 2010, not far from her last known position.

HMS *Enterprise* survived the rigours of the two Arctic expeditions that she had carried out in conjunction with *Investigator* and was still in use until the first decade of the 20th century. The purchase price of these two ships was nearly £50,000.

During the 11 years between 1848 and 1859, there were at least nine attempts to track down the Franklin expedition, mostly by sea but overland as well. The effort was led by the Royal Navy which sent a total of about 20 ships (5 of which were abandoned). Then there were some privately funded attempts, notably by Franklin's widow, and in 1850 an American sent two ships to take part in the search. These two expeditions became known as the first and second Grinnell searches after their sponsor, Henry Grinnell, a wealthy American philanthropist.

This gives some idea of how much money and effort were invested in ships alone to carry out all the voyages involved in the search for Franklin.

Although Ross's second lieutenant, **John Sibbald**, must have come as 'highly recommended' to the expedition this would not have been as a result of any polar experience. He had entered the navy in 1821. By 1828 he had moved up to become the mate on board HMS *Prince Regent*. Between 1830 and 1834 his ship was HMS *Nautilus*, and as with several other men from the Antarctic expedition, his tour of duty covered the coastline of Portugal and Spain down to Gibraltar, keeping an eye on the developments in the Iberian peninsula. By 1837 he had secured the rank of lieutenant on Sir Patrick Campbell's flagship, HMS *Edinburgh*. The post he held aboard *Edinburgh* would have been recommendation enough to secure his place on *Erebus* where he gained an insight into the scientific purpose behind the enterprise, and Ross would have required him to become conversant with the instruments used. When the ships arrived at the Falklands the knowledge Sibbald had gained about reading these instruments connected to the study of magnetism would be put to good use; he was delegated to look after the observatory set up at Port Louis while the two ships ventured to the remote and desolate coast around Cape Horn at the beginning of the fourth summer (1843). On the ships' return to Berkeley Sound Sibbald was transferred to *Terror*, replacing the ailing Lieutenant McMurdo. Sibbald retained this post for the completion of the voyage back to England. Later that year he was promoted to commander and then, in 1849, captain. For a few years after his promotion he was the inspecting commander of the coastguard based in Dundalk. When he retired from naval service he took a rather unusual appointment; he became the secretary to the governor of the Falklands, and travelled down with his old shipmate, Thomas Moore,

The Mendicity Society building in Red Lion Square, London.

who was to become the governor. Cape Sibbald in Victoria Land remembers him to the world.

Ross's third lieutenant, **James Frederick Lewis Wood**, has left behind just one reminder that he took part in the expedition. His name was given to Wood Bay, located along the coast of Victoria Land, and that is all that I can find to recall his presence on the expedition. Sometime after leaving the navy, he became involved in a charitable organisation, the Mendicity Society; in the larger British cities in particular its members devoted their efforts to assisting beggars. Some of these destitute men and women found it easier to gain a living from begging rather than submit to the rigours of the workhouse. James Wood became the secretary of the London branch, and it is possible that the fate of unemployed seamen driven to begging drew his attention to their plight – but that is my own speculation. His address and that of his family in the 1851 census would, however, confirm his association with this charitable movement; both were in Red Lion Square, Holborn.

James had only been married for three years when that census took place, but it would appear that he had been in a long-standing relationship with his wife, Ann Elizabeth, who was about five years his junior; their relationship must have started in the early 1830s because in 1851 the household consisted of three children: the eldest Frederick aged 17, Emma aged 15, and Elizabeth aged 11 – she must have been born after her father had set off on the expedition. An additional fact that emerges from the census of 1851 was that all three children and their mother had been born in Great Yarmouth in Norfolk. This might indicate where James Wood had started his relationship with Ann as early as 1834, when their son was born. An earlier census conducted in 1841 shows Ann Wood living in Great Yarmouth with her two younger children, but of the eldest child, Frederick, there is no mention.

Wood had been born in Blackheath (then in Kent) in 1805 and had gone to sea at the age of 15. A list of the ships he sailed on does not show his very early years in the navy and only begins with an entry aboard HMS *Prince Regent* in August 1826. (John Sibbald, too, had sailed on her at about the same time.) This post lasted until the following May, by which time he had obtained his mate's certificate. He continued to find employment in this capacity and listed are at least four other ships that he served on. Most of them appear to have been involved in coastal patrols searching for and arresting smugglers.

By the time he joined *Erebus* he had passed his exams and was now a lieutenant. Promotions continued to come his way; in October 1843, on completion of the expedition, he became a commander. His captaincy was awarded prior to his retirement in 1860. Four short years later he passed away at his last known address, 13 Red Lion Square. His will showed his estate valued at under £600, with possibly a small service pension. His widow appears in various census records right up to 1891 when she was shown to be living alone in lodgings in Paddington aged 77. A note of interest about one of Wood's relations; on his mother's side of the family, the Fitzmaurices, he was a cousin of James Ross. Roper Fitzmaurice served aboard HMS *Beagle* on her third cruise of exploration in 1837, when he also carried out the duties of naturalist and artist as she surveyed the coast of Australia.

Much of the story relating to James Wood comes from Tim Ridge, a distant family contact of his, and their family tree. Tim very kindly put most of the meat on the bones of the information that I had managed to collect from the official sources.

We have seen how the three senior officers aboard *Erebus* fared during their careers, but under them and answerable to them were the men who actually worked the ship. These were the warrant officers: the mates, the master, the boatswain, the gunner, the carpenter and the captains of the hold and forecastle. Then there were the petty officers, such the quartermaster, the officer's steward and the gunroom steward, but also including craftsmen such as the sailmaker, caulker, blacksmith, armourer and cook. Senior crew members held positions as captain of the maintop and captain of the foretop, and captain's coxswain. There was also a complement of seven marines and their sergeant. Unusually in naval vessels, but probably because of the anticipated rigours of the expedition, neither ship carried boys,[26] so it was able seamen who made up the rest of the crew. Last but by no means least were the civilian officers: the surgeon and his assistant, and the purser or clerk in charge.

The first of the warrant officers to sign on, as gunner aboard *Erebus*, was George Grant. However, before she sailed he received orders to transfer to HMS *Poictiers*, a ship not involved in the expedition. He was replaced by **Thomas Abernethy**, who had previously sailed on more than 13 other ships, one of them *Hecla* on Parry's 1824 attempt on the North-west Passage, overwintering in Prince Regent Inlet. This was Abernethy's first known experience of Arctic travel, and at the time he would also make the acquaintance of Ross, his future captain. The expedition ended in the second summer when *Fury*, driven ashore by massive quantities of dense pack ice, had had to be abandoned. Abernethy gained more Arctic experience as an able seaman during the summer of 1827 when *Hecla* sailed to Spitsbergen for Parry's attempt to reach the North Pole, again in the company of James Clark Ross. On the expedition's return Thomas married his first wife, Barbara, in 1829.

During times of war the role of gunner is obvious; he was in charge of the ship's armaments, including training the men who would use the guns. On the Antarctic expedition the ship still carried a range of firepower, but its use was primarily ceremonial and, as mentioned in Part One of this book, signalling. These peaceable uses still required a skilled presence when the guns were used, and the gunner would be on hand to administer the correct and safe way to carry out any orders given, not only firing but checking that the ordnance was safely handled.

Most of the tradesmen aboard could rely on having a mate to assist them in their tasks, which could be quite demanding, requiring at least a semi-skilled assistant to help with the heavier work. In the case of Thomas Abernethy, he should have been able to call on Jerimiah Quin, who had been taken on as the gunner's mate, but before sailing from Chatham Quin had been promoted to quartermaster, a position he held for the remainder of the expedition. Quin had a sister, Catherine, and – who knows? – she probably waved a fond farewell as the ships sailed from the dockside, leaving her to benefit from his allotment. So it appears that Abernethy had no dedicated help.

When a landing was attempted on any unknown shore he would be called upon to exercise another of his skills, that of handling the ship's boats in the sometimes turbulent waters they encountered in the regions they visited. On one occasion this skill would see him fulfilling the daring rescue of four of his fellow shipmates. Not long after leaving Kerguelen Island a rescue attempt had been made to save John Roberts, the boatswain of *Erebus*, who had been swept overboard in very rough weather. Two of *Erebus*'s boats were swung out and launched into a tempestuous sea. By the time they reached the spot where the unfortunate Roberts had last been seen, he had succumbed to the cold water and could not be found. Returning to the ship

26 Ships' boys were aged up to 18.

and preparing to be hoisted back on board Thomas Abernethy saw to his horror that the other rescue boat had been nearly swamped by a huge wave, throwing four men into the sea. With little thought for his own safety he encouraged his men to set out from the safety of the ship's side and go to the aid of their companions. The rescue was successful; both boats regained the security of the ship and all four men were saved. Henry Oakley, one of *Erebus*'s mates, also took part in the rescue.

In 1829, when James Ross was second in command of *Victory*[27] under the leadership of his uncle, spending a total of four years marooned in the Gulf of Boothia, we find the name of Thomas Abernethy cropping up again amongst the crew, this time as second mate. This was probably the most arduous experience in Abernethy's whole career. Instead of the anticipated two summers and one winter in the Arctic, they found themselves frozen into their winter harbour, unable to release *Victory*, for three whole winters. Freedom was finally secured by trekking for over 200 miles across the frozen sea and spending a fourth winter on Fury Beach, after which they sailed to the mouth of Prince Regent Inlet in boats abandoned by Parry in 1824. Then more by luck than judgement, they sighted a whaling ship which brought them back to England.

They did however establish several very important facts about the region in which they had spent so much time locked away from civilisation. It turned out that Boothia Peninsula was cut in two by the Bellot Strait, creating Somerset Island, which had previously been thought to be the northern part of the original peninsula. Somerset Island is about 160 miles long, and it was where the North Magnetic Pole was located at the time. Abernethy had been a member of the party that searched for it. Although Prince Regent Inlet led into the Gulf of Boothia it could not have formed a part of any North-west Passage as it was landlocked. They also established a long-term friendship with a group of Inuit who had previously had no contact with white men. This relationship enabled the two Rosses to barter fresh meat and fish to help sustain their crew and keep them free from scurvy for such a long time.

John Ross, returning to England in debt, had to find a way to pay his men for the nearly five years they had endured in the harsh polar environment with him. He petitioned Parliament and the Admiralty, explaining that he had been unable to earn money from the book he had hoped to write and he felt that the accomplishments of the expedition warranted a pay packet to be forthcoming from the government; the total wages bill amounted to over £4,500. Eventually this was sanctioned, and Thomas Abernethy was paid the princely sum of £32 14s 8d[28] – but neither of the Rosses benefited from the funds granted.

When the search for Franklin began in 1848, James Ross once more called on the services of Thomas Abernethy to sail with him, on *Enterprise*. Abernethy then took part in several further searches for Franklin and his men, one on *Felix* on a privately funded expedition under the 72-year-old Sir John Ross. This venture was nearly aborted before it set sail, when Abernethy and other members of the crew came aboard the worse for drink. Ross was not,

---

27 You may remember from Part One that this *Victory* was a privately-owned ex-Mersey ferryboat, not to be confused with HMS *Victory*.

28 £4,500 is approx £49,000 and £32 14s 8d, £3,500 in 2022.

however, a man to be deflected from his aim, and *Felix* set sail nevertheless, with a lot of headaches, bound for Greenland, then Canadian waters. They spent the winter of 1850 on the shores of Cornwallis Island. From there search parties were despatched in conjunction with the crews of the two ships under the command of Captain Penny. No signs of Franklin were found, and when the ice released the ships in spring 1851 Ross, lacking sufficient stores to spend an additional winter there, returned home.

Abernethy ventured into the Arctic the following year aboard *Isabel*, commanded by Lieutenant Edward Inglefield, on another privately sponsored search; this time the sponsor was Lady Franklin. *Isabel*, however, being insufficiently ice-strengthened, had to return to Britain before the onset of winter. On both these expeditions Abernethy held the post of ice master.

At the end of the *Isabel* trip he returned to his wife at home near the Woolwich naval dockyard, where he had been employed between voyages. Married in 1829, he had been absent for much of their married life, and his wife died just two years later. He packed his bags and returned to Peterhead, where he married for a second time, but died in 1860 at the age of 59. His gravestone in the old churchyard in Peterhead has a very simple inscription on it; for a man who had achieved so much for his country the words do not convey the true value of a professional naval veteran. His legacy to his widow was five polar medals.

William Keating Cunningham was born in 1809, and at the age of 20 signed up for the marines in Chatham. This was one of three depots in the country, the others at Portsmouth and Plymouth. When he signed on he was above average height at 5 feet 10 inches and in his full uniform would have been an impressive sight. As a private he took passage with other marines to join HMS *Revenge* in Portuguese waters. She was employed, as were many other Royal Naval vessels from time to time, in securing the Portuguese coast against attack from rival political groups who would have threatened British trade routes and the Portuguese monarchy.

He gained promotion to corporal on his way to becoming a sergeant in 1836, then in June 1839 he volunteered HMS *Terror*'s four-year voyage of discovery. After his return in 1843 he gained a further promotion, to quartermaster sergeant, but he never sailed again.

Crozier was so impressed with Cunningham during the expedition that he had his own watch suitably engraved and gave it to his sergeant for services rendered. Later, Ross would have been instrumental in getting a long service and good conduct medal awarded to Cunningham. On a more personal note, Cunningham married, but had no children; he lived in Chelsea from about 1861 to 1881, then moved to Gillingham, where he passed away in late 1884, aged 75.

Whilst Cunningham was aboard *Terror* he had under his command a detachment of six marines and a corporal. Their duties were mostly related to discipline and ensuring that good order was maintained throughout the ship. Other actions were searching for deserters when in port, issuing spirits to the crew, checking on the men's attendances at musters and divisions, and carrying out security and guard duties when the ship was berthed. Any sailors brought back on board after failing to return to the ship voluntarily were detained and then brought before the ship's captain for a suitable punishment to be dispensed.

By the time of Ross's expedition, flogging was not usually used in the navy unless the desertion was combined with a secondary offence such as stealing from the ship's stores. Loss of pay and restrictions on future leave would, it was now considered, suffice to bring the offender to his senses. The causes of desertion were many and varied. If a man failed to return by the allotted time and then after some days gave himself up, a sympathetic officer might allow his reinstatement after handing out some sort of punishment, and the sailor in question would be returned to duty – and later might achieve promotion to become one of the senior members of his watch. For an example of this, see Part Three, HMS *Fairy*, Thomas Farr.

Cunningham had a counterpart aboard *Erebus* by the name of **Samuel Baker**, who had at his disposal a similar squad of men. Baker's wife, Mary, would have drawn on his allotment of pay while he was absent for those four long years. The two units were depleted by the time they arrived back in England: a marine from each detachment was seconded to the observatory in Hobart. In addition to this *Erebus* lost George Barker, drowned at the stopover in New Zealand, and *Terror* lost William Talbot, hospitalised during the expedition's stay in the Falklands.

Returning to other members of the crew, a study of the muster lists reveals one **Cornelius Sullivan** as being promoted to the position of blacksmith and armourer following the desertion of Richard Stebbing when *Erebus* was in Hobart in October 1840. Both Abernethy and Sullivan had signed on at Chatham, and they completed all four years of the voyage. When the two ships returned to Hobart for the second time in 1841, extra hands were signed on to replace deserters and sick crew members, and amongst them was **Joseph Fitton**, a first entry but also a blacksmith and armourer. It would appear from the comments column on the muster lists that Cornelius Sullivan had been gauged as only Fair at his job, but Joseph Fitton received the plaudit of being Very Good. We must assume that Fitton's recruitment was to strengthen the blacksmithing department. Whereas the gunner looked after the ship's cannons and the ballistics, the armourer was responsible for taking care of the small arms and checking they were kept in a state of readiness; but all three tradesmen were capable of carrying out repairs when equipment was damaged.

The expedition had returned to Hobart for its second winter and recruiting took place as the ships were being readied for the following season when Ross hoped to resume his search for the South Magnetic Pole. A number of changes needed to be made to the crews due to the discharges and desertions that had taken place since their arrival in port. Among the new recruits was **James Savage**, who entered *Erebus* as an able seaman. He had originally come from Brighton in England, and at just 22 must have been one of the youngest crew members. He certainly gave a good account of himself, because by the end of the expedition he had become captain of the main top.

Searching through naval records as I set about writing these short stories of various crew members, I came across an interesting document. It was written by Cornelius Sullivan for the benefit of the young James Savage who joined the expedition in Tasmania in June 1841. They must have formed quite a close bond because Sullivan took the trouble to write in longhand a very detailed account of the first and second summers as the two ships penetrated the pack ice and sailed all the way down to the great ice barrier. His writing was carried out in a very firm style and is easily readable, unlike some old documents I have come across. Sullivan was capable of penning down his observations extremely well, and began his narrative just as the two expeditionary ships reach the newly discovered Victoria Land on 11 January 1840:

> At 7 o'clock in the afternoon we were under the Lee of the land, sounded in 250 fathoms of water – not a cloud to be seen in the firmament, but what Lingered on the mountains – Large floating Islands of ice in all directions. Hills, vallies and Land all covered with snow. The Snow topd mountains Majestically Rising above the Clouds. The Pinguins Gamboling in the water, the reflection of the Sun and the Brilliance of the firmament Made the Rare Light an interesting view.

His version of the events that took place spans the first and second seasons of exploration, until the ships dropped anchor in Berkeley Sound in the Falkland Islands. It was written on 15 sheets of lined paper with a total of about 4,500 words. At one point in his story he expresses the wish that he had been an artist or a draughtsman instead of the blacksmith and armourer. He goes on to tell of discovering a live volcano and hearing Ross naming it after their ship, likewise the second volcano that stood behind Mount Erebus being named after *Terror*. Nothing in the world could prepare him and his shipmates for the first glimpse they had of the ice barrier. Its height and length, although likened to the white cliffs of Dover, left them awestruck as they sailed south-east along its length for over 300 miles – and still it stretched away into the distance. Even from the masthead it was impossible to see beyond its topmost rim. He goes on to describe the search they made for the land supposedly discovered by the American exploring ships the previous year under the command of Lieutenant Charles Wilkes, and is very dismissive of their reports as *Erebus* and *Terror*, sailing across the area, sounded at least 500 fathoms.

During the second summer Sullivan reported that he was captivated by the sculpting of the icebergs they encountered as they sailed further south:

> To compare any sight ever my eyes beheld to this magnificent ice island one mile square as if the hands of man prepared it with splendid mouldings, cornices, porticoes, towers and columns, all natural architecture how wonderful is the works of nature.

As 1841 drew to a close all the officers and crew spent New Year's Eve out on the ice in which they had been trapped for several days, creating a public house out of ice blocks; later when all the other arrangements had been made, they had a celebratory party with games and pantomime for entertainment. A week later they were assailed by what Sullivan described as a 'perfect hurricane', which caught both ships broadside on and smashed them against the adjacent ice floes threatening to destroy the hulls and send the masts overboard. They were detained for a further two weeks in the closely packed ice, making it 47 days since they had first ventured into it. The time lost in forcing a way through the pack ice meant their stay at what was eventually to be their furthest south was short-lived. Both ships turned north on a heading that would take them to their next destination, the Falkland Islands.

When they had recrossed the Antarctic Circle and seemed to be making excellent progress, logging about 150 miles a day, on 13 March the terrifying line of icebergs loomed out of the deteriorating evening light. Sullivan takes up the story:

> It was blowing a gale of wind at this time, the watch was on the fore-yard taking in the last reef, the night was exceedingly dark we could scarcely see a hundred yards off. When low we were running into a cluster of ice islands at the rate of 7 knots. James Angelie cried out from the fore-yard an iceberg lay ahead. The mournful cry of all hands, all hands, soon brought our naked tars on deck. Before they could all get on deck both ships struck with such force we thought all was over…. The *Terror* put her helm hard a port and we put our helm hard a starboard…. Now the dreadful and memorable scene took place, a heavy sea elevated *Terror* with our bowsprit entangled across her bows, the bowsprit was snapped to atoms, fore topmast soon followed, booms, stays and every gear connected with the ship's forecastle was torn away at this time. We expected *Terror* would sink but she rose the victor to dispute the conquest, from this time we were the sufferers, the bowsprit carrying away saved our lives, five minutes longer would do the job but God decreed it not.

Once the two ships separated, it fell to the two captains to manoeuvre their craft to safety. Sullivan reported that by using all their sailing skills each commander achieved what can only be described as a miracle in gaining the relative safety of the lee side of the two icebergs that had so nearly brought about their demise. It was fully expected by both crews that the other had perished in this frightful encounter, and it would require the passage of several long hours before the pale light of dawn revealed that both ships were still afloat, and many more hours of inspection to assess the magnitude of the damage that had been inflicted. Sullivan even retells the expedition's story in a poetic version. He was certainly a talented man, and strangely this appears to have been his first journey aboard a Royal Navy ship. In the muster list his age was given as 31 and he hailed from Killarney in Southern Ireland. When he had set out from Chatham, he left instructions that his daughter, Mary, was to receive an allotment from his pay.

This was one of a number of instances when *Erebus* and *Terror* suffered severe damage to their steering gear, their masts and spars and even to their hulls. Sullivan's account highlighted the worst incident, when the two ships were negotiating their way out of the pack ice in the summer of 1842 after their second visit to the Great Ice Shelf. Once the crisis was past, temporary repairs were carried out at sea and on their arrival at the Falklands both ships were careened to enable the carpenters to inspect the hulls and, where necessary, to facilitate repairs. Spare masts and spars were stock items aboard all Royal Naval ships, as were rudders, but many a time jury rigs were improvised to help bring the ship in question to port. On one occasion whilst the ships lay at anchor at the Bay of Islands in New Zealand, a working party was delegated to go ashore and select several suitable tree trunks that could be used as spare masts. The choice of tree would have rested with the carpenter, who would have been expected to know which species would provide the most suitable timber for the job in hand. In extreme instances ship's carpenters would have been called upon to strip timbers from a wrecked ship and use them build another vessel to seek a passage to safety. The carpenter would need to have spent some of his training in a shipyard to gain the knowledge that would be necessary to carry out this specialised sort of work, and it is quite likely that this would have been true in this case.

The position of carpenter's mate aboard *Erebus* fell on the shoulders of **John Bennett**. Although he joined the crew in Hobart during the first wintering of the two ships, he had originally come from Dartmouth in Devon, so probably had some sailing experience; but he was still recorded as a first entry. He replaced Joseph Barclay, who had taken the opportunity of deserting before they sailed on the first attempt at reaching the Antarctic continent. Bennett completed the trip, and was graded Good.

The carpenter was a key member of the crew, especially on these early exploring ships that could suddenly find themselves in dangerous situations where damage to the ship would need expert knowledge to carry out repairs. In this role *Erebus* had on board **John Bromley**, and *Terror* had Thomas Honey, who I will come to shortly. They had been recommended by the Admiralty and both served their ships very well. Bromley had been active in the Royal Naval service since at least 1826 when he had sailed with Parry with Ross as second in command aboard *Hecla* on the expedition to Spitsbergen in the second attempt to find a passage to the North Pole by that route. As the carpenter Bromley would have been responsible for the modifications to the two ship's boats enabling them to be hauled out of the water and slid across any ice floes they encountered as they trekked northwards. The plan was to find a suitable anchorage for *Hecla* and from there sail their small boats north, penetrating the pack ice as and when it was encountered. The outcome was basically a failure as they only reached 82°45'N. Parry realised that the ice was drifting to the south nearly as fast as they were struggling north; his men were getting exhausted, and he had to be back aboard *Hecla* before any freeze-up. They turned back from what was to become the farthest north yet achieved, and reached their ship on 21 August 1827. Their record stood for nearly 50 years.

Following his return to England John Bromley continued in the navy. His last appointment was on HMS *Fisgard*. She was stationed at Woolwich docks and when he joined her she had been converted into a training establishment. This was probably the last of his ships, because he worked on *Fisgard* from 1847 until 1854, by which time he would have been over 61 years old. He had been born in Deptford in 1793 and he was still living very near to the Woolwich Dockyard when the 1871 census took place. He would have had many memories to pass on to his grandson, who lived with him during his retirement.

His wife, Phoebe, was named on his allotment papers during the expedition, but does not appear on the 1871 census returns.

A sailing ship is always going to need the services of at least one sailmaker, and **James Duffield**, aged 27 from Great Yarmouth, and **William Greenstead**, who had been born in Bromley in Kent, were recruited at Chatham for the task. However, on reaching Hobart Duffield had become so ill that he was transferred to the hospital there and should have been replaced, but the best that could be done was to enlist a sailmaker's mate, **William Perry**. He had been paid off from HMS *Winchester* in 1838 when she had visited Hobart, and this must have looked like his ticket home – but fate was to deal him a different hand; by the time the expedition reached the Falklands in 1842 he too had become unfit for service and was discharged to await a suitable vessel to take him home to England.

Whenever a ship was in port an inspection would always be made to check on any leaks that might have occurred in the hull. Traditionally as the ship was being built the planks were sealed with strands of old rope, oakum, kept for the purpose. Once the rope had been unravelled and pulled apart the caulker would use a selection of caulking irons of different shapes and a mallet to compact the rope into the gaps between the planks of wood. This was a tedious process as each gap had to be packed tightly with the rope strands. To create a watertight seal over the joint, a coating of melted pitch was spread across the exposed surface and allowed to cool. The caulker could apply this technique to the decking planks as well. But sometimes a ship would be subjected to so much strain that the decks would distort, allowing water to penetrate to the holds or cabins.

Two caulkers were taken on at Chatham. **William McDougal** was originally from Dundee, and the fact that he was the second man to volunteer and be signed on probably reflected his interest in this voyage of discovery. He was entered as a first entry, but it was significant that Dundee was very famous for its rope-making factories so he had probably gained the relevant experience there. Dundee also had a worldwide reputation for building some of the best whaling and sealing vessels in the world. Scott's ship, RRS *Discovery*, was built in Dundee specifically for his first expedition mainly because of the port's reputation for constructing wooden sailing ships likely to encounter icy seas. *Discovery*, now a museum open to the public, is berthed in Dundee.

The second caulker to join *Erebus* came from Hull, another seafaring port. **William Williamson** was, at 23. one of the youngest men aboard. Both of these men completed the expedition, as did **James Wilson** who had entered the service as a caulker's mate.

Now we come to the junior officers responsible for the day-to-day running of the ship. The principal of these were the mates, directly answerable to the officer of the watch. *Erebus* and *Terror* ran a three-watch rota – four hours on duty and eight off – for most of the voyage, so each watch would probably have had one mate and they could generally rely on a deputy as well.

The first mate on *Erebus* was **Alexander John Smith**. He had served with Ross on a previous voyage and was the most experienced of the three mates listed. He was the third of eleven children and had grown up with his brothers and sisters near Greenwich Docks until their father was bankrupted, due to a loan he had given which turned sour on him. This forced the family to move to a more modest house but shortly afterwards Alexander reached the age of 14 and joined the navy.

His interest in the navy probably stemmed from his early childhood, living close to all things naval and seeing for himself the hustle and bustle that attended one of the greatest naval institutions in the world. He travelled down to Portsmouth to find his first ship. This was HMS *Thetis* which was built as a 46-gun fifth-rate frigate. The voyage he was about to embark on was to last four years and it would take him to South America carrying out a series of patrols along the coast and visiting places such as Rio de Janeiro, Valparaiso and Montevideo. The ship's last port of call was Rio. Two days into the voyage home, in overcast weather, a call for all hands resounded along the lower decks, and men raced to their stations. The situation that faced them was dire; they were heading directly for a rock-strewn coast backed by steep cliffs, and it was clear that they were about to be wrecked. Men were leaping off the ship to try and save their lives. Smith was amongst them, and he managed to reach the cliff face but in the gloom he could not see how to reach safety. Having clung on for what must have seemed like ages, he was hailed from above by some of the crew on the clifftop, and they lowered a makeshift rope, enabling him to climb up and join them.

This incident was responsible for 22 men losing their lives. A court martial later established the two main causes to be that the ship was being navigated by dead reckoning and her captain and master had not carried out the standard procedure of taking regular soundings. The two officers concerned were punished by having two years deleted from their records, reducing their chances of promotion and their pension rights. *Thetis* had been carrying a large amount of bullion; although salvage operations managed to secure a good quantity of it, much was lost.

On his return to England Smith seems to have shrugged off the nightmare, as he embarked on HMS *Harrier*. She was set to travel halfway round the world to Singapore, calling at Cape Town, Ceylon and India on the way. This voyage kept him occupied from 1831 until 1835, by which time he had taken and passed the examinations to become a midshipman. This was soon followed by a job change, to third mate.

Alexander then gained vital experience, sailing around the Orkneys on a ship carrying out survey work, and at one juncture he commanded a small naval cutter.

For James Clark Ross's 1836 HMS *Cove* mission to rescue the stranded whalers, Smith had been ordered to join the crew. This was the first time that young Smith had worked under Ross's command, and although this would be his first experience of working a ship through the icy waters around Greenland, it must have stood him in good stead, because Ross's impression of him secured for him the position of first mate aboard *Erebus* when she set out for the Antarctic in 1839.

When Smith reported for duty *Cove* had already been victualled and refitted. Alexander was to experience at first hand just how good a captain his new commander was. They battled through some of the worst weather most of the crew had ever experienced, and the ship suffered an enormous amount of damage. The superb seamanship demonstrated by Ross brought them safely through the tempest that had struck them, but the damage inflicted was so great that they retreated to Stromness to lick their wounds and regroup for another attempt at carrying out the rescue they had been entrusted to accomplish.

During his time with the Antarctic expedition, Smith had left behind in Hobart his sweetheart, Sarah Read, and his ambition now was to return there and get married. So when the expedition was wound up and he was free to go on leave, he set off to see his family in Cottingham in Yorkshire. Here he could announce his intention of setting off once more – but this time to get married. Part of his plan was to take up a post at the observatory in Hobart which would enable him to continue in the navy and hopefully gain a further promotion. Probably with some help from his old commander, he reached Hobart and in 1844 wed Sarah. They had three children, and his promotion to commander duly came through; but in 1853 the navy relinquished control of the observatory to the civilian authorities.

After a visit to England with his family, where a fourth child was born, Smith set off back across the world, but now to the new state of Victoria in Australia. Here he would take up a civilian post and help administer the newly discovered, and burgeoning, gold fields. Thousands of people from all over the world were rushing to the area to try and make their fortunes, and lawlessness was rife. The local police force being inadequate, restoring law and order this was his first objective. He had left his family in Hobart with Sarah's family, but as he established himself and became respected, he found a suitable house in the township of Castlemaine.

As years elapsed Smith found himself drawn into local politics. He prospered, and purchased a farm where he could go and relax from the rigours of civilian matters, and it was here that in 1872 at the age of just 59 he passed away. His wife survived him by 28 years, as did six of their seven children. His death at such a relatively young age might indicate that the illness he had sustained on returning home on *Erebus* might have taken more out of him than anybody had realised.

The other two mates aboard *Erebus* were **Joseph Dayman** and **Henry Oakley**. Dayman's previous ship had been HMS *Excellent*, a 98-gun second-rate ship of the line, originally called HMS *Boyne*. She had been in active service since 1810 in the Napoleonic wars, but in 1834 she was taken out of frontline duties to become a training ship, renamed *Excellent*.

The main object of the expedition's 1840 visit to Hobart having been to set up an observatory, Dayman was delegated to help administer it, assisted by **Peter Scott**, the first mate of *Terror*. When the two ships departed to the south for the second time Scott continued to help run the observatory. In 1843 he was promoted to lieutenant, and from 1845 through to 1848 he served with Captain William Fitzwilliam aboard HMS *Columbia*, carrying out survey work along the North American coast. When Captain Shorland took over command of *Columbia* in 1849, Scott continued his service with her until 1853. Surveying work seemed to have been his forte; he continued it on HMS *Indus* then HMS *Nile*, right up until 1866, when he gained his captaincy. Census records show his wife to have been Esther, and his death is recorded in 1900 at the age of 84.

Private George Parr, a 23-year-old from Hunstanton in Norfolk, a member of the marines aboard *Erebus*, and **William Stevenson** from *Terror* were also delegated to look after the observatory in Hobart until they were collected and brought back to England later in the expedition. Their commanding officer, **Lieutenant Kay**, stayed on for several more years.

When the expedition arrived at the Falklands and Alexander Smith had been posted as a lieutenant, Henry Oakley gained a measure of promotion by taking Smith's place as first mate. Before the expedition he had been aboard HMS *Edinburgh*. Up to about 1837 she had been on a commission serving in the Mediterranean Sea. Oakley listed his occupation as master mariner in 1861 but when the 1871 census took place he had obviously retired from the navy and taken on the role of a ship's underwriter. By at least 1861 he and his wife Mary had moved to Cheshire, where they continued to live for a number of years. They had a daughter, Mary, and a son, Henry, three years younger, who was to become an architect. After their father's death sometime before the 1891 census, the two children were still recorded as residing with their mother.

When a ship was heavily manned there would also be a mate of the lower decks, but on the expedition ships the crews were numbered in their tens, not hundreds as in a man-of-war. The main duties that the mates carried out was to record the daily ship's log, noting any incidents that might have occurred during their watch and ensuring that all the men were at their stations, fit and well, and ready to carry out their tasks. Joseph Dayman was an excellent artist and surveyor when not involved in helping to run the ship in his capacity as mate he carried out surveying and drawing. His ability to draw charts would be put to good use by Ross when it came to writing his book about the expedition; many of Dayman's works were included. He prospered later in his naval career. When the expedition arrived home in 1843 he was promoted to lieutenant. He continued to find further employment in the navy and had commissions aboard HMS *Tartarus* and then HMS *Rattlesnake* which spent a lot of time in the latter half of the 1840s carrying out survey work in the Far East and Australian waters. As his career developed so did his promotions, first to commander in 1858 then to captain in 1863, 32 years after his first posting; his first entry into the navy had been in 1831 aboard HMS *Excellent*.

When underwater telegraphic cables were being laid, Dayman, with his surveying background, became involved; in 1858 he was serving aboard HMS *Gorgon*, surveying the route for the proposed cable across the floor of the Atlantic Ocean. *Gorgon* and *Valorous* worked in conjunction with HMS *Agamemnon* to plot and lay the first transatlantic cable, and Dayman was one of only nine men to be awarded a first-class medal; it was made of pure gold and weighed 5 ounces.

His penultimate command was aboard HMS *Firebrand*, destined for more surveying work in the Mediterranean Sea, and the culmination of his naval career saw him in command of HMS *Hornet*, sailing halfway round the world to the East Indies.

About the domestic side of his life there is not a lot to tell. His father was Charles Dayman who held the stipend at Great Tew in Oxfordshire and his mother was Flavia. This slightly unusual name might give some credence to the entry in the 1851 census that he was born in France. He was living with his brother at the time of this census. Just before he sailed in *Hornet* he was residing in St James's Square in Westminster as a lodger, and here his birthplace was given as Dover. He does not seem to have been married, and devoted 32 years of his life to the navy. He passed away in 1869.

Thomas Rawe Hallett held the post of purser aboard *Erebus*. This position was unique in that it did not usually entitle the holder to a naval salary. Instead he had the responsibility of purchasing certain consumable supplies such as tobacco, clothing, bedding and even candles for sale to the officers and crew for their personal use. Any profit he made from the sale of these goods was his and his alone. However, on this voyage there is evidence that he did actually receive a salary of £182. Hallett had come to know Ross in winter 1835, when they sailed together on HMS *Cove* attempting to relieve the whaling ships trapped in the ice near Greenland.

Terror had on board one **George Moubray** as the purser, given the title of clerk in charge.

As was usual for an administrative officer, Hallett had the services of an assistant, **John Watson**. Prior to sailing from Chatham with the expedition in 1839 Watson had spent two years up to 1837 in the Arctic aboard *Terror* under the command of Captain George Back. The ship had limped home in a desperate state having suffered from the ice in Hudson Bay during yet another failed attempt at finding the elusive passage across northern Canada.

By the time the Ross expedition arrived at Simon's Town in South Africa, Hallett had obviously had enough of Watson and the muster roll states quite clearly that he was discharged at the request of the purser as 'indifferent'. The expedition spent a few weeks at Simon's Town and here a second man, **William Plunket**, was taken on as the purser's steward, but by the time they reached Hobart Plunket would put in a request to be discharged due to his failing health, so a search commenced to find yet another purser's steward. **Charles Patterson**, aged just 20, from Marylebone in London, took on the role – but when the expedition returned to Hobart after exploring the Antarctic for the first time, he too was relieved of his position. The comment 'Indifferent' against his name paints a dismal picture as regards purser's assistants.

Thomas Hallett's fortunes took a turn for the worse after the expedition; he took on the post of purser aboard a new ship, HM Steamer *Eclair*. They were bound for the west coast of Africa to help capture any vessels trafficking slaves to the Caribbean or the Americas. After she reached her station some members of the crew became infected with some sort of virulent disease which swept through the ship's company. She was ordered home under extreme caution not to land any men along the route, and immediately she reached England she was quarantined. Hallett was amongst some of the earliest casualties, as was the captain. In fact, over half the crew had lost their lives before she set off for home waters. It is most probable that those who died before *Eclair* set out for England would have been buried at sea.

As Cape Hallett was named after Ross's purser, at least he has some sort of memorial. The cape was used as a base by the Americans during part of Operation Deepfreeze when they took part in the International Geophysical Year from 1957 to 1958. It was staffed by a joint team of New Zealanders and Americans for a number of years, but a substantial fire in 1964 reduced it to a summer-only base, then in 1973 it was abandoned.

The man selected as master and pilot of *Erebus* was **Charles Tucker**. According to the 1861 census returns he had a land-based job, as the harbourmaster at the Port of London.

This same census states that he was then aged 50. This would mean he had been born in 1811, so was only 28 when he joined *Erebus*. An interesting note about his pay is worthy of mention here. When he entered service with *Erebus* in 1839 he was given six months' advance salary before they sailed: £65/12/-.[29] Apart from knowing that he completed the four years successfully I cannot, however, find very much else that happened to him subsequently. One other feature of the 1861 census shows that he had a 10-year-old son living with him but no other family members, although he also had a housekeeper and a young servant girl. He was obviously doing reasonably well for himself.

Moving on down the list to the lower ranks of the petty officers, the information about their personal lives and subsequent careers becomes less readily available compared to that of the officers, but an exception to that statement was **John Diggle** who became one of the quartermasters. This position had initially been filled by David Hennessey, but a few weeks after signing on he requested to be relieved of the post. John Diggle was offered the position and continued in that capacity for the duration of the voyage. Prior to his involvement with the expedition he had been sailing on HMS *Wolf*, and had been discharged from her in March 1839, when she arrived at Portsmouth. He was a Londoner by birth and aged 30. He had a number of years of sailing experience to his credit, and was one of the earlier recruits to be mustered. *Wolf* had returned home from what appears to have been a long commission. Her log details her departure from Plymouth in 1834; she called at Madeira and Rio de Janeiro then on to India via Cape Town and Ceylon. Singapore features on her list of ports visited. China was touched as she collected despatches destined for the 'Supreme Government' (whatever thar might have been). Her voyage lasted from 1834 to 1839, most of it in Far Eastern waters. Diggle would have seen many different ports along the way in addition to the apprehending of Malay pirates while in the seas around the Malay peninsula in 1836. Just before he set out on *Wolf* he was in Stoke Damerel in Devonport[30] and managed to fit in a wedding to Mary Ann Johnson.

His first venture to sea was aboard HMS *Confiance*, a paddle-driven ship of just under 300 tons launched in 1827; in 1830 she set sail from Woolwich bound for the Mediterranean with mail for the servicemen stationed in the garrisons that Britain maintained there. As she passed Cape Finisterre a French troopship hailed her for assistance; dismasted and with a damaged hull, she was in grave danger of sinking. She had on board 500 French soldiers plus her crew; many lives were at stake. Lieutenant Belson, the commanding officer of *Confiance*, immediately attempted to take her in tow, but the severe weather compounded the problems. A second line was sent across after the first had parted – and after nearly a week *Confiance* brought the stricken French ship into Lisbon. As a result of the action taken by the little paddle steamer, no lives were lost. In recognition of Belson's act of humanity the French king, Louis Philippe, had a gold medal struck in his honour, suitably inscribed to indicate the valiant action.

Diggle also sailed on HMS *Talavera*, carrying out blockade patrols off the Dutch coast during hostilities between Belgium and the Netherlands.[31] The establishment of Belgium as

---

29 Equivalent to about £7,250 in 2022, according to https://www.in2013dollars.com/uk/inflation/1839.
30 Stoke Damerel was then part of Devonport but is now part of Plymouth.
31 This *Talavera* was not the one that accompanied HMS *Victory* into battle at Trafalgar.

an independent state was one of the conditions of the settlement at the end of the Napoleonic wars, and it was supported by Britain.

When the expedition to Antarctica was completed, Diggle returned to his wife in Devonport and presumably spent some time with her. When in 1845 the navy started recruiting for the Franklin expedition he volunteered for this venture.

A point of interest at this juncture; I have a book called *Sir John Franklin's Last Expedition* by Richard Cyriax. In it is a list of all the men who took part. I recalled the names of a few of them, and John Diggle is one of these, probably because his name is a little stranger than most. I ran a check on all the 128 men who sailed with Franklin and found 13, including Francis Crozier, who had accompanied Ross down to the Antarctic; 3 from *Erebus* and 10 from *Terror* perished in the bleak, frozen, open spaces of King William Island sometime around 1848.

Finding out that so many men from the first expedition, having so recently endured the stresses of spending four years in the Antarctic, had volunteered to seek out the North-west Passage gave me a most uncomfortable and unsettling feeling. It was this above all else that prompted me to write about the lives of as many of the crewmen as I could so that their part in Ross's expedition became more widely known.

A footnote to the life and death of John Diggle came to light many years after the tragic event of 1848 had been played out in the Arctic. His parents, John and Phoebe, had written a letter in January of that year to their son, probably guessing the worst and that disaster had struck the expedition yet in hope that some of the crew members might be saved. There had already been newspaper articles predicting the worst, and it was in the light of these revelations that Diggle's parents penned these lines.

> Dear Son
>
> I Wright these few lines to [you] in hopes to find you and all your Shipmates in both Ships Well as it leaves us all at Present thank God for it but our fears his wee shall never see you again seeing the account in the Newspaper how you have been Situated what with been frozen inn and having that Dreadful Disorder the Schervey which us in little hopes of seeing you again but wee trust in God. when HMS *Plover* Reaches you our thoughts will be Flusternated and Joyful news it will be for us to hear on her Return to England that you and all the Crew are Well.
>
> Please God it may be so.

The letter continues with wishes for a safe return from other family members and friends, and ends with these few words of love.

> Dear Son I conclude with our Unbounded Gratitude to you.
>
> Your Loving Father and Mother
>
> John & Phoebe Diggle and God Bless you.

Although he had held the position of quartermaster on *Erebus* for the whole expedition, on Franklin's expedition he was appointed as the cook aboard *Terror*. His shipmates from *Erebus* on the Ross expedition were Richard Wall, who retained the post of cook aboard *Erebus*, and James Rigden, who was made captain's coxswain.

The muster list showing all the men who were employed as quartermaster aboard *Erebus* takes a number of twists and turns; this chart shows how the situation changed as the expedition progressed:

Name	Entry date	Leaving date	Positions held + dates
James Rigden	2/5/1839	23/9/1843	A.B. 29/5/1839 Captain's Coxswain 27/4/1841 A.B. 26/9/1841 Captain of F/top 12/7/1843 Quartermaster
Jerimiah Quin	2/5/1839	23/9/1843	Gunner's mate 29/5/1839 Quartermaster
John Diggle	6/5/1839	23/9/1843	A.B. 14/7/1839 Quartermaster
James Angeley	18/5/1839	Drowned 2/4/1842	A.B. 28/10/1840 Quartermaster
Samuel Glover	27/5/1839	Deserted 27/10/1840	A.B. 27/6/1839 Quartermaster
James Rogers	1/7/1839	23/9/1843	A.B. 25/9/1839 Quartermaster 8/10/1841 A.B.
Edward Baxter	28/10/1840	Sent home sick 29/11/1842	A.B. 9/10/1841 Quartermaster
John Stewart	4/7/1841	23/9/1843	A.B. 30/11/1842 Quartermaster

So in addition to John Diggle there were no less than seven men who filled this position at various times during the expedition. Samuel Glover managed to get as far as Hobart, then absconded. He was replaced by James Angeley, who was drowned after being lost overboard as the two ships forged their way through terrible weather to reach the Falklands in April 1842. Angeley had come directly to *Erebus* from HMS *Poictiers* when the expedition ships were being overhauled at Chatham.

Edward Baxter from Scarborough signed on during *Erebus*'s first visit to Hobart and received his promotion to quartermaster on 9 October 1841 following the demotion of James Rogers at the Bay of Islands in New Zealand. Rogers, from Boston in Lincolnshire, must have shown some potential because he had sailed from Chatham as a quartermaster; the reason for his demotion is, however, not given in the records.

Baxter's health failed him by the time they arrived at the Falklands and he had to be repatriated to England aboard a merchant ship, *Governor Halkett*. His place was taken by John Stewart from Dunfermline in Scotland; he joined *Erebus* as a first entry when she spent her second winter in Hobart, and he completed the tour of duty.

James Rigden became one of the quartermasters as *Erebus* and *Terror* arrived in Simon's Town in May 1843. John Diggle and Jerimiah Quin both held their posts for the four-year duration of the expedition.

In 1839 **Jerimiah Quin** was a 31-year-old sailor who had just been discharged from HMS *Pelican* and was number 11 on the muster roll indicating his enthusiasm to join the expedition. *Pelican*, a wooden sailing ship of just under 400 tons, not far removed from the weights of *Erebus* and *Terror*, had been built in 1812; immediately after helping guard a convoy of merchant ships sailing to England she was detailed to assist in the capture of *Argus*, an American raider which was interfering with British shipping around the coastline of Great Britain. Two days later *Pelican* cornered the raider and after a short engagement *Argus* struck her colours. This had all taken place well before Jerimiah Quin's involvement with *Pelican*, but it shows just how the Royal Navy was being called upon to regulate the high seas. *Pelican* is recorded as being in service along the coasts of Africa during the years 1834 to 1839, when Quin would have been aboard. He was discharged at the end of the Ross expedition still with the rank of quartermaster.

He had been born in 1804 or thereabouts in the disreputable London borough of Shadwell, now Tower Hamlets in the East End. A record of his sailing days shows him to have been at sea for over 20 years, between 1823 and 1849, holding various posts including captain of the main top, captain of the forecastle and, of course, quartermaster aboard *Erebus*. The extremely hard life in the Royal Navy started to take its toll, however, and he spent several periods in a naval hospital – in his case a hulk moored at Woolwich called the Dreadnought Seamen's Hospital after the ship. The original *Dreadnought* was replaced from time to time but all the ships used thus were given the name HMS *Dreadnought*.

In the end the hospital became land-based and was run as part of St Thomas's Hospital, devoted to the treatment of sailors suffering mainly from tropical diseases. When the National Health Service was created in 1947 St Thomas's was included, and even today it has a ward called Dreadnought; seamen abroad are if necessary repatriated to the UK for immediate treatment there.

There are several references to Quin's incapacity at the hospital, the first as early as 1833, followed in 1852 and then again in 1861, when he was being treated for ulcerated legs. The final entry takes place in 1871 when at the age of 66 he again found himself in hospital, but by that point the hospital had moved to a land-based building near Whitechapel. I cannot find any record of Quin being married, and he died in 1875.

Returning to his naval career, he can be found in 1846 as a member of the crew sailing out of Plymouth on HMS *Mutine*. She had been sent to the Cape of Good Hope on her first voyage to carry out search and apprehension missions connected to the slave trade. Once this assignment was completed, she returned to England having suffered some damage to her hull, and underwent major repairs before being despatched to the Mediterranean in January 1847. It would appear that Quin, having completed the African run, was also part of this second voyage. The ship visited various ports around the Mediterranean and in 1848 anchored off Venice to weather out a storm of some magnitude – but she succumbed to the ferocious wind, and was driven ashore, a total loss. Although the majority of the crew were saved, five men died, and the remainder suffered from the low temperatures that were prevailing at the time. Many of the men had frozen extremities, so it was not unlike the results of losing a ship in icier polar seas. Quin survived this tragedy but was probably left reflecting on how lucky he had been compared to the sailing he had done in a really frozen environment. At the court martial consequent upon the ship's loss Quin would probably have been called as a witness during the hearing. The court found in her officers' favour, and no charges were brought.

HMS Dreadnought, *the naval hospital ship from 1831 to 1857 under the auspices of the Seamen's (now Seafarers') Hospital Society. She had fought at the Battle of Trafalgar as a 98-gun second-rate ship of the line.*

Henry Braddick Yule shared the post of pilot with **Charles Tucker**. Yule has a small testament to his career. He was born in 1811 and there is a gravestone in the Holy Cross churchyard at Shipton-on-Cherwell giving this information. There is also an inscribed brass plaque within the church revealing his naval appointments as he passed from 18-year-old sailor through his promotions and finally to his demise at age 66 on Christmas Day in 1877. By the time of his retirement in about 1862, he had achieved the rank of staff commander. His first ship is listed on the brass plaque as HMS *Druid*, a 46-gun frigate first commissioned in the 1820s. The list dates his second ship as HMS *Warsnipe*, followed a year later by HMS *Dublin*, then HMS *Quail* in 1833. He sailed in a total of six naval ships prior to the Antarctic expedition, so would have gained plenty of experience before being offered the post of second master and pilot aboard *Erebus*. Following his return in September 1843 he took a post in some survey work being carried out across England as part of the study to produce an accurate map of the country, possibly the same survey that Ross had been involved in. His next appointment was aboard HMS *Porcupine*, where he served as master. She was steam-powered but she retained two masts; the Royal Navy had not yet reconciled itself to the fact that steam propulsion was going to supersede wind power. Most of her time was spent in towing other ships out of the Thames and Medway docks to reach the open sea.

By the time he took on his last appointment as staff commander, he had become involved in the training of seamen in all things mechanical for use on ships as the navy became more and more dependent on steam-powered vessels. The training took place aboard HMS *Fiscard*, a retired 46-gun frigate moored at Woolwich. As the training of artificers became more important, a permanent facility was built on land at Chatham, taking the name HMS *Fisgard*. On a more personal note, in 1844 he married Rebecca Byrne at St Martin-in-the-Fields in London. On his retirement the family moved to Shipton-on-Cherwell in Oxfordshire. His wife continued to reside there after his death, and their son Charles became the rector.

Henry Braddick Yule, Staff Commander RN. HMS *Druid* 1829. HMS *Warsnipe* 1831. HMS *Dublin* 1832. HMS *Quail* 1833. HMS *Seaflower* 1836. HMS *Prospero* 1837. South Polar Expedition – HMS *Erebus* 1839 to 1843. Surveying Service – HMS *Porcupine* 1844. HMS *Comet* 1849. HMS *Fisgard* 1854–1862.His eldest son, Henry Braddick, was domestic chaplain to the Duke of Maryborough, 1871, vicar of Hampton Gay, Oxon, 1871, and rector of Shipton-on-Cherwell, 1874.

Continuing with other men who held responsible positions aboard *Erebus*, we can take a look at the post of the boatswain. He would have played a very important part in running the ship. It was his responsibility to superintend any work carried out on the ship's working gear: anything from anchors and chains to stays and yards. Cables, cordage, canvas, ship's boats and their rigging, and so many other items came under his remit. Another of his duties was to pipe up the crews to be ready to carry out the officer's orders. He was in other words, a key figure in the smooth running of the ship once she had put to sea.

John Roberts was signed on as the boatswain of *Erebus*, but as we have recently read he met with death by drowning after the ships had departed from Kerguelen. Prior to the expedition Roberts had been serving aboard HMS *Victory*. At the time she was stationed in Portsmouth Harbour as 'the Port Admiral's ship'. This meant that any court martial brought against a serving member of the navy would be carried out aboard her. Prior to this posting little is known of John Robert's career, but he must surely have served in several more active positions.

His place was taken by **Robert Beeman** who Ross had ordered to be transferred from HMS *Terror*. His initial recruitment to *Terror* had followed a period aboard HMS *Poictiers*. He was one of the many men who signed on to the expedition following their discharge from that ship. She seems to have had a lively time during the war against America in the early part of the 19th century, capturing several foreign ships. Towards the end of her naval service, and in particular the period just before so many men were discharged from her and joined the expedition, she appears to have lain at Chatham as a hulk; sailors awaiting a new position would be able to live on her until they moved to their next ship, hence the major exodus from her to *Terror* and *Erebus*, where 13 sailors signed on. Beeman continued his working life after the expedition by becoming the foreman of riggers at Woolwich, and progressed to master of riggers at Chatham. He continued gaining promotion, and in 1865 was the chief boatswain at Chatham, a position he held until his retirement in 1870.

He features in three censuses. First in 1851, at around the time when he joined the management at Chatham Dockyard; he had taken up residence nearby in Gillingham, with his wife Eliza and four children. Then in 1870 he had reached retirement and at the age of 61 he could start to look back on a very successful career. His wife was still by his side as was one of his sons, 17-year-old Thomas, who had started an apprenticeship as a shipwright. Beeman survived until the 1891 census but by only a few months, dying that year at the age of 81. By that time not many of his contemporaries from the Ross expedition would still be alive.

The unfortunate death of John Roberts created another change of personnel, in that **Edward Mann** from Rochester in Kent, who had been on *Erebus*, found himself delegated to *Terror* for the remainder of the voyage; on signing on he was 29, and his wife's name was given as Elizabeth Ann. When first recruited he had been given the position of boatswain's mate, but now he found himself promoted to acting boatswain, replacing Beeman, who had been transferred to *Erebus*.

Mann's previous ship had been HMS *Pelican*. Like *Poictiers* and many other Royal Naval ships *Pelican* had seen plenty of active service during the wars with France and America, but in peacetime seems to have been reduced to routine patrols round the coasts of Africa. She had just completed one such mission in May 1839, having been away for nearly five years, and when recruiting started for the Antarctic expedition she was stationed at Chatham. Eight other seamen from *Pelican* joined Mann on *Erebus*. He had entered *Pelican* as an able seaman at the age of 26 in 1835, and by the time the ship had completed her commission he had attained the rank of boatswain's mate.

When the Antarctic expedition returned to Woolwich in 1843 he soon found further employment, and by October 1844 he was bound once more for Australia, New Zealand,

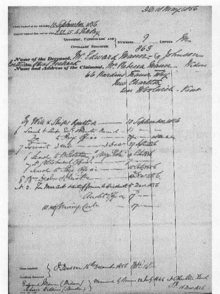

Left: Edward Mann's will, dated 10 September 1856 claimed by his widow Rebecca. Right: Edward Mann's service record with a note about the Lloyds Patriotic Fund.

China and Singapore, aboard HMS *Daedalus*. Her return to England gave him a chance to be at home for about 18 months, signed on as a boatswain second class, based at HMS *Agincourt* at Devonport. Then he spent a further year on HMS *Fisgard* at Woolwich.

He continued to seek employment in the navy and in 1852 found himself once more headed to Australia on HMS *Firebrand*. He was then sent to the Black Sea in 1854, now with the rank of boatswain first class, to become involved in the Crimean War. *Firebrand*'s captain was killed in action leading an attack on a shore battery, and on 18 May 1856 Mann lost his life in the same conflict whilst serving aboard her, but from what cause is not stated. He left a different wife, Rebecca, back home in England, and in 1856 she filed a claim for his pension and back pay of £22 15s 6d. I also have a list of the ships in which he served and on it there is a footnote; this just states 'Lloyd's Patriotic Fund 12 Mar 64'.

The Patriotic Fund had been created in 1803 by what was to become the world-famous insurance broker Lloyd's of London. Its primary function was to award financial support to men in the armed services for acts of bravery beyond the normal call of duty; this was expanded later to include support for injured soldiers and seamen and their dependent families in the event of any hardship that had overtaken them.

Within a year of its conception it had received donations from various sources that amounted to nearly £175,000. Later, swords would be given, mainly to officers, as a token of the service they had rendered to their country in times of military action. The higher the rank the more expensive the sword, up to £100 in value at the time. In 2008 Bonhams the auctioneers sold one of these swords for £84,000; it had been presented to the captain of

HMS *Spartan* in 1810 which had been in action in the Mediterranean. The footnote does not elaborate on whether Edward Mann's widow received any remuneration from the fund, but it could indicate that he died after performing an act of bravery.

Two of the most interesting men on *Erebus*, and the two about whom most is known, are the surgeon, **Robert McCormick**, and his assistant, Joseph Hooker. As you will have learnt from this book, McCormick, naval surgeon on several other Arctic expeditions, had sailed with Ross before, and his experience in the icy realms of Arctic was the reason why he had been selected.

Royal Naval protocol aboard expedition ships had developed to the point where the surgeon and his assistant were expected to fulfil not only their medical remit but also scientific studies connected with natural history. On the Antarctic expedition this was a bonus for McCormick. For many years he had borne a grudge from being unable to fulfil his ambition of being the chief naturalist aboard HMS *Beagle* on her second voyage of discovery under Captain Fitzroy; this was because on board at the same time had been Charles Darwin who, although travelling as a gentleman and not a naval officer, had been given all the opportunities of going ashore and carrying out the duties that McCormick regarded as his by virtue of his position as surgeon. His frustration built up to the point when, on reaching Rio de Janeiro, he felt compelled to request a passage back to England. His later life seems to have followed a similar pattern; whenever he came up against the hierarchy of the naval authorities and promotions were being handed out he was rebuffed or passed over, and other surgeons were promoted.

Born in Runham near Great Yarmouth in 1800, he lived to 90. Because his father, Robert McCormick senior, had died while he was still very young he did not join the service until he was 21. After he had attained a suitable medical qualification – he had spent two years studying medicine at Guy's and St Thomas's hospitals in London – he entered the navy as an assistant surgeon. McCormick senior had been serving in the war against France and at the time of his death his ship, HMS *Defence*, was returning from the Baltic Sea where she had been in action, when she went aground on the coast near Jutland and was destroyed. Only 14 of the nearly 600 crew were saved. Many years later in Sydney, Australia, while on Ross's Antarctic expedition, McCormick met up with a retired naval surgeon, Sir John Jameson, who spoke to him about his acquaintance with his father when they had served together in the Baltic Fleet; Sir John recalled trying to dissuade McCormick senior from returning to England aboard *Defence*. Her role was to escort the badly damaged HMS *St George* back to a home port, but both ships foundered en route, one trying desperately to save the other.

Robert McCormick had first sailed with James Clark Ross on William Parry's *Hecla* expedition to Spitsbergen heading towards the North Pole. It was during this trip that McCormick had developed his fascination for flora and fauna, finding much of interest on Spitsbergen. His next assignment took him for another spell in the Caribbean which brought on the yellow fever, when he was repatriated to England. Having recovered, he applied for the position of surgeon on *Beagle*, which turned out, as we have just seen, an unfortunate affair.

When Ross was equipping *Cove* to rescue the whalers trapped off the Greenland coast *Terror* was commissioned to accompany her and McCormick was given the post of surgeon, but before *Terror* could sail most of the whaling ships had returned and he was stood down with the rest of the crew.

His participation in the Antarctic expedition is well documented in Part One of this book; however, he yet again managed to ruffle feathers, finding fault with several of Ross's other officers.

On the expedition's return he was awarded an honorary fellowship of the Royal College of Surgeons; but as far as professional promotion was concerned he was both overlooked and critical of the recognition that other men received. He had always yearned for a command of his own and in 1852, while he was the surgeon aboard HMS *North Star* under the command of Captain Pullen, that ambition was realised for a very short time when he commanded one of the ship's cutters – bearing the proverbial name *Forlorn Hope* – manned by six oarsmen. They searched the coastline of Wellington Channel seeking the lost Franklin expedition, but found no trace.

In 1857 he received the Arctic medal in recognition of his time there, and his final promotion came in 1859, when he was appointed deputy inspector general of hospitals – but he never actually served in that capacity. Following his retirement, he spent the last 20 or so years of his life in obscurity, alone with his collection of stuffed birds and animals collected during his foray south with *Erebus*. These days we might see this unfortunate man as one seriously lacking social skills.

One of the brightest stars to emerge from the expedition was **Joseph Dalton Hooker**, the assistant surgeon on *Erebus*. Like McCormick he came from East Anglia, and he grew up in his birthplace, Halesworth in Suffolk. His father, William Jackson Hooker, was very influential throughout his life and steered him towards a lifetime of studying natural history based on his own career. Hooker senior became the director of the Royal Botanical Gardens at Kew, and he would be followed in this post by his son Joseph.

When Joseph's father became a lecturer at Glasgow University the family moved from Halesworth to Glasgow, and by the time Joseph was seven he was sitting in on his father's lectures, so infatuated was he with the natural world of plants and their worldwide distribution.

From childhood he was an assiduous collector of plants and insects, encouraged by a similar-minded father. When he left school, he chose to enrol for a medical degree, as this was the only course that included in its curriculum the study of plants used in medicines.

His father, William, found out about the forthcoming expedition and made a point of contacting Ross to find out more about its natural history aspects. The position of

Left: Joseph Dalton Hooker, assistant surgeon on Erebus. Right: Robert McCormick, surgeon.

senior surgeon had already been taken, but it appeared that an opening existed for an assistant, and William immediately proposed that Joseph be considered for the post, explaining that he was studying for a doctor's degree. Ross promised to consider Joseph for the vacant post if he successfully completed his exams. Joseph not only succeeded, but also managed to fit in a course on astronomy, which had the additional benefit of teaching him the basics of navigation.

By the time he graduated in 1839 he was aged 22; the prospect of gaining travel to distant parts of the globe became a reality and led him to taking on the role of assistant surgeon aboard *Erebus*. Joseph's father paid for most of the scientific equipment his son might need during the four years he would be away.

Once his appointment to the expedition had been confirmed he received from the Admiralty a long list of the duties he would be expected to carry out. When the ships arrived at any destination Joseph Hooker was to take every opportunity of getting himself ashore, be it on some remote volcanic atoll or the more spacious environs of Tasmania or the Bay of Islands in New Zealand. His studies of the samples he acquired had to be examined for any medicinal or commercial properties they might reveal.

His knowledge of plants including mosses and lichens was quite remarkable for one so young, but it was his passion. In addition he spent many hours poring over and dissecting the marine life brought up in the dredges and trawls sampling the seabed, even sharing the great table in Ross' cabin as they both worked into the early hours.

One of the stipulations laid down for all the members of the crew and especially the officers before the expedition set sail was that all notebooks, artwork, records and specimens were to be handed over to the naval authorities when they arrived back in England. Joseph wrote voluminous letters home to his father to keep him informed of all the interesting observations he made and detailed descriptions of the samples he collected. He even sent home seeds from some of the rare plants he came across. This tactic must have worked, because there do not appear to have been any official reprimands. Charles Darwin became a close friend, too, during this period and he also benefited from the young Hooker's enthusiastic correspondence.

Unlike the expeditions mounted by other nationalities, the British researchers were always provided with the best equipment required to carry out the research set for them, but reliance was placed on the surgeon, his assistant and the officers and crew to master all the techniques that they would need to use. The captain's role in all this was vital as he strove to encourage and direct his budding scientists.

Postal services were gradually becoming more reliable and it was possible for a sailor to receive letters from relatives at home by forewarning them when and where he might be at certain times during the voyage. Homeward-bound mail could convey this information, and if any outward letters failed to arrive in time they would be sent on to another destination, sometimes taking the best part of a year to arrive. There were ships designated to carry out this function of delivering and collecting mail on a fairly regular basis, used by private, commercial and government agencies. Joseph Hooker, for one, took full advantage of the postal service to keep his father and other correspondents up to date with his activities.

All the time Hooker was away exploring he was not spending much of his salary but on his return he soon needed to consider his position in the navy. It would provide some certainty of income, and Ross had intimated that he might be able to assist with a posting that had the prospect of a scientific nature. After due consideration Hooker continued his naval connection on half-pay and this together with a government grant of £1,000 towards the cost of writing up his copious notes from the voyage, allowed him to produce a series of superbly illustrated volumes that he entitled *The Botany of the Antarctic Voyage of H. M. Discovery Ships* Erebus *and* Terror *1839–1843*. The first two volumes were published between 1844 and 1847, and others followed over a number of years. His literary output was phenomenal, including, as it did, books, articles, leaflets and even a series of magazines. He continued to write into the final year of his life.

Although reticent about his artistic skills he managed to produce some excellent pictures of the natural history that would eventually make up his collection. His fascination with the voyages of James Cook and the travels of Sir Joseph Banks would lead him to carry out his own expeditions to remote places across the world, seeking out new plants and inferring how they came to be found in so many different locations.

In 1847, with the first two volumes of his Antarctic work completed, Hooker was once again seeking adventure overseas. This time he set off for India, or more precisely the Himalayas. He was absent for nearly four years, in which time his travels took him through Bengal, Bhutan, Sikkim and Nepal. He even ventured over the border into the forbidden country of Tibet. At one point of the journey through Sikkim he and his companion were arrested and imprisoned, but fortunately were soon released without any harm coming to them. Returning to England in 1851 he had amassed another collection of plants to disseminate, and now had to set about writing up his notes again.

He made several more overseas trips connected with botany, and in particular worldwide plant distribution. In 1860 he travelled to Palestine. In 1871 he spent three months in Morocco. His final overseas journey took him to the United States of America in 1877. All the time he spent travelling was taken up with collecting plant material and seeds to bring back to Kew Gardens, where he now had taken over the role of director following his father's death. He spent 20 years as the head of Kew, building on his father's legacy.

By the time he reached 80 he had outlived all the officers who had accompanied him on *Erebus* and *Terror*. All the prominent plant collectors that roamed the world in the 19th century consulted Hooker, and even the great Charles Darwin sought his opinions.

The visits from famous people didn't stop at botanists, either; when Robert Falcon Scott was preparing *Discovery* for his first Antarctic expedition he too came to visit; it was of course Ross's expedition nearly 60 years before that had first breached the frozen ocean to reveal the Antarctic continent and the great ice barrier, and Scott acutely aware of Joseph's participation in this venture, wisely consulted him. In 1910, when Joseph was approaching the age of 93, Scott tried to persuade him to raise the white ensign aboard *Terra Nova* before he set off on his second expedition to Antarctica, this time to conquer the South Pole. Although sound of mind, Joseph politely declined the invitation on the grounds of frailty.

Left: Nitophyllum Smithi *and Right:* Veronica Bentham. *Just two of the hundreds of superbly detailed pictures drawn by Hooker.*

In 1908 the South Magnetic Pole had finally been reached. During Shackleton's Antarctic expedition, three of his men succeeded in dragging a sledge several hundred miles to establish its position. James Clark Ross had set his heart on achieving this, and if he had still been alive he would have had a wry smile on his face to know that at least it was a British expedition that had achieved the task he had set for himself all those years ago – and that one of his junior officers was still alive to learn that the task had been accomplished.

Working down the list of crew members, we find **Richard Wall**, ship's cook, who successfully completed the whole expedition. At 40 years old he would have been one of the older crew members, so it is strange to find him entered as a first timer. He had actually been with both the Rosses when they led their privately funded *Victory* expedition into Prince Regent Inlet and wintered in the Gulf of Boothia for those four long years between 1829 and 1833. According to John Ross' book about this expedition Wall was listed as the harpooner. He must have enjoyed life aboard the various discovery ships because next time his name occurs it is on the muster list of *Erebus* as she sailed under the command of Sir John Franklin in 1845. James Ross seems to have had an affinity for him, as after their return in 1833 Wall became a servant at Ross's residence in Blackheath.

Wall perished, of course, with the other members of the Franklin expedition. He left behind his wife, Hannah. How she coped after his death was confirmed by the Admiralty is not apparent – nor, for that matter, can I find any data about the way, if any, that the others who were left behind might have been provided for.

To cook for over 65 people, Wall would have needed some help, and this came in the form of stewards who were allocated to the various messes. Ross had his own cook, however, who would probably have sailed under him before, because it was a position of trust as much as anything else. **Thomas Boddington** carried out this role, and remained for the duration. His previous ship had been HMS *Winchester*, which discharged her crew in April 1839, and he had stayed in Chatham, probably waiting to sign on for the new Antarctic expedition that was about to commence recruiting.

The crews' messes would be designated according to the watch they were on. The lieutenants' mess was called the gunroom, and here they would dine and relax, and when in port would be able to entertain visiting dignitaries or officers from other vessels. They had just two men marked on the muster list as their stewards: the first was **Henry Martin** who was discharged even before they set sail, and the second man, **John Lewis**, deserted at Simon's Town.

The junior officers such as the mate and the gunner would dine in the young gents' (midshipmen's) mess, which was looked after initially by **Edward Smith**, a first entry from Chatham, aged just 21. He got as far as Hobart after the long voyage through the tropics down to Simon's Town, calling at the various island groups on the way, but there he fell ill and was sent to hospital. When *Erebus* came back to Hobart for the second time he was replaced by **George Pine**, originally from Tiverton in Devon and had signed the register as a first timer. He obviously withstood the rigours of the remainder of the voyage because his name appears on the list of those signed off when the vessels returned to Woolwich.

As explained earlier, although the two ships had been provisioned for long periods at sea they called in at various ports when it was possible for the men in each mess to buy at their own expense fresh vegetables, fruit and any fish, fowl or other meats they could obtain by purchase or hunting. Ship's biscuit, notorious for weevil infestation, must have been at the very bottom of their choice of food, especially as it was common practice on the part of the person issuing them to use up any old stock before starting on a new batch. The other staples of shipboard diet would have been salt pork and beef, together with pea soup and preserved potatoes. A large round steam pudding popularly referred to as plum duff was a firm favourite when cooked properly, but when overcooked it was seriously considered for use in cannons.

Some of the most important seamen were the captains of the various watches who trained and led by example the hands whose job it was to man the rigging and set the sails. These leaders were captain of the main top, captain of the foretop, captain of the forecastle, depending on the part of the ship that they worked on. **George Scott** and **James Rigden** were the two longest-serving captains of the main top. Turning to the foretop, we find **Thomas Marshall** and **William Waddup** holding their posts for the duration.

The captain of the forecastle was tasked with looking after and leading the sailors working for'ard. Important equipment such as anchors and their chains, ropes, sails and other working impedimenta connected with the forecastle came under his remit. **Edward Fawcett** and **James Woodward** carried out the duties of looking after the forecastle all the way out and back home.

There is one other captain who has not yet been mentioned; the captain of the hold. He was directly answerable to the first lieutenant, who had overall command of the stores carried in the hold. Whilst *Erebus* was stationed in Hobart in 1840, her captain of the hold, **Edward Bradley**, lost his life, as mentioned earlier, during a routine cleaning operation, when Bradley was suffocated by fumes and died before help could be administered. He was 45. When a crew member had allotted some of his wages to next of kin and at whilst he was away from home he died, I assume the dependant would have continued receiving the benefit of the man's wages until his record had been brought up to date.

His place was taken by **William Brimson**, who was promoted from able seaman. He, the 37th man to sign on, was a 27-year-old from Gascombe in the Isle of Wight. His previous ship had been HMS *Spartiate*[32] which, many years before he sailed on her, had been a French man-of-war captured by the British under Nelson at the Battle of the Nile. She went on to take part in the Battle of Trafalgar. From 1835 onwards *Spartiate* was held at Plymouth dockyard 'in ordinary': coming to the end of her useful life she had on board a skeleton crew to maintain her until a final decision was made as to her future. It was during this period that Brimson was stationed aboard her.

A fascinating story emerges about one of *Erebus*'s able seamen, **Robert Devese**. Most of the details have been retrieved from a document stored in the National Archives, which lists the ships he sailed on from a very early age. He had been born in Portsmouth in 1814, and after joining the navy at the age of 16 he sailed aboard HMS *Aetna* along the coast of Africa on surveying duties. Her captain was Edward Belcher, who came to prominence when Franklin was being sought. Transferring to HMS *Revenge*, Devese spent the period between April 1831 and January 1834 taking part in the Royal Navy's programme of protecting British business interests along the coast of the Iberian peninsula as Portugal struggled with political problems that had beset her royal family.

Devese then shipped out on HMS *Russell* as she departed from England in July 1835, staying on board until January 1839, the ship again looking after the trade with Portugal where political unrest was still causing problems for the British Empire's expanding overseas trade. Devese's discharge from *Russell* in January 1839 meant he could enlist for the Ross expedition; I suppose the promise of double pay would have been an enormous attraction to him, as it would have been to all those signing on. At this juncture he would have still been single, as it was his mother, Elizabeth, who was receiving his allotment whilst he was away on the expedition.

As I have stated before, little or no mention of either of the ship's crews appears in the books written after the expedition was completed, and it was not until Devese sailed aboard HMS *Excellent* in 1847 that we start to get some idea of the man himself. *Excellent*'s muster roll describes him as a man of average height, 5 feet 6 inches tall with a dark complexion. This

---

32 An interesting note here about one of *Spartiate*'s officers, Lieutenant Clepham. After the Battle of Trafalgar he was presented with the ship's 'Union Jack flag' (Nelson's phraseology) by the crew in recognition of the esteem his men held him in. This same flag was discovered 100 years later by a descendant and, believed to be the only surviving Union Jack from that battle, was sold at auction, fetching the princely sum of £384,000.

was complemented by dark brown hair and hazel eyes. There were no distinguishing marks on his body such as pockmarks or tattoos. Throughout his naval career he received the highest of plaudits from his commanding officers. The comments column in most of the ships he served on was Very Good. He had four tours of duty aboard *Excellent*, and when he sailed on her in 1852 he had been promoted to second master. He retained this position until he left the navy in 1858 to take up a civilian occupation.

Three years later his family appeared for the first time in the census records. He now had a wife, Sarah, and a young son and daughter, living in his home town of Portsmouth. There is an unusual circumstance surrounding their property in that it appears to be some sort of co-operative. Not only did the members of his family live with him but there were two cobblers and a bootbinder plus two unemployed seamen. The property itself is listed as a beer house, for which Robert Devese paid 12 shillings a year rent. Ten years later, in 1871, he had only his wife living with him, and they had moved away from the first house. Although he was listed as a naval pensioner in 1861, the occupation column on the 1871 census return has him down as a drainage labourer. The following year he died, at the age of just 56. How sad that a man who had given his working life to the navy, visiting some of the remotest parts of the Earth and experiencing so many dangerous and exciting times, should finish up doing such a menial job.

Although the later years of **John Newman** are obscured by time, we do know of an incident in his naval career that brings to life the reality of how hard it was to serve in the Royal Navy. He was signed on to *Erebus* as an able seaman and the record shows that he was Irish by birth with his age given as 31. He had been sailing with the navy since at least 1831. His previous ship was HMS *Pelican*. He served the full term of four years with Ross on *Erebus* and then continued to find employment, first on HMS *Poictiers* but very soon embarking on HMS *Blazer*, where he took up the post of second master. He spent the next three years with her, then in 1847 he entered service on HMS *Fisgard*, the training vessel that many of his contemporaries from the expedition gave their time to.

In 1853 he again set sail, this time on HMS *Archer* to patrol the African coast for slavers. But on 12 May 1853 his decision to go back to sea changed his life for ever; as he was helping to set up the jib-stay he was knocked down from the rigging. There is a written record of the accident and a subsequent report about the extent of his injury and his discharge to Simon's Town hospital:

> He was struck with great violence by the foot of the foresail and thrown off the head gratings against the foresail tack cavil[33] where he sustained a second blow on nearly the same part of the shoulder – an examination of the right shoulder discerned a drop below the level of the other, movement was limited and accompanied with much pain.

---

33 A large cleat for heavy lines such as sheets or braces.

There are further notes of the medical treatment he received at the hands of the ship's surgeon and his discharge to hospital nearly six weeks after the accident. The initial treatment onboard was to strap him up to reduce movement and so reduce the pain; he was allocated a crib in the sick bay so that he would be more comfortable at night.

His stay in hospital lasted several months, but he was apparently collected from Cape Town early in 1854 to return to England. His life after this incident has not been recorded, but at least he had completed a sufficient number of years in the service of the Royal Navy to earn him a pension.

The names of the men on *Erebus* as yet unmentioned are too numerous and the information about them too sparse for me to go into any detail – and 'detail' is the appropriate term, because they signed on as ordinary seamen and to a greater extent their place in history has been obscured by time and lack of historical information relating to them. About half of them completed the whole journey whilst others experienced a range of fates such as being discharged from the service early, deserting, falling ill and finishing up in hospital, or later signings on, joining at various ports of call along the way. At the start of the expedition *Pelican* and *Poictiers* supplied most of the original signatories. This in itself would have assisted the crew to settle down quickly to the routine of the expedition, providing as it did a core of experienced seamen, many of whom already knew one another, to train the starters.

At the start of the voyage in 1839, 48 brave souls signed on as crewmen, 32 of whom had the luck to be with the expedition for every day of the round trip – and the stamina to endure it. In all, during the four epic years it took to complete this particular circumnavigation of the world 70 men signed on as crew for Erebus, 22 of them joining the ship as the voyage progressed.

It comes as no surprise that the majority of the two crews hailed from seaside towns such as Portsmouth, Dover, Sunderland, Fishguard, Hull, Dundee, Boston and Great Yarmouth. These towns and many others, breeding grounds for sailors, are ample evidence of our maritime history.

A whole host of ships' officers had helped to hone men such as these into the mightiest naval force the world had ever known, and sailing on some of Britain's most historic ships brought them the experience that would prove to be the key to the success of this historic journey that would one day open up the vast unknown southern continent to the likes of Scott, Shackleton, Amundsen, Mawson and so many others of the Golden Age of Exploration.

Travelling as supernumeraries aboard the two ships but not apparently named on the muster lists were several army personnel who would be set ashore at either St Helena or Simon's Town. **John Henry Lefroy** was a lieutenant in the Royal Artillery. Ever since he had joined the army at the age of 14 in 1831 he had shown an interest in scientific matters, and this came to the notice of one of his superior officers, **Colonel Edward Sabine**, a leading figure in the field of magnetic

Sir John Henry Lefroy, KCMG CB FRS. He founded the Royal Canadian Institute in Toronto.

studies. As a result Lefroy was selected to accompany the Ross expedition to set up and manage the running of the observatory on St Helena. He took with him three soldiers from his regiment, led by **Corporal Robert Fulcher**. They took up residence while the observatory was being constructed in the house that had been built to accommodate the deposed Napoleon Bonaparte. Lefroy continued to run the observatory for the best part of three years, but in 1842 he was sent to Toronto to supervise the new magnetic and meteorological unit being built there. During his time in Canada he travelled widely, employing men supplied by the Hudson's Bay Company, to take a series of measurements at over 300 sites to gain a fuller picture of the geomagnetic fields all the way from Montreal to the Arctic Circle, and then continued further west, covering an estimated 5,000 miles in the process. He married his first wife in Toronto in 1846, and continued with his scientific work which led him to be instrumental in establishing the Royal Canadian Institute of which he was the first vice president in 1851 and president the following year.

He and his family returned to London and he was promoted to inspector general of the army schools. Amongst other duties he carried out after leaving the army in 1870 as a major-general were governor of Bermuda followed by administrator of Tasmania. Knighted in 1877 he lived for a further 13 years, marrying again after the death of his first wife in 1859.

Simon's Town was the destination for the next observatory, and it was the turn of **Lieutenant Frederick Marow Eardly-Wilmot**, another Royal Artillery officer and friend of Lieutenant Lefroy. He too was assisted by a small detachment of Royal Artillery soldiers led by **Sergeant Weir**, and they commenced building the observatory soon after disembarking from *Erebus* at Simon's Town in March 1840. The buildings had to be iron-free so as not to influence the instruments – copper, brass and zinc fixings were essential building materials, all of which had been shipped out from England – and it took nearly a year before the measurements could be started.

Eardly-Wilmot returned to England at the end of 1842 on leave, but was back in charge during a period in 1843. Because of his training as an artillery officer, the governor of the Cape Colony requested his secondment to an army unit that was currently employed safeguarding the colony's frontier against attacks by the Xhosa tribe, and a little later by unrest amongst the Boer settlers who had many disagreements with the British colonial authorities. These disagreements would eventually lead to all-out war between the two sets of colonists, which became known as the Boer War. His time in Africa came to an end in 1847 when he was posted back to England to the Woolwich Academy. By the time he was stationed there he had been promoted to captain, and he eventually reached the rank of major-general. He passed away in 1877. Interestingly a near relative of his became governor-general of Tasmania, succeeding Sir John Franklin. He served there from 1843 to 1846, and died in Hobart a year later.

HMS *Terror's* senior lieutenant was **Archibald McMurdo**, of Scottish parentage; he was born in 1812 and joined the navy twelve years later in Dumfries. A year after he joined the navy he found himself serving on various ships of the line including HMS *Superb* and HMS *Melville*, and in 1828 he sailed from England aboard HMS *Blonde*, a 46-gun frigate; on this voyage she was bound for the Mediterranean, where action was taken to help a French armed force capture a Turkish-held castle and in the process further the cause of the Greeks in their struggle for independence from the Ottoman Empire.

At this time he earned his mate's ticket, and this led to him being sent aboard HMS *Alligator* which was provisioning for a commission to the Far East. Various destinations were visited and one of them saw him in action near the Bay of Islands (which he would subsequently revisit in 1841as Ross's expedition made its way towards the Antarctic). A whaling ship had been wrecked on the New Zealand coast, and the survivors, captured by local Māori, were being held for ransom. Probably because of several misunderstandings an armed conflict took place. The result was the release of the hostages, and for this action McMurdo went on to receive promotion to lieutenant in 1836.

That year, McMurdo was taken on by Captain George Back, heading for the Arctic in command of *Terror* to try and establish a route through Hudson Bay to the North-west Passage. As mentioned earlier, heavy ice caused the expedition to be abandoned, and *Terror*, seriously damaged, had to make her way home. By superb seamanship the ship reached Ireland, where Back beached her to prevent her sinking.

In 1837 McMurdo sailed aboard HMS *Volage* on a mission connected with the start of the opium wars that Britain inflicted on Imperial China. At some stage during this mission McMurdo's health deteriorated and he had to be invalided home.

His next assignment was Ross's Antarctic expedition. He was probably selected as the first lieutenant because of his experiences in Hudson Bay two years earlier. But when the expedition arrived at the Falklands in September 1842, the two surgeons pronounced him unfit to continue due to an abdominal illness which was possibly a recurrence of the sickness he had contracted while aboard the *Volage* in the Far East four years earlier. Despite this setback he continued in the navy, and on his return to England was promoted to commander. This led to his first command in 1846, that of HMS *Contest*. She had recently been launched, and her first commission was to patrol Benguela, on the west coast of Africa. This is now part of Angola and the famous Benguela Current takes its name from the region.

When *Erebus* had been closing with the coast of Africa in March 1840 on its way to Simon's Town, Ross had noted in his book that they were experiencing an upwelling of cold water in this same region:

> March 8th. By 1pm the next day, the temperature of the sea had fallen from 70° to 56.5°, that of the air being 65°, and the mist unpleasantly cold to our feelings. … We had expected to have found an elevation both of the air and sea on our approach to the African coast by reason of the radiation of heat from its shores: but the cause of the depression became evident on the morning of

the 9th, when, having sighted Cape Paternoster at daylight, we found we had to contend against a current increasing in strength and coldness of temperature as we neared the land.

This ties in with the fact that there is a strong cold current now known to force its way up the west coast of Africa – and it was in these seas that in 1846 that Commander Archibald McMurdo found himself patrolling in the Royal Navy's attempt to stop the slavers carrying out their despicable trade in human beings. A number of naval ships were employed in this operation, and they certainly experienced some success during the many years it was in operation. Although Britain had abolished slavery in 1833 other countries still plied the vile trade.

Ross and Crozier held McMurdo in high regard, and as a result he had what is now one of the best-known features of Antarctica named after him, McMurdo Sound. It continues to be used today to identify the main American and New Zealand bases on the continent; there is in addition an ice shelf carrying his name, and a dry valley as well.

Archibald McMurdo eventually rose to the rank of rear admiral in 1867, and on his retirement in 1873 became a vice admiral. He died two years later, in 1875.

With the repatriation of McMurdo from the Falklands some reorganisation of the senior officers became essential. Sibbald transferred to *Terror* to become her senior lieutenant. Smith had now received his promotion aboard *Erebus* to the rank of lieutenant and Oakley, the mate, became an acting lieutenant because Bird had been raised to the rank of commander. To complete the promotions, Wood now assumed the role of senior lieutenant on *Erebus*.

There is another lieutenant we have yet to take a look at, and that is **Charles Gerrans Phillips**. His name was appended to a cape in the Antarctic by Ross and Crozier. He was one of the most popular of the officers on the expedition, and certainly a favourite of Robert McCormick, the surgeon; every time they made a landfall the two of them would be among the first to get ashore and start exploring. Having joined the navy in 1820 Phillips made steady progress, and his promotion to lieutenant in 1838 came at an opportune moment, enabling him to apply for the position aboard *Terror* for the Antarctic expedition.

Having returned with the two ships to Woolwich in 1843, when he and all the others were paid off, he soon found his next assignment, aboard HMS *Helena*, and proceeded to the Cape of Good Hope.

When the search for Franklin was at its height Captain Sir Ross was asked by Lady Franklin to help find her husband, or at least any record of what had happened to him and his expedition, which had by then been missing for nearly five years. She had commissioned a ship, *Felix*, and Lieutenant Phillips volunteered, to become second in command aboard her. They set sail in 1850 but after a winter spent on Cornwallis Island and time taken during that winter to explore across the island *Felix* returned to England without finding any trace of the missing ships and their crews.

On his return Phillips was pleased to find he had been promoted to commander, and soon found himself in command of his first ship, HMS *Polyphemus*, bound for the West African coast to deal with the slave trade. In 1853, while still aboard *Polyphemus*, Phillips was asked by the local chieftain to support him against an insurgent bunch of warriors. The attackers were intent on capturing Lagos (in what is now Nigeria) and defying the treaty that had been enacted to help stop the slave trade. With the co-operation of two other naval vessels Phillips bombarded the attackers' stronghold and dislodged them whilst the loyal supporters of the local chief pursued the enemy to complete the overthrow of the rival faction who had been intent on maintaining their terrible trade.

The navy was rapidly turning to steam-driven vessels; first fitted with paddle-wheels and then screw-propelled. *Polyphemus* became involved in some of the trials carried out to determine which system was the better, and became well known in naval circles a few years after Phillips left her. There appears to be some controversy in historical records as to whether she competed in the famous 1845 'tug of war' episode or just speed trials, but ultimately of course it was screw propulsion that was chosen.

Returning to Phillips' career, we find that his experience with steam propulsion resulted in him being given command of HMS *Urgent*. Built in 1855, she had just been commissioned into the navy as a screw-propelled troopship, and he was her first commanding officer. His orders were to proceed from Portsmouth with an embarkation of over 1,100 troops destined for Malta. This turned out to be a rather unpleasant trip, not from the point of view of the sailing conditions but more from one of unfortunate events that eventually led to a court martial against Phillips and the ship's master.

The master, Mr Braund, had been in charge of the navigation as their ship approached Valletta Harbour after nightfall, and the court heard how it was essential for any ship approaching at night to change direction when she was well past the light beacon displayed on Cape St Elmo. Braund had not adhered to these instructions but had turned too soon, resulting in *Urgent* running aground. Luckily no serious damage was caused and after being refloated she entered the harbour to discharge the troops safely. Then there was a second incident when they returned to Spithead three weeks after leaving Malta. This time it involved a small trading vessel which was struck by the much heavier *Urgent* and suffered so much damage that she looked as if she would founder.

The findings of the court concluded that no blame could be laid against Commander Phillips, but the master received a severe rebuke.

A couple of weeks after the verdict, Phillips took *Urgent* back to Malta with another consignment of troops and a large quantity of stores. These were destined for the Crimea, to support Britain, embroiled as it was there in conflict with Russia.

This voyage was to prove as trying as the previous one, in that *Urgent* required a tow into Gibraltar for repairs to her boilers. The repairs enabled her to complete the troop transport, but she had to limp back to Britain, and on arriving at Portsmouth went straight into dock for an overhaul of her machinery.

Phillips retained command of *Urgent* right up until June of 1857, and after his retirement he became an honorary member of the Meteorological Society. He passed away in 1871 aged 67; at the time of his death he was living in London.

As you will be well aware of by now, when *Erebus* and *Terror* stayed at Hobart in 1840 the main objective was to set up an observatory to continue the series of magnetic and solar observations that had been undertaken since they left England. In command of the Hobart observatory was the third of *Terror*'s lieutenants, **Joseph Henry Kay**. It appears he was related to Sir John Franklin by marriage, as his mother was the sister of Franklin's first wife, Jane Porden. His father, Joseph Kay, was a well-known architect. Anyway, Joseph certainly resided at Government House for the duration of his stay at the observatory. His assistants were drawn from the crew members of *Erebus* and *Terror*; they were Peter Scott, the first mate on *Terror*, and Joseph Dayman, the mate aboard *Erebus*. Two marines were also delegated to help staff the station because round-the-clock observations would be required. **George Parr**, the younger of the two, was aged just 23 when he left England; he came from Suffolk. The other man was **William Stevenson**, aged 35, who hailed from Nottingham.

After his return to England, Parr was sent to New Zealand to take part in one of the wars against the Māori and suffered a serious injury but survived to continue in the service of the navy. The census of 1861 shows a George Parr being aboard HMS *Mercury* at Chatham, but she was not on active service and would soon be decommissioned to be broken up. Parr's home was in Hunston in Suffolk but at the age of 55 he can be traced to Gillingham in Kent where he was residing as a naval pensioner living with his first wife, Jane, and three of their children. Ten years later the 1871 census lists him as a boatbuilder and Greenwich pensioner, but now apparently married to Sarah. The last census that he features in is the one for 1891; the children had left home but Sarah, now aged 60, was still alive, and at 74 he listed himself as a naval pensioner.

Another snippet about his life turned up in a short article in *The Times* of Monday 25 April 1904. It transpired that at a meeting held in the town hall in Chatham he was toasted as the senior veteran at a reunion of retired Chatham naval pensioners. He had the honour of sitting between the two most senior officers present, Major-General Sir Reginald Hart VC, and Rear Admiral R.W. Craigie, the superintendent of the Chatham dockyard complex. Parr lived on until 1910, dying at the remarkable age of 93 – exceeded only by Sir Joseph Hooker, who passed away at the age of 94 in 1911.

Returning to Kay, he was just 25 when he took on the role of commander of the observatory. His promotion to lieutenant had come just five months before he set out aboard HMS *Terror* and just 12 years after he had joined the navy at the age of nearly 13. Prior to the expedition Kay had gained sailing experience in HMS *Fly* in the West Indies and on the American Station in the mid-1830s. Before that, he had found himself setting out in HMS *Chanticleer* between 1828 and 1831 on an extensive exploring and surveying voyage along the South American coast as far down as the South Shetlands and Deception Island. The next step was to cross the South Atlantic and revictual the ship at Simon's Town in South Africa before setting out in a north-westerly direction, touching in at St Helena and Ascension Island as they crossed the Atlantic for the third time. *Chanticleer* then proceeded northwards along the coast of Brazil, towards Venezuela and ultimately Panama. They spent time here exploring the Panamanian isthmus, and the captain, Henry Foster, carried out a survey up the Chagres river. He travelled in a native canoe, and as they returned to *Chanticleer* he tumbled into the water. Unable to swim and with his heavy naval uniform, he was soon lost to view and his body was never recovered. The ship's first lieutenant, Horatio Austin, took command and sailed *Chanticleer* back to England.

Foster's orders had included the requirement to look into a number of subjects, among them the study on magnetism. Young midshipman Kay had soon shown his aptitude for the scientific aspects that the expedition hoped to investigate, and this would be the main reason why he was selected to accompany the Ross enterprise. The Royal Society provided the scientific instruments, as it did for most of the exploring ships that sailed from this country. *Chanticleer* had her rigging modified during her refit and an extra mast was stepped, converting her from a brig to a barque. Whilst taking part in the voyage, which was to last for three years, Kay kept a journal for the first 12 months, and it has survived to the present day, courtesy of the Scott Polar Research Institute in Cambridge. For a relatively young man he was very observant, noting down details that others would have ignored and consequently his journal makes a very interesting read.

After three strenuous years at sea *Chanticleer* was in need of a major overhaul, so was not ready to carry out the next scientific journey that had been planned. This task fell to HMS *Beagle*, the ship that will always be associated with Charles Darwin. *Beagle* made three voyages of discovery and it would be the second voyage, between 1831 and 1836, that set Darwin on the path to his major natural historical work, *On the Origin of Species*.

Upon Kay's discharge from *Chanticleer* he embarked for the next three years in HMS *Rainbow*, destined for the Mediterranean. Under the command of Sir John Franklin, his uncle, it must have been a plum appointment for Midshipman Kay, and would probably have had some influence on his being chosen for the Ross expedition. Kay's promotion to lieutenant came shortly after his return from *Rainbow*, just in time for his appointment on *Terror*. (It was following *Rainbow*'s voyage, too, that Franklin was offered the governorship of the Tasmanian colony.)

When Ross and Crozier returned to Hobart for a second winter Kay was still active at the observatory, and he would continue to command the staff there for another five years; but by 1847 he was starting to fret that he had been overlooked for the promotion to a full captain that he had set his heart on. He had in the interim period married. Finally, the first step to becoming a captain came his way with advancement to commander in 1849; by 1853 he had resigned his position at the observatory and returned to England – and, as mentioned earlier, this heralded the death knell for the observatory; the navy had handed over its running to the local government and with a lack of funds it was soon closed down.

On his return to the southern hemisphere in 1855 it was not to Tasmania but to Victoria in Australia that Kay headed. There he took the position of clerk to the Executive Council and continued in that capacity until he retired in 1865. (Alexander Smith, too, had chosen the state of Victoria to live and work after leaving the navy.) Kay gained the final promotion of his naval career by becoming a post captain. He lived out his retirement in Australia and passed away in 1875.

Thomas Edward Laws Moore had been in the navy for 17 years when he was offered the post of mate aboard *Terror*, and after the expedition he went on to earn a number of other promotions. Having joined the navy in 1832 and been away with *Terror* for the four years of the expedition, he soon found himself promoted to lieutenant. The Admiralty felt that further exploration to the southern hemisphere was deemed necessary to follow up Ross and Crozier's highly successful voyage and fill in some of the areas they had not been able to cover.

A suitable ship, *Pagoda*, was made available and Lieutenant Moore, in command, was assisted by **John Brodie** as her master. She set sail from Simon's Town in January 1845 heading west, and after a few days turned in a more southerly direction. They had initially hoped to find the elusive Bouvet Island, but they were no more successful than Ross. The ship crossed the Antarctic Circle and achieved a furthest south of nearly 68°S. Moore was thwarted, however, in making a landfall, and as the ice cover increased so did the frequency with which they encountered icebergs, giving them little alternative but to turn back north and head for warmer waters.

This was to be the last known British expedition to venture so far south without the aid of steam power. *Pagoda* had been at sea for six months on this voyage and on her return Moore moved on to other commissions. Her next voyage was to be her last. In 1846 as she neared Mauritius she foundered.

Other ships that featured in Moore's career were *Winchester* and *Caledonia*, but only for short commissions, and then in 1848 the Admiralty began the series of searches for Sir John Franklin. Moore gained further promotion, this time to commander, and his Antarctic experience made him a prime choice to take part in the search. He was given charge of HMS *Plover*. She was destined to sail 17,000 miles to take up her station on the Alaskan coast near Point Barrow and act as a rendezvous for the various ships that visited that northern part of the American continent as they joined the Franklin search. Moore stayed in the area until *Plover* was withdrawn in 1854, but for the last two years he became a supernumerary when Captain Maguire was sent to relieve him. At this juncture he had attained the rank of captain, but on his return to England he found himself on the half-pay list with no future prospects.

He was, however, elected a Fellow of the Royal Society for services rendered to science in the field of magnetism. In 1855 he was offered the governorship of the Falklands, and he stayed there until 1862. It appears that John Sibbald accompanied Moore, taking his family down to the South Atlantic Island group. In 1869 Moore took a well-earned retirement, and the rank of rear admiral was bestowed on him, then at the age of 53 he passed away at his home in Plymouth. Several geographical features commemorate his presence in the colder regions of the world, notably Moore Channel and Port Moore located near Point Barrow in northern Alaska; and in the Antarctic one can still find Cape Moore at the entrance to Smith Inlet.

Charles Molloy was engaged at Woolwich as the third mate aboard *Terror*. It would appear that he had received his mate's ticket in July 1837 whilst serving aboard HMS *Cornwallis* on a tour of duty that took her to the North American and West Indies stations, returning to

Portsmouth in June 1839 just in time for him to enrol for duty on *Terror*. When *Terror* arrived in Tasmania, however, he became so ill that he had to be repatriated to England, and he played no further part in the enterprise. The 1851 census showed that he had forsaken further naval service and had become a grocer, working with his wife Susannah in a shop in Woolwich. At that point they had five children.

Molloy seems to have been born in 1810 and his wife in 1817. When they got married is not certain, but in 1851 the eldest of their children was ten; this would tie in nicely with his return to England from Tasmania. Susannah continued to run the grocery business until at least 1881, but without her husband who passed away in 1871. Many of the records for the name of Molloy have an Irish connection but the only baptism record I can find that fits with other information I have places him as being born in Kent, and in fact the 1851 census record gives his birthplace as Woolwich in Kent.

'Talented' was the byword for some of the men who took part in the expedition, and this description certainly applied to **John Edward Davis**. Although he was designated as second master on *Terror* he performed many other tasks. Born in Gosport in Hampshire in 1815, he was destined to join the navy as did so many young men from coastal towns. His father had been a sailor for many years and now he followed him and his older brother Henry into the navy as soon as he left school at the age of 12. He had attended Burney's Naval Academy which had been set up with the express intention of giving boys an education that would fit them for a life at sea. His first ship was HMS *Pearl* and she was commissioned to survey part of the Irish coast. On the completion of this trip he then signed on to HMS *Samarang* which sought broader horizons. They went to South America, again for surveying purposes. Returning from the likes of Rio de Janeiro and Montevideo, his appetite seems to have been whetted for foreign travel and a few weeks after returning to Portsmouth he was off again. Now aboard HMS *Blonde* under Commodore Francis Mason he would see again some of the ports he had been to on *Samarang* but would now be based at Valparaiso in Chile where the navy maintained a permanent presence. While on this station HMS *Beagle* entered the harbour under the command of Captain Robert FitzRoy and with Charles Darwin aboard as the naturalist. The *Beagle* was about to set off for the Galapagos Islands and then continue her voyage around the world. FitzRoy had bought a small yacht, the *Conception*, with the express purpose of completing the survey of the Peruvian and Bolivian coasts and he had chosen one of his junior officers, Alexander Usborne, to be in charge of her. He approached Commodore Mason for the loan of John Davis. This was agreed and Davis was transferred to the muster list of *Beagle*. His role on *Conception* was to assist with the survey work. This is what he had been trained to do whilst on his previous two ships. After they had completed their task Usborne was instructed to sell the yacht and return to Britain with his crew of Davis and seven seamen. He arrived back on English soil in time to receive promotion to become second master. Two days after Davis packed up his belongings *Beagle* sailed for the Galapagos Islands never to return. During his time aboard *Beagle* he had shown his aptitude for art, and this, combined with a solid grounding in naval surveying work, made him an ideal candidate for Ross's forthcoming expedition. His artwork graced the pages of James Clark Ross's book about the expedition, and today his drawings can fetch a four or even a five-figure sum when they come up for auction. He also drew most of the charts from the surveys that were carried out. Later in his career he joined the navy's hydrographic department in 1863 for 14 years, until his retirement in 1876.

The following year was to be his last, and he died in Greenwich, where he had lived with his wife, Mary. They had had eight children, and their eldest son, Percy, had co-operated with his father to publish what was probably the first set of azimuth tables.[34] Both men had been honoured with memberships to scientific societies: Davis senior became a Fellow of the Royal Society and Percy became a Fellow of the Royal Astronomical Society.

We have seen that the navy had two titles for the officer responsible for the finances and stocking of the ship: usually purser but in some cases clerk in charge. On board *Terror* the latter position was held by **George Henry Moubray**. He was only 29 when he took on this very important role, and it would appear from his subsequent appointments that his expertise lay within the organising side of naval life.

After his return to Woolwich in 1843 he took posts of the same nature aboard at least two other naval ships, HMS *Terrible* and HMS *Daring*. The latter was built as one of several of her type, and entered service in 1844 as part of an experimental squadron used to carry out sea trials, part of a development programme set up by the Admiralty to assess new and modern design features for use in the Royal Navy's combat role around the globe. By 1846 he was listed as a captain of Greenwich Hospital and found himself on half-pay. This was quite normal on reaching the higher ranks when there were no vacant commands available, but his aptitude for figures and organisation soon led him to a new posting. The approaching war with Russia in the 1850s meant that the War Office and the Admiralty were involved in the transportation of thousands of men and their equipment to Turkey as part of the military build-up in preparation for the forthcoming hostilities. Moubray was selected to help set up the supply depot at Constantinople (now Istanbul). He held the important post of naval agent and storekeeper, and once the flow of men and materials had been organised he transferred to Malta, where he carried out a similar task; Malta was the primary staging post for stores and soldiers shipped out from England.

At the end of the Crimean War in 1856 Moubray transferred back to England, and in the 1861 census we find him living in Portsmouth with his Austrian-born wife Eliza, 15 years his junior, and five children. Moubray had been born in Jamaica; his father, also a naval captain, had fought at the Battle of Trafalgar. Later, Moubray was to move to Greenwich, where he was paymaster in chief until his retirement. He passed away in 1887 aged 76, and his wife outlived him by over 20 years.

Regarding **John Robertson**, *Terror*'s surgeon, little – unlike his counterpart aboard HMS *Erebus* – seems to be known about his later life. He did accompany the newly promoted Captain Bird aboard HMS *Investigator* when in 1848–1849 the ship was used as part of a two-pronged search, with HMS *Enterprise*, looking for Franklin's missing expedition. Robertson was the surgeon on this voyage and probably continued his career in the navy until his retirement or,

---

34 Azimuth tables allow the navigator to determine the angle of the sun in degrees from due north and that, with the date and time of day, enables calculations to be made to fix a ship's position.

David Lyall, the assistant surgeon on Terror, *and his headstone in Cheltenham cemetery, Gloucestershire. He died in 1895.*

as many naval surgeons did, took an administrative role within the naval organisation.

His assistant, **David Lyall**, however, became far better known; as mentioned earlier he had made a lifelong friend of Joseph Hooker, and they kept in touch throughout their lives. Botany was the subject that fascinated the two men, and it took them all over the world. After returning to England in 1843 Lyall was promoted to surgeon in 1846, and the next year saw him aboard HMS *Acheron*, one of a new class of vessels combining sail and steam power, as she set off to carry out an extensive survey of the New Zealand coast. Her captain, John Stokes, having been on the *Beagle* when she had carried out a similar task around South America, had got to know Charles Darwin, so Stokes and Lyall had many common interests, and whilst the ship was being used for surveying Lyall would have been able to get ashore to continue his botanical studies and build up his collection of New Zealand flora.

Lyall's next assignment saw him setting off as the senior medical officer in Captain Belcher's squadron as they too sought the missing Franklin party; their expedition set out in 1852 with four ships: HMS *Assistance*, HMS *Resolute*, HMS *Pioneer* and HMS *Intrepid*. Belcher spent a second winter continuing the search, having been supplied by relief ships in 1853, which also shipped home the sailors who were considered unfit to continue. By the time the summer of 1854 had arrived he was faced with a terrible dilemma, as his vessels were still trapped in the ice. He took the risky decision to abandon them. Fortunately, two supply ships, plus *North Star*, arrived in time to evacuate the crews of the icebound four.

Any naval officer in charge of a ship and losing it faced a court martial. Belcher's defence was the threat to his crews' health posed by staying any longer in the Arctic regions; he deemed this more important than continuing a search for men who had been missing for over eight years. Lyall was of course called upon as a witness; he substantiated his commander's submission, and Captain Belcher received a caution. Belcher continued his career in the navy and eventually became an admiral.

Lyall was awarded the Arctic medal in 1857 in recognition of his work caring for the men on the expedition. These included the crew of HMS *Investigator* who had been rescued from their stricken ship. For more about that exploit, see her entry in Part Three.

Lyall was kept busy with subsequent appointments, the first of them on HMS *Pembroke*. She was part of the naval squadron despatched to the Baltic as part of Britain's plan to thwart Russian expansion into Scandinavia. Then, following the Treaty of Paris at the conclusion of the Crimean War in 1856, Lyall found himself helping a naval contingent to secure the boundary between the USA and Canada. This gave him an opportunity to help carry the survey overland, and he took full advantage of this to add many plants to his collection.

Gradually his rovings ceased and in 1866 he married Frances Rowe, 21 years his junior, and took up shore appointments at Pembroke Dock amongst other sites, always in a medical capacity. Just before his retirement in 1873 he became deputy inspector general of hospitals and fleets. His retirement took him to Cheltenham where he died in 1895, his wife having predeceased him by three years. He was survived by two sons and a daughter. A tombstone marks his grave in the cemetery in Cheltenham.

One of the remarkable facts to emerge from the two muster lists, especially that of *Terror*, was the number and type of men who, having survived the Antarctic, volunteered to sail on her again, into the wastes of the North-west Passage. Ten of them, including Captain Crozier from *Terror* and three men from *Erebus*, took part in that fateful expedition. Many of the other officers from Ross's Antarctic venture were involved in the various rescue attempts, but none of them actually served on either of the two expedition ships; apart from Crozier, those that did participate were exclusively from the lower ranks. Why did neither Franklin nor Crozier manage to attract any of the senior officers who had played such key roles in the success of the earlier expedition? The fact that many of them took an active part in the rescue operations could perhaps be seen as their way of paying tribute to the men they had sailed with who then lost their lives in the Arctic.

Trying to build up pictures of the lower-deck crew members of either ship lost in the Arctic is very difficult due to the dearth of information. Official census records only started in 1841 (and that census was a very basic one) and as censuses are held only every ten years it was 1851 before the next one. By then the Admiralty had declared the men dead. So it is impossible to trace most of the crew members who took part in both expeditions: they would have been in the Antarctic for the 1841 census and dead by 1851.

This means that birth and baptismal notices are virtually the only records of any use; these can, when combined with the ships' muster rolls, be a good source of information as to where the sailors were born and how old they were when they signed on. This does have its limitations, however, because in national records a Christian name can be common to more than one person with the same surname.

Take **Thomas Honey**: he was an experienced naval carpenter, and when *Terror* arrived in Simon's Town on her way south he transferred to her from HMS *Melville*. I originally believed that as the muster roll for *Terror* showed him to be 28 in 1840, when he joined, he would have been born in about 1812. But Judith Upton and another source of information indicated that he was born in 1802. The conflict of dates meant I had to be aware of stating any career or personal details about him. I found that two years after Honey's return in 1843 from the Antarctic, when Franklin was preparing to set sail, Honey was accepted by him as carpenter. However, on board *Terror* as she headed towards the Arctic was another man with the surname of Honey; he was listed as the blacksmith and his Christian name was Samuel, but his age was not recorded. One might infer that they were brothers. I had only the births, baptisms, marriages and deaths records held by Ancestry to work with, and these had 18 records for men named Thomas Honey born from 1806 to 1816 (I was still working on the assumption that Thomas was born around 1812). Of those 18 entries there were just 5 births; the rest were men who had died during those years, so could be ignored. Then I did the same for Samuel Honey but over the wider time scale of 1800 to 1816; for that name I found 16 entries.

In the navy's description books, as mentioned earlier, details were given of a man's height, complexion, colour of hair and eyes, and any distinguishing marks such as tattoos or evidence of having had smallpox; but in the case of Thomas Honey I could not find these details. It was becoming increasingly difficult to link the two men, and there was not enough information for me to write a factual account of the two men's earlier lives and where they had come from. This illustrates the problem I have been constantly been faced with when putting together a plausible history of individuals and trying to throw light on men who lived good lives but have never had written records to show how good they were.

One of the other sources of information I referred to above provided me with positive proof that Thomas had been born earlier than I had thought; it was supplied to me by Judith Upton, the secretary of the Cornwall Online Parish Council Project. Thomas Honey was actually born in 1802 in Devonport. He married Margaret Spargo in the September of 1830. Their first child died in infancy but they had another, young Thomas, born in 1838. Honey embarked on HMS *Melville*, bound for South Africa in October 1839 and arriving there just before Christmas. When she sailed for Singapore on 30 April 1840 he had left her, transferring to *Terror*. This was to be good news for that ship, because she was in dire need of a carpenter: **William Rich**, her original carpenter (who had signed on at Chatham, leaving behind his wife Elizabeth), had been sent to hospital; and **Alexander Turriff**, the carpenter's mate, a 24 year-old Scotsman from Aberdeen, had deserted, along with at least nine other men.

Honey's skills would be severely put to the test after he embarked. The real test would come during the southern summer of 1840–1841 as the ships headed into the icy wastes of Antarctica. The prospect before them was daunting. Both of the commanders and quite a few of the officers and crew had gained experience sailing in similar conditions in the Arctic; the principal difference now was that in this, the remotest part of the world's oceans, no possible rescue could be mounted and they would have to depend entirely on their own resources.

The carpenter's craft is one of the oldest known, and it has to a large extent been through the carpenter's skills that the human race has moved from its most primitive state to where it is today, and the spread of humans to all the habitable areas of the world is attributable to our ability to fashion wood into seaworthy vessels.

These skills would be put to the test in the months ahead. To start with, there was always routine maintenance; the ship's boats, for example, would often require attention, and modifications to the fabric of the ship itself were sometimes needed. Companionways had to be kept in good order to avoid accidents, and hatch covers had to be watertight to stop seawater soaking the tweendecks. Spars, masts, blocks and the many other wooden items that were integral parts of the ship's working equipment constantly needed to be maintained to the highest order. Thomas Honey and his counterpart on *Erebus* executed their duties admirably.

*Facsimile of Margaret Honey's
headstone in the cemetery at
Stoke Damerel.*

Danger was never far away. Ice and icebergs, raging seas, uncharted reefs and sandbars would all play their part in the future of the expedition; any one of these threats could put all their lives in jeopardy, and repairs to any damage sustained would need to be accomplished in the most unpleasant of circumstances. The carpenter was deemed important enough to be a warrant officer, putting him ahead of the blacksmith, sailmaker and cook in terms of his importance to the ship.

When Thomas Honey was discharged in September 1843 he was assigned to HMS *Ocean*, a hulk at Woolwich. There are no records of his going on any other voyages before he set out again on *Terror* to the Arctic two years later; in the interim he returned to Devonport, resuming family life. How and when he found out about the Franklin expedition is not known, but he volunteered for it even though his wife was pregnant with their second child. The expedition sailed before the baby was born, so he missed the birth of his daughter – and he never saw her, his wife and their small son ever again.

The crucial information supplied to me by Judith was that Thomas Honey's wife Margaret left a small epitaph to him, and it is this that confirms his age, and when and where he was born.

So now I know my first opinion was wrong, and I am grateful for the help I have received from Judith Upton.

We can have a look at the other tradesmen on board, and one who would often work closely with the carpenter was the caulker. *Terror* set out without this post being filled, but they did have **John Lane** as a caulker's mate, and on their arrival at Hobart they were able to recruit **John Irvine** as their caulker. He was 30 at the time, and came from Whitehaven in Cumbria. How he had reached Hobart is not known, but what does show up on the muster list is the fact that by October 1841 he had been demoted to able seaman. He completed the mission, but was only rated as Fair in the comments column.

John Lane held his place of caulker's mate until October 1840, then took on the role of carpenter's mate. Did he perform both roles? We don't know, but they would have complemented one another, especially when the ship suffered her structural damage.

Moving on to others from *Terror* who took part in what was to become known as the Franklin Mystery we have **Thomas Farr**. He had signed on at Chatham as an able seaman, but by the time the expedition had reached Tasmania he must have been having second thoughts; it is recorded that he deserted on 6th November 1840 but just three days later he returned to the ship and asked to be reinstated. By diligence he received his first promotion in 1842, firstly to captain's coxswain and then in February 1843 to captain of the foretop, retaining this post for the remainder of the voyage.

William Jerry seems to have been content to remain as an able seaman. **David Sims** from Lincolnshire, too, remained as an able seaman. **Thomas Jopson** had been Crozier's steward in the Antarctic and presumably he was asked to carry out the same function when they sailed north in 1845. He had been born in Middlesex in 1819, and had been only 22 when he had joined *Terror* in Hobart on her second visit there in 1841. **William Smith** is of course not an uncommon name, so this entry has question marks all over it, in that on Ross's expedition he was one of the mates aboard *Terror* but the William Smith who sailed to the Arctic is listed as the blacksmith, an unlikely change of occupation. Then there was a **Thomas Johnson** who progressed from able seaman to quartermaster during his voyage to the Antarctic, but the Thomas Johnson who sailed north was listed as the boatswain's mate, and this on its own is far from conclusive evidence that this is the same man. The muster list confirms he was born in Wisbech in Cambridgeshire, which in the middle of the 19th century was a small and thriving inland port on the River Nene. It was here that he would have gained his experience of handling sailing ships and small boats and although listed as a first entry he very soon became the captain of the maintop, then quartermaster as they sailed into Hobart in October 1840. Trying to establish if he accompanied Franklin led me to the article 'The Men Who Sailed with Franklin' by Ralph Lloyd-Jones, published in *Polar Record no 41*. Lloyd-Jones asserted that Thomas Johnson did in fact sail north on that fateful voyage. and he gave the following information about our erstwhile explorer: he stood 5 feet 8 inches tall, had hazel eyes, a sallow complexion and dark hair, and his previous voyage had been Ross's expedition to the Antarctic. I have failed to find any census records that would indicate Johnson's presence in the United Kingdom after the Ross expedition so it would appear that he lost his life with the other 128 men in the Arctic.

The position of quartermaster, like a number of other petty officer positions, was held by various members of *Terror*'s crew. One, **James Grimes**, was like Johnson a first entry and he, alongside **James Cleat**, held the post from her departure from Chatham in 1839. He served in this capacity until February 1842, when he became the captain's coxswain. His place of birth was given as Radcliffe in London, and at the start of the expedition he was 23 years old.

The hospitalisation of any of petty officer would entail a promotion of another man, as when John Lumsden was invalided during the second visit to Hobart, and James Cleat took his place as acting gunner. Discipline and performance played a part in the commanding officer's thinking; the efficiency of running the ship would have been paramount in his decisions.

The next two men, **William Johnson** and **Luke Smith**, are stronger possibilities for matches. They had both signed on during *Terror*'s second visit to Hobart and went on to complete the journey, so could well have struck up a friendship which carried over to the Franklin expedition. For this they both signed on as stokers for the voyage north, a position that would only just have become available, because *Erebus* and *Terror* had been fitted with auxiliary steam engines.

The final man who I can be sure took part in both expeditions was **James Rigden**. He had started off aboard *Erebus* in 1839 as an able seaman, and by the time the ships sailed homeward in 1843 had risen to second master. He was one of only two *Erebus* men who sailed on her on the Arctic voyage, the other being Richard Wall, mentioned earlier. Taking part in this second voyage Rigden signed on as the captain's coxswain but of course we have no way of knowing whether he had a new opportunity to be promoted. We do know he was born in Deal in Kent about 1809 and at his baptism he was given the full name of James Frederick Elgar Rigden. His pay allotment was in the name of his mother, Frances, but other than that I could find no known facts about him.

The same goes for the many other seamen who made up the bulk of the men who sailed north in *Erebus* and *Terror*, and it is sadly outside the scope of this book to deal with them.

Having seen the involvement of the crew members and some of their officers in the Franklin expedition, both participating in it and carrying out some of the searches that took place, we can now have a look at the men who continued their naval careers but who must have been touched by the events unravelling in the Arctic as it became more and more apparent that a major disaster had occurred. No positive news had returned with the searching ships; they had found no messages or cairns, just the three graves on Beechey Island, where the expedition had obviously spent its first winter.

Terror had an armourer called **William Riggs**, who had started his naval service in 1826 at the age of 20 and from his naval record he seems to have visited many parts of the world on ships engaged in exploration. His first ship, HMS *Success*, sailed south from England early in 1826 on her maiden voyage. Her destination was New South Wales, where she was to carry out surveying work. She was away for five years, returning to England in April 1831. While she was in Australian waters two incidents stood out: the first was being stranded on a reef that resulted in her having to be careened for repairs to her hull, and the second – the one that Riggs would probably recall best 12 years later, when he went back there on *Terror* – was a visit to Sydney in 1841. He lived to the good age of 74, dying in the Medway region of Kent in 1880.

Some family records have helped me as I describe the fortunes of William Riggs. These were very kindly passed on to me by David Taylor, who extracted the details from the family tree he had constructed, and they include many fascinating facts that I feel privileged to share. William, 5 feet 7¼ inches tall, had a dark complexion and a distinguishing mark on his neck. His eyes were grey and he had brown hair. So says the entry in his records when he gained his ticket in 1846. He had progressed to armourer the year before he sailed with Crozier on *Terror* in 1839. Subsequently he became involved in the Franklin search. Firstly, HMS *Plover* and then HMS *Herald* took him on as their armourer whilst they sailed all the way round Cape Horn to the northernmost point of Alaska as part of the Admiralty's plan to search eastwards along the coast of the North American continent in the hope that Franklin might still be making his way through the North-west Passage. On Riggs' return from what proved to be an abortive mission he once more set out to take part in the search, this time westwards into Lancaster Sound on *North Star*. She had been sent out to take supplies to the squadron of Royal Naval ships led by Captain Belcher. As mentioned earlier, after two winters locked in the ice Belcher was forced to

HMS Heron *and HMS* Plover, *stationed in Kotzebue Sound in northern Alaska as part of the Franklin search carried out from the Pacific Ocean.*

abandon his ships, and *North Star* helped bring all the crews back to England.

One of the facts I learnt from David Taylor was how the allotment system worked, and I have explained this at the start of Chapter 4. In this instance it was Riggs's mother who was the beneficiary. Although he was one of 13 children he apparently had none of his own, although he did get married. He moved from the Plymouth area, where he had grown up, to be closer to the ports on the Medway from where he most frequently sailed.

In contrast to the story of William Riggs there is a paucity of information available relating to **George Knight**, the blacksmith on *Terror*. He was 25 at the beginning of the expedition and listed as a first entry; although he was recorded as being born in Braken Ash in Norfolk, it is most probable that he would have had some mercantile sea experience before joining the Royal Navy. His birthplace, now Bracon Ash, is about 6 miles south of Norwich, quite a distance from the sea, but he would have gained experience in small ships on the River Yare, navigable from the North Sea to Norwich. His naval record shows that he served for at least six more years. His final known ship was HMS *Melampus*, which he joined in the East Indies. The record shows that he had transferred to her from HMS *Medea* somewhere in the Far East in November 1848, and that he was discharged from *Melampus* in August 1849 – almost certainly not in an English port, though, as she appears to have been sailing around the East Indies for some time after he was discharged.

On *Terror*'s muster list for there is no evidence of anyone assisting Knight in his duties as blacksmith, so a member of the crew would have been delegated to work the bellows and fetch quenching water and fuel for the furnace. After his tour on *Terror* Knight continued in naval service; on HMS *Cyclops*, a paddle-wheel sloop of just under 2,000 tons he took on the role of stoker, but by the time he sailed on his next ship, HMS *Medea*, he had resumed his original occupation of blacksmith. Whether he married is not known, but his mother was listed on his allotment entry for the Ross expedition. Then he disappears from any records I can access. The 1851 census reveals a George Knight incarcerated in Brixton Prison. This man was also a sailor, but the birthplace given was Southwark in London, so probably not our man – and after that, nothing.

Promotions took place from time to time during the voyage to help ensure that the crews were kept up to strength and to maintain efficiency. **James Cleat** was a good example of this. Initially he had signed on as an able seaman but even before they sailed he had been upgraded to quartermaster. Like a number of other men, he had joined *Terror* from *Poictiers*, and at the age of 32 he would already have seen a number of years' service at sea. His new position would have required somebody with plenty of experience, which his earlier voyages would have given him. He held the position of quartermaster until the expedition returned to Hobart in April 1841, when he became acting gunner. **John Lumsden** had held this post since the beginning of the voyage from England but had to go into the hospital at Hobart. Cleat took his place, which raised him from petty officer to warrant officer.

However, by 1843 when the two ships sailed into Simon's Town, Cleat's own health had deteriorated, and he finished up in the hospital there. HMS *Winchester* was lying at anchor in Simon's Town and William Lewcock was transferred from *Winchester* to *Terror* as her gunner.

Further details relating to James Cleat, both before he joined the expedition and after he was sent to hospital, are obscure. There is a January 1807 baptismal record of his name at Kirkwall in the Orkneys, which would tie in with his stated place and year of birth in the muster list; and he left behind a wife, Sarah, when he sailed with *Terror*. Both the 1851 and 1861 censuses show a master mariner several years younger whose birthplace is given as South Shields, but this sailor spelt his name Cleet. This is sufficiently conflicting evidence to discount a positive connection between the two men.

John Lumsden, the gunner James Cleat replaced in Hobart in 1841, seems to have made a speedy recovery because the 1851 census shows his wife, Jane, and six children, the eldest of them 10 years old, residing in Stepney. Bear in mind that John Lumsden was in hospital in Hobart in April 1841. He was not present at home when the censuses of 1851 and 1861 were taken, and by the 1881 census he must have died, because Jane is marked down as a master mariner's widow. The inference, then, is that he resumed his naval career and was absent for the 1851 and 1861 censuses.

The *Terror*'s third gunner, **William Lewcock**, can be traced more clearly. He had sailed into Simon's Town aboard HMS *Winchester* and following his transfer to *Terror* he completed the voyage back to England and was discharged with the rest of the crew in September 1843. The record of his association with the Royal Navy goes back to November 1833 when for four years his ship, *Jaseur*, was patrolling the Bay of Biscay region. This was a period of civil unrest in Spain and Portugal, with their South American colonies wanting independence. Portugal being one of Britain's oldest allies, her interests were often looked after by the Royal Navy intercepting revolutionary shipping.

Each change of vessel up to Lewcock's association with the expedition showed him progressing along the path from able seaman to eventually become gunner's mate aboard HMS *Winchester* on her voyage to Simon's Town. After he was discharged in September 1843 he continued to find employment as a fully-fledged gunner and sailed in a further ten ships up to December 1854. One of these, the 18-gun HMS *Cruizer*, became involved with seven other Royal Navy ships in attacking a pirate stronghold on the coast of Burma (now Myanmar). So it was not only Africa that had a slaving problem; it appears that pirates were carrying off the natives of Burma and other neighbouring states into slavery, and Britain took it upon herself to intervene. As the gunner aboard *Cruizer* Lewcock would have been in the thick of the action, and two men were wounded in action. All told, 10 sailors were to lose their lives in the successful attack and of the further 16 wounded several died later from their injuries. Lewcock's last commission, on HMS *Royal George* in 1853, brought about his involvement in the Baltic as part of Britain's efforts to stop the Russians' Baltic Fleet from participating in the Crimean War.

After his retirement from the navy he continued to find useful employment at sea, and the census records for the middle of the 19th century show him as the master of a small trading vessel, *Linda Flor*, working out of Penryn in Cornwall. As he was aged 44 in 1861 it would mean he had been just 26 when he took over the demanding and highly responsible role of gunner from James Cleat. Ten years later his career still had a nautical flavour but he was no longer at sea; he was a shipping agent, living in Ipswich with his wife, Amelia, and a small daughter, so unlike any of his former shipmates on the expedition, far away in Hobart, he features in the 1841 census.

Although the 1841 census gave just the names of the head of the household, their family members, their occupations and their ages, this is enough for us to confirm that Lewcock was the same man as the one in the 1851 and 1861 censuses; he had been born in Orford in Suffolk in 1817. The census for 1881 portrayed him as a ship's broker. For this he would have had the responsibility of dealing with businesses importing and exporting cargoes, and in addition he could find himself dealing with the buying and selling of ships. Now aged 62 he had worked hard, and was probably getting ready to retire. The birth, marriage and death records show that he passed away at his home near Ipswich in 1888.

The sailmaker was obviously an essential component of a sailing ship's crew. **Robert Inch** was only 22 when recruited as a first entry, a few years younger than the two men he was to work with. As we have seen, though, a first entry doesn't mean a man with no experience; Inch hailed from Peterhead in Scotland, which then as now was a very active seaport, and this was where he would probably have learnt his trade. On numerous occasions during the voyage sails were ripped apart by the storms they endured, and under very stressful conditions this team of Robert Inch and his two mates, John Owens and James Harris, would have been required to work aloft refitting new sails or standing precariously on a heaving deck carrying out repairs, lashed by waves coming over the side as the rest of the crew fought to control the ship.

John Owens was reduced to able seaman in January 1840, just four months into the voyage. Few details emerge about his life outside the expedition; he was from Beaumaris in North Wales, and had signed up having been recently discharged from HMS *Flamer* at Portsmouth. The other sailmaker's mate, **James Harris**, was also from Wales, but in the south-west of the country; his home town was Milford in Pembrokeshire. The naval dockyard there probably gave him his first taste of the sea but his entry in the muster list shows that he was a first entry. Both men completed the four years the expedition took, as did Inch, and in the case of Harris we can trace him to the 1871 census, when he was in Bedminster in Somerset. As he listed his occupation as a sailmaker, he may have made the grade eventually. By the time of this census, both men would have been in their early sixties, but I cannot find any other information about this particular John Owens – there are far too many of them. I do know that James Mobbs and John Owens had been shipmates on a previous voyage, and they had both transferred to *Terror* from *Flamer* when she docked in Woolwich on her return from the West Indies.

James Mobbs was the captain of the hold for only a few months, but then, demoted in May 1840, needed to be replaced. The man chosen was **Andrew Johnson**. He had joined *Terror* at Chatham in June 1839 and a couple of weeks later was offered the position. His birthplace was stated as Guernsey in the Channel Isles and his age at entry was 28. I am inclined to think he had been employed in other branches of the seagoing fraternity simply because of his rapid promotions. Be that as it may, I cannot find any further evidence of his naval career except to say that he must have performed the duties of captain of the hold satisfactorily, because he stayed in that post for the duration of the expedition.

The crews of both ships contained men from all over the United Kingdom, many from seaside towns, and the next volunteer for a place on *Terror* was **Archibald Stewart**, born in 1809 in Campbeltown on Kintyre in Argyllshire. He was described as 5 feet 8 inches tall with a dark complexion and dark brown hair. His eyes were hazel, and he had no distinguishing marks. He had an up-and-down-and-back-up type of voyage, by which I mean he initially came aboard as a first entry and like many of the early entrants was soon given a more responsible position, in his case captain of the forecastle. For no stated reason, a year later he was demoted to able seaman – not for long, however, because six months later he was made captain of the foretop. This role lasted from February 1842 to February 1843, when he was made captain of the forecastle again. The overall impression he gave his commanding officer was Very Good. I have not been able to trace his personal life after the expedition, but he certainly carried on serving in the navy for a number of years, signing on to HMS *Superb* for six months then moving on to HMS *Illustrious*. Both these ships were in reserve – but HMS *Britannia*, his next ship after that, took him, like many of his contemporaries on the expedition, into the theatre of war that centred on the Black Sea and the Crimea around 1853.

Thomas Abernethy sailed on board *Erebus* as the gunner, and on *Terror* there was an able seaman called **William Abernethy**; born in about 1816, he was at least 13 years younger than Thomas. They both came from Peterhead, and it turns out that they were brothers. We have seen how the elder of the two had been a stalwart of so many important Arctic expeditions, but in contrast William appears to have only been to sea with the Royal Navy just this once. In fact, on his return to England he enlisted with the coastguard, and for the next 27 years, to 1870, made this his life. Census records plot his life after he retired; he lived in Peterhead, his home town, with his wife, Jane, and after she died he remarried; his second wife was Eliza. On the census returns he stated his occupation as retired naval pensioner, and on the last one in 1881 he was down as a retired coastguard boatman. For the last ten years of his service as coastguard boatman he was in fact the man in charge of the boat used for patrols at sea.

A man with a long connection to the navy was **Charles Gregory** but his stay with *Terror* lasted only a few months. He came aboard at Chatham in August 1839, but in March the following year, while the two ships were anchored in the bay at Simon's Town he was invalided to Melville Hospital, prematurely terminating his expedition. He did however make a full recovery and went on to sail for another 13 years on board ships such as HMS *Excellent* and HMS *Cyclops* plus at least six or seven others, as gunner's mate. Then a gap appears in his history until 1861, when he can be found as the gunner's mate on HMS *Victory*, moored in Portsmouth Harbour. After his retirement he settled down at Portsea in Hampshire with his wife, Emma, three daughters and two sons.

Isaac Munday was just 21 when he enlisted to sail in *Terror* in 1839. This made him the youngest member of the expedition crews at that time, and the fact that he nominated his father Isaac as his dependent would indicate that he was unmarried. Like so many of his crewmates he had been aboard *Poictiers*, but in what capacity no mention was made. During his four years on *Terror* he was the gunroom steward. This position would have seen him looking after the domestic requirements of the lieutenants and other senior warrant officers. When not involved in this aspect of the voyage he could be called upon to help to sail the ship.

The life he chose for himself after arriving back in England shows that he must have had a caring nature, because whilst many others in the crew carried on sailing the seven seas looking for adventure, Isaac turned his attention to looking after his fellow sailors; census records reveal that he took every opportunity of working in hospitals. In Gosport, not far from where he was born, was Haslar Hospital. It had been built in the reign of George II, and the original plan of the building had been a closed quadrangle, but huge overspend dictated that only three of its sides were built; even so, at the time of its construction it was the largest brick building in Europe. Originally designed for naval casualties, it soon catered for soldiers as well, especially those wounded in major conflicts such as Waterloo It was the largest hospital in the country devoted to caring for wounded service personnel, and it continued to function as a major centre for wounded sailors and soldiers right through both world wars; when the RAF was formed, it also looked after airmen. Now it is redundant and plans are afoot to create a lasting memorial to all those that worked there.

Isaac, our lowly sailor from HMS *Terror*, became an attendant there for many years, then he and his family moved to Great Yarmouth, where he took up a post in the naval hospital there, but now as a cook. By the 1891 census he had taken retirement and at the age of 73 lived out the remainder of his life with his wife Olive by his side. He passed away in 1895 having served his country, travelled to one of the least known parts of our planet and spent the rest of his life caring for others. The inclusion of his story here gives an insight into the varied lives that these intrepid adventurers led.

Robert Chilcott's mate's licence.

Robert Chilcott, who joined *Terror* in Hobart as she returned from that first encounter with the Antarctic continent, was even younger than Munday, his birth being in October 1820. He was one of 1841 five recruits taken aboard *Terror* in Hobart in 1841. Robert completed the voyage, so visited the far south twice before returning to England, as did the other new crew members. His association with the sea continued, and in 1863 he was awarded his mate's certificate. By this time he had moved up to Liverpool with his wife Priscilla, six years his junior. The family lived in the Toxteth region and continued to reside there for a number of years, bringing up a family of three daughters and two sons. Both his mate's and his master's certificates were awarded in Liverpool. The census records for 1861 and 1871 would indicate that he was away at sea, as Priscilla was listed as a mariner's wife and his name was not on either return. Finally, he can be found on both the 1891 and 1901 returns, his sailing days over as the censuses state that he was retired. His long association with the sea finally came to an end with his death in 1907, aged 86.

Following Chilcott's career, we can see that it was almost the complete opposite of Isaac Munday's. Whereas Munday chose a more domestic form of employment after the expedition, Chilcott typified the life of a sailor who carved out a life for himself at sea, striving with some success to improve his station. He achieved his goals by sheer hard work from humble able seaman in Hobart, rising through the ranks to become a master whose responsibilities would have allowed him to sail and navigate his own ship.

At this point I feel that you will have had sufficient information relating to the lives of some of the more interesting seamen who dared to venture into this unknown world of danger. Many more of them survived and continued to serve their country to the best of their ability, but their details are too brief and their stories would end up as just a catalogue of ships' names and census records, with little of personal interest.

In addition, in many cases their names were too common and the muster lists gave insufficient details to identify them in later years. From the examples already covered it would seem probable that most of them continued working in the navy, the life they were most at home with. What is certain is that most of those who ventured into the vastness of the Southern Ocean came home, and later in their lives would have been able to regale their families and friends with some amazing stories.

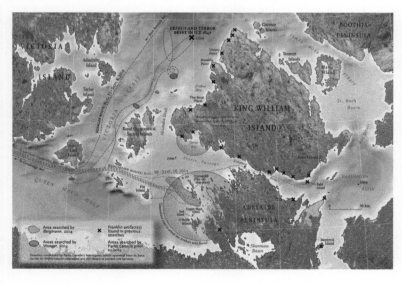

King William Island, where the wrecks of Franklin's two ships, Erebus *and* Terror, *are located.*

One final piece of the jigsaw needs to be put in place to sum up how this expedition was interlocked with another of a similar nature. I am of course referring to the Franklin expedition which took place just two years after the conclusion of the Antarctic expedition. The most notable person to participate on *Terror* in both expeditions was of course Francis Crozier, her captain. One warrant officer followed him – Thomas Honey, the carpenter – and four petty officers: John Diggle, formally from *Erebus*, who became the cook; Thomas Johnson, who became the boatswain's mate; Thomas Farr, who became the captain of the maintop; and Thomas Jopson, who followed Crozier to retain the post of captain's steward. As mentioned earlier, two new posts were created to look after the recently installed engine, and **Luke Smith** and **William Johnson** became the stokers; and finally William Jerry and David Sims stayed as able seamen. In addition to the men who followed Captain Crozier onto *Terror* three petty officers joined *Erebus* again; William Smith stayed on as blacksmith and Richard Wall retained his post as cook, while James Rigden took the position of captain's coxswain. All told, 12 seamen from the Antarctic expedition joined Crozier for the attempt on the North-west Passage and never returned.

PART THREE

THE SHIPS AND THEIR SAILORS

In the third and final part of the book I tell the stories of the ships in which those brave men sailed.

The history of the Royal Navy is a long one, steeped in traditions and legends that go back over 1,000 years. Over the centuries it has always played a major part in our island's fortunes by being there in time of need. The earliest records of an organised English navy go back to the reign of King Alfred, according to the Saxon chronicles of the 9th century. Alfred is reputed to have had a small number of specially designed ships built to counter the continual threat posed by the feared Viking longships. There are no known pictures of exactly how Alfred's ships looked, but apparently they were a much larger version of the longships and could carry many more men. But therein lay their weakness: the Viking ships could and did sail up river estuaries to attack the vulnerable towns and villages on their banks. But Alfred's ships were not as manoeuvrable, and in the shallower waters that suited the Viking ships Alfred's became stranded on mudbanks and sandbars left by retreating tides, allowing their enemy to escape.

The constant threat to the population and security of his kingdom was probably the reason why Alfred decided to take the Vikings on at their own game. The story goes that in about 896 nine of Alfred's ships confronted a smaller number of Viking ships in an estuary on the Channel coast, possibly in Hampshire or Dorset,. The Viking attack was well under way, and three of their ships had already landed their raiding parties. The other three attempted to escape, but only one succeeded. When the men from the English ships attempted to attack the men ashore they found themselves fighting hand to hand; and amidst the mayhem some of the Vikings managed to beat a retreat. The shallower draught of their vessels allowed them to launch their ships and start to make good their escape, but as they had lost many of their men in the skirmish the ships were undermanned and were soon cut off by the Saxon ships. This resulted in the eventual capture of two of the longships, and the third was eventually wrecked further down the coast.

Sea battles, however, as we have come to know them in more recent times, with cannons and gunpowder playing a significant part in naval warfare, would have to wait several centuries. In Alfred's time his navy would, like those of the Greeks, Romans and Phoenicians, be used for transporting soldiers rather than engaging enemies at sea – and when an armed conflict did occur on the high seas it would finish up in hand-to-hand combat, as two opposing ships would grapple one another, enabling boarding parties to fight their way onto the enemy ship to try and gain control of it.[35]

As our island nation developed its navy, it became more and more difficult for our enemies to attack us, and ever since the Norman Conquest Britain's wooden walls have been instrumental in defending our country against threats from overseas.

When William of Normandy landed on the Sussex coast in 1066 his navy had been the means by which he transported his army across the English Channel and as we know from our history books he prevailed over King Harold at the battle of Hastings – but the outcome was in doubt until the end, and if the Norman fleet could have been intercepted our history books would have told us a very different story. 'If' is the key word; we all can recall instances in our lives where after the event we have said, 'If only …'.

Moving on to the Middle Ages, another king would instigate a programme of ship building. Henry VIII had shocked Catholic Europe with his seizure of monastic estates in this country and antagonised it by his declaration of a Protestant faith within our shores, and defying the papal authority of Rome by divorcing his first wife, Katherine of Aragon. Henry, realising that his political enemies at home and abroad were plotting an invasion, implemented a programme of defensive measures. The plan was to build a number of substantial fortifications along the channel coast and augment these with a radical redesign of his navy to incorporate all the latest technology available at that time.

The Tudor dynasty was instrumental in persevering with this policy, and Queen Elizabeth I took it to its peak during her reign. She was admirably supported by some of the finest seamen of the era: Lord Howard of Effingham, Francis Drake, Walter Raleigh and Sir Richard Grenfell. The coming – and going – of the Spanish Armada was the pivotal naval engagement of her reign, and opened the way for the ascendency of the Royal Navy. Looking back through the pages of history the defeat of the Armada provided England with an unrivalled opportunity to take control of the seas in a way no other nation had ever done before. Other nations would challenge England's supremacy and then fall back in dismay as the English won sea battle after sea battle. With the coming of the Industrial Age, businessmen were quick to realise that overseas markets had opened up to them, and supported by the Royal Navy this country dictated world trade as no other country ever had before. Great Britain set up trading stations, creating a toehold in many parts of the world, then established colonies in the New World, Asia and Africa, creating a vast, powerful and supremely dominant empire.

Into the 20th century, and the oceans of the world were still Britain's domain – but other nations were catching up fast, and the two world wars left Britain virtually bankrupt. It was trade that had been Britain's lifeblood, but America had become the major trading nation. For over 300 years the British had been unbeatable, and that was almost entirely to the credit of the Royal Navy; not just the ships that were an integral part of it, but also the men, with their determination, bravery and devotion, who sailed in those ships. This book is dedicated to those men and their ships.

---

35 Interestingly, despite the long-range weaponry of a millennium later, Nelson was still to famously declare: 'No captain can do very wrong if he places his ship alongside that of the enemy.'

The two ships that took part in what became known as the James Clark Ross Expedition of 1839 to 1843 were, as we have read in the earlier parts of this book, HMS *Erebus* and HMS *Terror*. There is, however, another story, one which has until now been hidden from view. This story relates to the ships that the 120 or so sailors who took part in Ross's expedition had been crew members of prior to 1839. The names of these almost forgotten vessels can be found in just one column in the muster rolls of *Erebus* and *Terror*.

By 1839 the Royal Navy had been judiciously reducing its complement of ships and naval personnel; as with all peacetime military establishments cuts had become inevitable. Many of the ships built during the Napoleonic wars and those used against the newly independent United States of America were coming to the end of their useful lives and were not being replaced. Britain still had many overseas commitments and still needed an active naval force; due to the strategy employed by John Barrow, the second secretary to the Admiralty, the navy continued to flourish. When he retired in 1845 he was knighted for 40 years' loyal service to the navy. During his time at the Admiralty he had used the skills and the ships that lay at his disposal to initiate a series of exploratory voyages to survey and map the unknown regions of the world and at the same time keep key officers and men in useful employment.

The Arctic and the North-west Passage were prominent in his list of search areas. It was a natural progression, then, to the setting up of the Ross expedition; there was now a pool of very experienced officers and crew members with polar experience. The navy had learnt how to build ships of supreme strength to withstand the rigours of the ice, even spending winters locked in it, and navigators needed to know more and more details of the Earth and its magnetic fields to overcome the limitations encountered sailing the world's seas. The time was exactly right to get answers to some of the questions that scientists were posing.

Below are some notes about the ships that helped unravel the geographical and scientific mysteries that in the 19th century needed to be overcome. Some facts from Parts One and Two are repeated here.

The year-dates relate to each ship's commission within the Royal Navy, and within each description I have named the sailors I can identify as being on both that ship and Ross's Antarctic expedition.

HMS *Algerine*, 1829–1844, a 10-gun wooden sloop built at Chatham, was 90 feet long and weighed 230 tons. Her guns were all mounted on her weather deck, and her crew numbered about 50 men and boys.

Richard Stebbing, discharged from *Algerine* in December 1833, signed on to *Erebus* as armourer. He deserted at Hobart in 1840.

Algerine's first commission found her just off Cape Frio on the coast of Brazil near Rio de Janeiro. It was here that on the night of 5 December 1830 HMS *Thetis* had been wrecked on the rocky coastline. *Algerine*'s task was to help salvage as much as possible of *Thetis*'s cargo: a large amount of bullion, and gold and silver coins. *Thetis*, having just completed her tour of duty on the South American station, had set off homeward bound from Rio when in a storm and navigating by dead reckoning she came to grief. *Thetis* lost 22 men in the disaster and at the subsequent courts martial her captain and master were held responsible for not carrying out standard procedures; they were each penalised by two years deleted from their sailing records.

The salvage operation took nearly a year, and for the whole of that year a crew of men, billeted on the cliffs above, had to work their way down to the sea using steps cut into the cliff face. The wreckage was in danger of being swept out to sea, and a series of nets were cast across the cove where *Thetis* had started to break up, to prevent as much cargo as possible from being lost in deep water. To help retrieve the gold, a series of cables were suspended from strategic points along the cliff face, spanning the cove. From these cables the men would lower into the water a large, weighted open-bottomed metal tank as a diving bell. It held enough air for the one or two men inside it to search the seabed for a short time. The tank (and the men) would then be hoisted to the surface and moved to a new area, the air being replenished, and thus little by little the sea bed was searched.

Using this simple but time-consuming operation much of the cargo was saved and brought safely back to England. *Algerine* completed her commission on the station and arrived back in England in 1833, when Richard Stebbing was discharged. He would have had much to talk about with Alexander Smith when they sailed together on *Erebus* – Smith had been aboard *Thetis* when she foundered.

After a refit *Algerine* sailed from Plymouth in September 1834 to visit the Cape of Good Hope, docking there in November. Her ultimate destination was the Far East Station, and under the command of her captain, Lieutenant-Commander George Stovin, she sailed for India and Ceylon. At one point there was a confrontation between Stovin and the mate, Charles Cardew, together with the master, Michael Heath. This resulted in Stovin being confined to his cabin on the allegation that he was unfit to command the ship due to his continuous insobriety.

This action by the mate and master would ultimately lead to a court martial once the crew had been brought back to England. After a lengthy hearing, Stovin was placed at the bottom of the promotion ladder with a recommendation that he never take command of another ship, but the case against the two warrant officers took an unusual turn; they were dismissed from the service and had to serve three months in Marshalsea Gaol near Southwark. It had a notorious reputation as being a vile and overcrowded establishment where the lives of the inmates were not high on the agenda. Interestingly, if *Algerine* had had a squad of marines on board at the time of the altercation, part of their role would have been to support the commander at all times. The inference is that there were no marines present on this voyage. Not only did the local newspapers cover the story of the proceedings, but when *The Times* printed several articles about it, it became national news.

Algerine, with a new commander and crew, completed her tour of duty in the Far East. In the early 1840s she was engaged in several operations during the conflict with China. When she was disposed of in 1844 she was still a relatively young vessel and the fact that she was sold rather than broken up probably reflected that.

HMS *Arrow*, 1823–1852, was a 10-gun wooden cutter/ketch built in Portsmouth dockyard. Her length was 64 feet and she weighed 160 tons.

James Giles was discharged from her in May 1842 and joined *Erebus* shortly afterwards, when the expedition reached the Falklands. He had started off as an able seaman but was to become a captain of the foretop before being discharged on the ship's return to Woolwich.

Arrow had been designed and built as a revenue cutter, so had an armament of two 6-pounder guns supplementing her eight 6-pounder carronades – all very useful for close encounters, as her main task would have involved the apprehension of smugglers. Fifty or so men would be required to man her, some of them marines.

While James Giles was a member of her crew she was stationed at Rio de Janeiro and had visited the Falklands several times between 1839 and 1844. Her captain on this commission was Bartholomew Sullivan, and he had chosen to take his pregnant wife along with him. After she gave birth to their first son they christened him James Young Falkland Sullivan. Sullivan senior was knighted in 1869 for his service to the navy.

While *Arrow* was visiting the Falkland Islands, where James Giles had effected his transfer, Ross despatched her to Rio. He needed her to bring back some much-needed stores and a spare bowsprit to replace the one on *Terror* that had been broken when the two ships collided following their dramatic encounter near the icebergs as the two expedition ships headed north from their second visit to the ice surrounding Antarctica.

Arrow was decommissioned in 1852 and her fate is not known.

HMS *Barham*, 1811–1840, started life as a 74-gun third-rate ship of the line. She was built at the Blackwall yard but in 1826 she was reduced to 50 guns over two gundecks.

Two members of her crew, **Alexander Gunn** and **William Riggs**, who had both completed four years of service on her, were discharged in April 1838 and signed on for the Antarctic expedition. Gunn deserted *Erebus* before she sailed, but Riggs became the armourer on *Terror*.

Barham had been the flagship on the West Indies and North American stations until in April 1829 she went aground on some sandbanks. Once she was refloated careening was required to check the damage, and the only facility available for that was at Curaçao. The damage turned out to be quite serious, and cost an estimated £4,000 to repair.

Her last commission saw her patrolling the coasts of Spain and Portugal, and going into the Mediterranean, in pursuit of foreign shipping that might interfere with British merchant ships and their trade with Portugal. Her fate was to be broken up in 1840.

HMS *Caledonia*, 1808–1856, was a first-rater with 120 guns on three decks, built in Plymouth dockyard. Her armour consisted of 32 × 32 pounders on the lower deck,

34 × 24 pounders on the middle deck and 34 × 18 pounders on the upper deck. These were supplemented by an assortment of carronades. At over 2,700 tons, she was one of the largest wooden ships in the navy and was the leading one of her class.

Thomas Roberts joined *Terror* at Hobart in 1840 as an able seaman but a year later he deserted and his place was taken by **David Penivarden** who successfully completed the voyage. After the conflict with France ended in 1814 *Caledonia* seems to have spent much of her time in routine patrols in the English Channel and along the Spanish coast, where there was always the possibility of apprehending blockade runners bringing goods into the Iberian ports against British commercial interests.

There was to be at least one other connection between the expedition and *Caledonia*: in 1843 **Thomas Edward Laws Moore**, who had been the mate aboard *Terror*, then received his promotion to a full lieutenant and was posted to *Caledonia*.

By 1856 she was at the end of her seagoing life, but the navy still found work for her. At Woolwich was *Dreadnought*, which had been used as a hospital ship for many years and needed replacing. *Caledonia* was selected to take on the role – and the name – of her predecessor, a function she carried out for many years until 1875 when she in turn was broken up.

HMS *Castor*, 1832–1902, was built at Chatham Dockyard and carried a crew of 275 officers and men. She was armed with 36 guns, ranking her as a fifth-rate. Her naval career spanned 70 years before she was broken up in 1902.

There was only one member of the expedition, **Able Seaman Henry Paradise**, who had served aboard *Castor*; he played a very insignificant part in the expedition, however, as he deserted at Hobart in 1840. An incident that took place while he was serving on *Castor* involved a collision with the revenue cutter *Cameleon*; she sank off the coast near Dover with the loss of many crew members' lives. The inquiry resulted in the lieutenant of the watch being dismissed from the service due to negligence.

Between 1839 and 1841 England found itself embroiled in a war between Egypt and the Ottoman Empire. Britain took the side of the Turks, helping to force Egyptian troops to withdraw from what is now Lebanon but which at the time of the conflict formed the coastal region of Syria. Following the resolution of the crisis *Castor* spent time in the Far East, then in 1845 became involved in quelling a Māori uprising in New Zealand. In the ensuing military action, an attack on the Māori stronghold at Ruapekapeka, a number of British sailors lost their lives.

At 2 a.m. on 26 February 1852 a few miles out of Cape Town, disaster struck HMS *Birkenhead*, an iron-hulled paddle-wheeler transporting soldiers, some accompanied by their families, to Algoa Bay. She hit an unmarked submerged rock which tore a massive hole in her bow. On the order to reverse away from the rock she suffered further damage, and enough of her watertight compartments were breached to result in her going down very quickly.

The way in which the soldiers on board gallantly stood aside as the women and children were put into the lifeboats came to be known as the Birkenhead Drill. But problems with those lifeboats resulted in the death toll coming to nearly 500 souls, most of them soldiers of the Queen's Royal Regiment and the 74th Regiment of Foot. *Castor* was one of the ships despatched to rescue survivors. Today a lighthouse stands near the scene of the tragedy.

Castor later became a training ship stationed at North Shields until, after 70 years' service in one form or another, she was sold for scrap.

HMS *Chanticleer*, 1808–1871, was built on the Isle of Wight for survey work and fitted with 10 guns. Later she was transferred to coastguard patrols, with the number CGWV 5 instead of a name.

Joseph Henry Kay sailed in *Chanticleer* as a first-class volunteer aged just 13 when she left Spithead on 27 April 1827; 12 years later he joined *Terror* as one of her lieutenants and, as you will have read, was left in Hobart to run the observatory set up there. As a very young man he entered the Royal Navy and found himself on a voyage of discovery that would potentially take him round the world. His father, an eminent architect, had seen to it that his son had had a comprehensive education. This stood him in good stead because during the voyage he kept a very comprehensive diary which many years later was published by the Hakluyt Society, edited by Ann Savours and Anita McConnell.

Chanticleer's early life saw her in action just after she was commissioned. Operating in the North Sea, she intercepted several armed Danish ships and put boarding parties aboard to bring them back to Britain as prizes. On one occasion she found herself outnumbered and had to beat a hasty retreat, but she survived the wars against France and was then laid up at Sheerness.

There had been several naval expeditions carrying out scientific work; two of the disciplines that had stimulated most interest were magnetism and the precise shape of the Earth. The Royal Society was actively trying to mount yet another expedition; as most of the data to hand had come from the northern hemisphere its members felt that research needed to be carried out in the southern.

The Royal Navy was drawn into the discussion primarily to provide a suitable ship and crew. Its attention was drawn to *Chanticleer* lying redundant at Sheerness, and soon she was being converted to accommodate the expedition members. This required the removal of her gunnery, creating space in the holds for the equipment and building in laboratories for the scientific staff. These would be civilians – quite unusual for a Royal Navy vessel, as the surgeons and other officers would normally have been the men conducting the scientific research. *Chanticleer's* captain, Commander Henry Foster, had been appointed because he had gained a reputation second to none regarding the work already carried out in the Arctic. He had sailed with Sir William Edward Parry aboard *Hecla* in 1824 and 1827. He had also been with *Griper* when she had explored around Greenland and Spitsbergen in 1823. On all these voyages he took part in the pendulum and magnetic experiments, and so was a natural choice to continue the process. Joseph Kay became involved in Foster's experiments, and his aptitude for them would eventually lead to him being sailing with Ross to Tasmania and the observatory in Hobart.

Chanticleer was away for the best part of three years, visiting the western and the eastern seaboards of the Atlantic; then she ventured as far south as the South Shetland Isles. Tragedy was to strike the expedition, however, when Foster fell out of a native canoe and was drowned. Her first lieutenant, Horatio Austin, brought her back to England, but *Chanticleer* was now deemed to be too badly worn for any further expeditions, and the cost to refit her too high. Her replacement was *Beagle*.

Chanticleer was confined to the role of a customs ship until 1871, when she was sold out of the service and broken up.

HMS *Cornwallis*, 1813–1957, was constructed of Indian teak in the dockyard at Bombay. She was a 74-gun third-rater with three decks: her main gun deck had 28 × 32 pounders, her upper gun deck 28 × 12 pounders, and on her quarterdeck and forecastle were a complement of 32-pounder carronades.

In 1836 her commission saw her sailing down the coast of the Iberian peninsula to the Tagus, where the Royal Navy had its floating headquarters. From here she took part in escorting a fleet of merchantmen across the Atlantic and then patrolling the Gulf of Mexico before returning to Britain in 1839. **Thomas Marshall** and **Edward Lancefield**, who had served on her during that time, were discharged in July, and enlisted on *Erebus* for the four years of Ross's expedition.

In the early 1840s *Cornwallis* was out in the Far East, getting involved in the wars with China. The Treaty of Nanking, marking the end of the Opium Wars, was signed aboard her.

Back in Britain she had a major refit, and a steam engine was fitted to her as part of the navy's continued experimentation with this form of propulsion. Paddle steamers had been in use for a number of years but with the successful design and trials of propellers it soon became clear that larger ships needed to be used as test beds. To accommodate the steam engine, her guns were reduced to 60. The costs soared to over £25,000.

Completed and trialled by 1855 she took part in the Crimean War under the command of the Duke of Wellington's nephew, George Wellesley. Her active years were numbered, and by 1865 she could be seen acting as a jetty at Sheerness. Converted to use as a base ship she lingered on, and could still be seen right up to 1957 at Sheerness. This was to be her final posting; after 144 years she was sent to the breakers. Her teak construction probably contributed to her longevity. Only *Victory* and *Trincomalee* have lasted longer.

HMS *Curaçao*, 1809–1849, was a fifth-rate vessel with 36 guns, built at Northam. In 1831 she was reduced to a 24-gun brig at Chatham.

Joseph Busbridge saw service on her between the time she was re-commissioned in 1831 to when he was discharged in July 1835. He went on to become the cook on *Terror*, but in February 1841 was reduced to able seaman. Interestingly, his captain's comment after the expedition paid off the crew was Very Good!

The 1831–1835 voyage was to take *Curaçao* all the way to the East Indies, where so many other Royal Navy ships were sent. Britain was actively employed in building up its commercial interests in that part of the world, and these had to be looked after. The East Indies and all across the seas surrounding that region were famous for the spice trade. Rubber was also starting to become a raw material for the new industrial age, and the Malay peninsula was a prime source of this commodity. Tea plantations were supplying the domestic market in Britain with this relatively new beverage, and of course India was the jewel in the crown of the British Empire; ships sent out to the Far East could call in at the Indian and Ceylonese ports for repairs and provisioning. The Dutch had for many years maintained an exclusive grip on the Spice Islands, but with the spread of British influence confrontation was never far away – as, too, was the ever-present threat from pirates.

On one of her subsequent passages *Curaçao* touched at the Pitcairn Islands, where her surgeon was able to dispense some much-needed relief to help combat a flu epidemic. Her picture appears on a stamp issued by the Solomon Islands in 1970 and the conclusion may be drawn be that she called there at some time and perhaps performed some kind of good deed as at Pitcairn.

Back at Chatham Dockyard in 1843 she was used in an experiment to trial a mast that had been manufactured in sections then glued and laminated. This was put to the ultimate test a year later when she was dismasted in a storm, and on her return to Chatham tests were carried out to determine why the mast had failed. Much to everybody's surprise it was found that the mast had sheared off not at the laminated join but elsewhere, and when the joint was inspected even men with wedges and sledgehammers found great difficulty in breaking it apart.

Her demise took place in 1849 when she was broken up.

HMS *Enterprise*, 1848–1903, when laid down was to have been a merchant ship, but was bought by the Admiralty while she was being built, to be used for exploration. Weight 470 tons.

Sir James Clark Ross captained her during the early searches for Franklin.

Dr John Robertson was her surgeon, also during the searches for Franklin. He had been surgeon on *Terror* from 1839 to 1843. **Thomas Abernethy** sailed with Ross and Robertson on *Enterprise*, and had been the gunner on *Erebus*.

Once the Admiralty took over the construction of *Enterprise* she was modified to withstand the ice of the Arctic regions and equipped to start the search for Franklin. Ross sailed her north in 1848 and spent the winter on the north-east part of North Somerset Island, together with her sister ship *Investigator* (more about her below). During the dark days of winter the search was continued across the land using man-hauled sledges. One of Ross's companions on these forays was a Lieutenant Francis Leopold McClintock, who about ten years later found the only written record ever recovered, just a few brief details about the lost explorers. But on this expedition no signs of the lost men were detected – or even, as Ross had hoped, any Inuit – so they had to wait for the ships to break out from Leopold Harbour, their winter refuge. Release finally came on 25 September – but that was far too late in the season to continue the search, and with some of the two crews showing signs of scurvy it was time to turn for home.

Between 1850 and 1854 *Enterprise* spent the best part of four years, including three winters, under the captaincy of Richard Collinson, patrolling the islands north of Canada, trying to find traces of the lost expedition. When Collinson sailed back to civilisation, however, he had very little to report. *Enterprise*'s intended consort for this voyage was once again *Investigator*, but in the first summer the two ships became separated and carried out their own searches; for more about *Investigator*, see below. *Enterprise* was sold out of the service in 1903 and had an ignominious end to her once illustrious life, as a coal hulk at Oban in western Scotland.

HMS *Excellent*, 1810–1859, started life as HMS *Boyne*, a second-rater with 98 guns, built in Portsmouth . In 1834, when she became a gunnery training ship, she was renamed *Excellent*.

Some of the men listed below spent time on *Excellent* before the Antarctic expedition, and others were transferred to her after it:

George Moubray, clerk in charge (purser) of *Terror*

Joseph Dayman, mate on *Erebus*.

Charles Gregory, an able seaman on *Terror*.

William Lewcock, an able seaman on *Terror*.

Thomas Marshall, captain of the foretop on *Erebus*.

Robert Devese, an able seaman on *Erebus*.

As *Boyne*, she took part in a number of conflicts against French men of war, one of which was portrayed by Vincent Courdouan; it shows *Boyne* and *Caledonia* pursuing the French *Romulus* in 1814, having fought a gun battle with her in which all three ships were badly damaged. *Romulus* managed to effect her escape by sailing close enough to the coast to prevent the two British ships from bracketing her.

As a gunnery training vessel *Excellent* was stationed at Portsmouth. The name *Excellent* had been given to an earlier vessel used for gunnery training, and when that *Excellent* was taken out of service in 1859 her name was transferred to the new ship. In the Royal Navy this name-transfer practice continued to the end of the 20th century.

HMS *Fairy*, 1826–1840, was a Cherokee class brig/sloop with 10 guns, built at Chatham. She was mainly used on coastal survey work, locating shifting sandbars and other hazards to shipping plying home waters.

Thomas Farr was a member of her crew during one of the surveys she carried out; he was discharged from her in June 1838. He joined *Terror* as an able seaman and when the expedition reached Hobart decided he had had enough and ran – but within a few days he surrendered himself and was taken back on. Later in the voyage he progressed to captain's coxswain, and towards the end of the expedition he became a captain of the foretop. His wages on this voyage were allotted to his mother, Sarah, and I am left wondering whether the thought of potentially leaving her destitute would have influenced his decision to return to the ship.

Early in the life of *Fairy* she was to be found in 1830 in the Caribbean taking part in some salvage work, and on the completion of this her crew could expect to be paid salvage money but this was more than likely to be before Farr sailed on her.

By 1840 *Fairy* was back in home waters, resuming her survey work. Towards the end of the year she departed from Harwich and expected to be at sea for no more than a couple of days. But on 12 December a short message was issued by the Admiralty.

> We are sorry to state that there is every reason to fear that the Fairy, surveying vessel, Captain Hewett, has been lost, with the whole of her officers and ship's company. It appears she left Harwich on the 15th ult., for the purpose of surveying some neighbouring sands, and must have encountered the late tremendous storm. It was ascertained before she left Harwich that she had no design whatever of proceeding above a few hours' sail, having only on board at the time two days provisions; but she has not been heard of.

A subscription was raised for the relief of dependents, and when it closed there was the sum of £2,262 to distribute. Her wreck was discovered 18 months later about 13 miles off Lowestoft after a fishing vessel brought up a spar identified as hers.

HMS *Favourite*, 1829–1905, was built in Plymouth and when she was launched had an armament of 18 guns. She served in several different capacities.

Samuel Coffin, discharged from *Favourite* in September 1841 at Bay of Islands in New Zealand, became an able seaman on *Erebus*. When Coffin joined *Erebus*, *Favourite* was already at the Bay of Islands as part of her commission that saw her depart from Plymouth in September 1837.

Prior to New Zealand she had visited Tonga to try and find a peaceable solution to a dispute between two rival factions on the islands: the inhabitants who had been Christianised and the remaining 'heathens'. When *Favourite* anchored in the bay feelings were running very high, and her commander, Croker, led a party of marines and crew ashore to put an end to the dispute. The record states that his tactics were, unfortunately, of the mailed-fist type, and as a result he and two of his men were killed; fifteen men were seriously wounded and six more received minor injuries. When the local Hampshire newspaper and other publications published their accounts of the conflict they all drew attention to the unnecessary waste of British lives in an event that could have been resolved by removing from Tonga the missionaries that appeared to have been at the root of the problem.

Favourite then sailed to New Zealand where Coffin left her, and her role now was to shuttle between Hobart and Sydney, collecting mail and stores for the colony in New Zealand.

After her return to England she was sent down the coast of Africa to join a squadron of Royal Naval ships based in Sierra Leone. Early in February 1849 she was part of a combined action to launch an attack by ships' boats on a fortified settlement where many slaves were being held prior to their despatch to the Americas. This action was carried out without the bloodshed that had accompanied the earlier episode; there were no casualties amongst the assailants and the mission, destroying the settlement, was adjudged a complete success.

Favourite's active life was to come to an ignominious end; by 1859 she was detailed to become a coal depot at Devonport docks. She lay there for 45 years and was sold for scrap in 1905.

HMS *Flamer*, 1804–1858, was an Archer class gunboat; she had been built by Joseph and Thomas Brindley at their yard on the Medway after the war with France had been resumed in 1803 on the breakdown of the Treaty of Amiens.

She weighed about 200 tons and was armed with 12 assorted guns. Her relatively shallow draught enabled her and her sister ships to operate near the coast and in estuaries where ships of the line would have grounded.

James Mobbs signed on to *Terror* as captain of the hold, but within a year found himself reduced to able seaman.

John Owens was given the job of sailmaker's mate, but like Mobbs soon found himself reduced to the ranks. Both men, discharged from *Flamer* in June 1839, remained with expedition until it returned to Woolwich in 1843.

Only one naval action seems to be recorded that *Flamer* took part in, and that was with three other Royal Naval vessels when in 1812 they were patrolling the Norwegian coast and engaged a similar number of Danish ships. The British disabled one of the Danes and captured two others, but lost them when they went aground on some sandbars.

HMS *Gorgon*, 1837–1864, was a paddle-wheeler with a wooden hull and an armament of six guns. Her steam engine was rated at 300 hp. She had been designed by Sir William Symonds, who had made a radical change to the way the engine was harnessed to the drive gear, making the engine much more efficient and reducing its weight by about 60 tons. His design meant that the crankshaft was now mounted above the steam cylinders to drive the paddle-wheels, which measured 27 feet in diameter.

While she was in commission she had several changes in her role as a naval vessel.

Joseph Dayman was the mate on *Erebus* and when he completed the expedition he received several promotions until in 1858 he was given command of *Gorgon*, when she became well known in naval circles due to her part in laying the first transatlantic cable. Not everything went smoothly, however; cable technology was still in its infancy, and the stresses that the cable were subjected to soon brought about its destruction. However, before the failure occurred it was possible for Queen Victoria to send a congratulatory message to US President James Buchanan. The messages, sent by Morse code, took many hours to pass from the sender to the recipient, and commercially it was a pending disaster but that is another story. Meanwhile, the crews of the ships involved had all received a medal struck to mark the occasion, and they were feted in New York as well.

Gorgon participated in the support given by Britain during Uruguay's civil war to gain independence from Brazil. Its independence had been declared in 1830 but both Argentina and Brazil still posed a threat to its borders, hence the Royal Navy's presence.

Gorgon also took part in the Crimean War, despatched to the Baltic. When peace descended again *Gorgon* and her crew were delegated to assist Sir Charles Thomas Newton at Halikarnassos in western Turkey, the location of the tomb of Mausolus,[36] one of the Seven Wonders of the Ancient World. Her remit was to transport many of the statues and other archaeological finds to Britain.

Gorgon's last trip was as a peacemaker to Madagascar in 1863 and when she returned home she was decommissioned but had one more duty to perform. HMS *Osborne* had returned to Greenhithe with some of her crew ill with smallpox. *Gorgon* acted as the isolation hospital ship until the medical authorities were satisfied the infection was under control. She was sold to a breaker's yard in October 1864.

HMS *Investigator*, 1848–1853, had the same start to her life as *Enterprise* in that she was bought by the Admiralty while she was under construction. She was built in Greenock, near Glasgow, and her initial weight was 420 tons, slightly smaller than *Enterprise*.

Lieutenant Edward Bird had been the first lieutenant on *Erebus* under Ross, and after his promotion to captain he took command of *Investigator* when she sailed north with *Enterprise* in 1848.

---

36 The origin of 'mausoleum'.

When *Investigator* returned home in 1849 with *Enterprise* she was readied again for Arctic service; this time, though, she was despatched to the Bering Sea to assist *Enterprise* by approaching from the Pacific end of the icefields. Her new captain, Robert McClure, promoted from lieutenant on *Enterprise*, rounded the Horn then entered the passage from the Pacific Ocean, and *Investigator* spent the second and third winters frozen in. McClure and his crew abandoned her in April 1853, rescued by Captain Kellett, who had fortuitously sailed into the passage from the Atlantic. McClure and his crew made their way by sledge to Kellett's ship and eventual safety.

Kellett's exit through Lancaster Sound back into the Atlantic meant that McClure and his crew had technically speaking passed from the Pacific to the Atlantic, so, despite the 1818 repeal of the Act of Parliament that had set up the original prize, they received the £10,000 reward for the first people to find a North-west Passage, the captain of course getting the lion's share, and his officers and men proportionate amounts of the remainder.

Investigator sank where the crew had left her. Although the Inuit helped themselves to abandoned stores, they never seem to have found her, and in 2010 she was discovered by a team from Parks Canada. Divers carried out an inspection, and it seems that due to the cold she is in a good state of preservation.

HMS *Melville*, 1817–1873, was in commission with the navy for over 50 years. She was built, with a complement of 74 guns, based on the design of a Danish ship, *Christian VII*, captured in 1807. Her construction was of Indian teak and she was built in Bombay by the East India Company.

Thomas Honey became the carpenter on *Terror* and later lost his life on the Franklin expedition.

Archibald McMurdo sailed in *Melville* as a midshipman, and went on to become a lieutenant when he joined *Terror*. In 1873 he retired as a rear admiral.

Like most of *Melville's* contemporaries in the navy, she sailed to a number of ports around the world; when McMurdo was aboard she was in the Mediterranean, calling at Gibraltar and Malta amongst other ports.

During her 1832 cruise to the Far East a crew member fell overboard, on 30 April 1835, and a rescue attempt was made with disastrous results. Amidst deteriorating weather a ship's boat was launched but it capsized, throwing its crew into the water; two officers and eight sailors died as well as the man who had fallen overboard in the first place.

Back home, *Melville* was fitted out as the flagship for the West Indies and American stations, and sailed to her new commission in 1836. Then after returning home she was despatched to Simon's Town in 1837, where Rear Admiral George Elliot took her as his flagship until 1841. Ross's expedition arrived at the cape on 17 March 1840 and before they set off a few weeks later they had recruited Honey. McMurdo was already on board, from the expedition's departure from England in 1839.

During the opium wars with China *Melville's* casualty list lengthened; she lost 16 of her crew and 4 marines as a result of an enemy engagement.

The navy were in need of a hospital ship based in Hong Kong and with hostilities at an end in that area she was commissioned in 1857 to undertake that role. The Admiralty then decided to sell her, and the sale raised enough money to build a land-based hospital in Hong Kong.

HMS *Ocean*, 1805–1875, was built at Woolwich. She was apparently a one-off, and even as she was being constructed she was extended and strengthened, to eventually carry 98 guns disposed over three decks. A full complement would see her carry nearly 750 men.

William Williamson served on *Erebus* as the caulker.

George Grant, a gunner of many years' experience, took on that position on *Erebus*.

John Bromley became the carpenter on *Terror*.

All three men had been discharged from *Ocean* in September 1939, so were recruited just before the expedition sailed.

Ocean's inaugural commission was as part of the force blockading the French fleet in Toulon and generally keeping the peace in the Mediterranean area.

Williamson, Grant and Bromley only seem to have been stationed on her because she was at the time being converted for use as a guard ship at Sheerness. Whilst still berthed at Sheerness she became a coal depot before being broken up in 1875.

HMS *Pelican*, 1812–1865, was a Cruizer class brig/sloop armed with 18 carronades, effective at close quarters. She was built at Topsham by a company called Robert Davy. She needed a complement of 120 men to fully crew her.

A total of ten men discharged from *Pelican* in 1839 took up positions aboard *Erebus*:

Edward Mann, purser's mate; **John Williams**, caulker; **James Rigden**, quartermaster; **James Lewis**, able seaman; **William Simmonds**, able seaman; **Jerimiah Quinn**, quartermaster; **Thomas Elwood**, able seaman; **Samuel Barber**, able seaman invalided at Simon's Town; **David Hennessey**, quartermaster, who requested a discharge at Hobart; and finally **John Newman**, who was discharged before even sailing.

Pelican was the last of the Cruizer class still in service when the decision was taken for her to be sold in 1865. She was tasked with escorting a convoy of merchant vessels sailing to Britain from the West Indies in 1812, and soon afterwards she was sent to patrol the Irish Sea on the lookout for the American raider *Argus*, which had been interfering with shipping in that area. Tracking down the raider *Pelican* intercepted her in the very act of seizing a merchantman and after a short engagement in which a number of men on both sides were killed including the commander of *Argus*, the Americans struck her colours and surrendered.

Some years later *Pelican* was policing the African coast looking out for slavers when the future members of *Erebus*'s crew were aboard. Her captain at this time was Brunswick Popham, and under his command a number of slavers were apprehended – with the notable exception of *Venus*. It was known she had on board about 1,100 slaves, and her escape drew forth a scathing letter to the Admiralty.

It was a common practice for many of these slave ships to fly the American flag as this would enable them to evade the patrol ships; the law of the high seas forbade them to stop and search any vessel under American colours. Captain Popham felt it incumbent upon himself to draw the Admiralty's attention to this loophole.

Coastguard duty would bring *Pelican*'s active naval service to a close. She was based at Shoreham in Sussex between 1850 and 1865, and now had to be called by her new name, CGWV 29. She escaped being broken up and was sold to a private buyer.

HMS *Poictiers*, 1809–1857, was a Vengeur class third-rater with an armament of 74 guns distributed over three main decks, plus the forecastle and poop deck.

Poictiers supplied 19 men in all to the expedition, mainly because she was being used as a holding ship at Woolwich with sailors awaiting new positions.

Of these, 13 went to *Erebus*: able seamen **John West**, **Robert Bates**, **Thomas Evans**, **George Harris**, **Joseph Smith** and **William Watson**; **Edward Bradley**, the captain of the hold who died at Hobart; **James Angeley**, who drowned near the Falklands; **William Waddup**, the captain of the foretop; **George Scott**, the captain's coxswain; **James Woodward**, the boatswain; and **John Kerr**, who was discharged at Woolwich.

On *Terror* the following signed on: **James Cleat**, the gunner who was invalided at Simon's Town; **William Tyler**, an able seaman invalided at Hobart; **William Smith**, the boatswain's mate; **John Wilkinson**, the purser's steward; **Robert Beeman**, the boatswain; and **William Rich** the carpenter, who was invalided at Hobart.

The disparity in number between the 13 men who signed on for *Erebus* and the 6 who sailed with *Terror* seems rather strange, especially when the muster rolls for both ships reveal that *Terror* received far more first entrants.

Poictier's most active period was during the years of the hostilities between America and Great Britain in 1810 and 1813. The engagement with USS *Wasp* was her greatest success, due to the fact that she rescued another British ship in the same conflict. She went on to help secure a number of foreign vessels, usually in conjunction with other Royal Naval ships. By the end of 1813 the war with America had to all intents and purposes ceased, and *Poictiers* returned to a mundane life, patrolling the naval stations in and around the Atlantic Ocean.

After she was broken up in 1857 her figurehead was salvaged and sent to a small museum in Chatham docks. It eventually fell into disrepair but a commission was given to have the remains copied, and today it can be seen at the Blue Town Heritage Centre at Sheerness in Kent.

HMS *President*, 1829–1903, was designed and built as a 60-gun fourth-rate ship of the line. She was launched in 1829 but not commissioned until 1832.

John Duffield was the sailmaker on *Erebus* until 1840, when he was hospitalised at Hobart. He had been discharged from *President* in June 1834.

President had an interesting lineage. In 1815 the Royal Navy had captured an American man-of-war of the same name, which was used by the navy for a couple of years then dismantled in 1818. The Admiralty decided that the American ship's design was worth copying and in 1824 the keel was laid down for the British version. But her construction was delayed, and even after her launch in 1829 it would take a further three years before she received her first commission. Her armaments were reduced to 52 guns: 30×24-pounders on the upper deck and 16×24-pounder carronades on the quarter deck, plus 6×24-pounders.

Duffield took part in *President*'s first overseas trip, to Halifax in Nova Scotia between 1832 and 1834. On her return she went into dock for the usual refit after time away from home, then she was despatched to Cape Town to become the flagship there, relieved by *Melville* in 1837.

President spent several months visiting China and Japan, both just opening up their markets to foreign traders. The outbreak of the Crimean War brought her back to the war zone in the Black Sea and here she was engaged in a gunnery battle with a Russian shore battery. A tragic incident occurred aboard her after the joint force of British and French ships withdrew. Her commander, Rear Admiral David Price, went to his cabin and committed suicide due to his guilt over the large number of casualties the fleet had suffered when it had failed in a land offensive.

In 1860 *President*'s role was reduced to reserve at the docks in London. She continued to fulfil this position throughout the next 40-odd years when she was dubbed *Old President*. She was broken up several months later, but her figurehead was, like that of *Poictiers*, renovated in 2015. The cost was borne by the Worshipful Company of Fishmongers, and today it can be seen adorning the present RNR ship HMS *President*, to commemorate the bicentennial anniversary of the capture of the original American ship in 1815.

HMS *Racer*, 1833–1852, was only about 110 feet long and weighed in at 430 tons. She carried 2 × 9-pounder guns and 14 × 32-pounder carronades. Her relatively shallow displacement allowed her to operate up estuaries and in shallower coastal waters. She would have required about 110 men to operate her in war at sea. Racer was also the class name for the nine ships built to the same lines.

Thomas Jopson, discharged from *Racer* in August 1838, took the position of captain's steward on *Terror*. His disposition towards Captain Crozier was such that when Crozier was asked to be second in command of the Franklin expedition Jopson applied for and got the same post on *Terror*, neither man, of course, dreaming that this would be their final voyage.

Racer was operating from the West Indies station when Jopson was on her between 1836 and 1838, and an extract from *Racer*'s log dated 28 September 1837 for three days gives a very matter-of-fact résumé of what transpired in a tempestuous period when the survival of the ship and her company hung in the balance.

The incident took place while *Racer* was near the Cuban coast, about a mile from Cape Antonio. The wind was steadily building up to gale force, and worse was to follow. By midday on the 29th the sea had risen to the point where hatches were battened down, sails were reefed and the helmsman could no longer keep her head into the wind without help. The waves crashed over the ship's sides, driven by what was now a Force 12 hurricane whipping the surface of the sea into a state where the water in the air obliterated all signs of the land they were afraid of being driven onto. Spars and rigging were strewn across the decks. At 7 p.m., as it was just getting dark, a powerful gust took hold of the ship and the next moment she was on her beam ends with her topsails in the water. Seawater flooded into the hull, but she wallowed and gradually righted herself. Her foremast was broken and the topmast had lost a complete section. Rigging was lying across the decks, making it very difficult for the crew to clear the debris. When the hatches had burst open she had taken on about 5 feet of water in the holds, which had to be immediately pumped out by the exhausted sailors. A young lad was injured so severely that he died soon afterwards. The hurricane reached its peak at midnight, so there was to be no rest for the crew as they and the officers fought to regain control of the ship. By 7 a.m. on the 30th when the crew were mustered it was found that two men was missing; they must have been swept overboard during the night. As the wind dropped and the danger receded, a burial service was conducted for the young seaman, who went to his lasting rest.

After a refit, *Racer* was again active in the early 1840s, this time helping to deal with slavers. By 1852 her useful life seems to have come to an end and she was sold out of the navy.

HMS *Rattlesnake*, 1822–1860, was in a class of ships originally called frigates then reclassified as corvettes. In the 1820s, when *Rattlesnake* and others of her class were built, a number of design modifications to the hull were used to increase their speed. The number of boats was increased as well, when she was employed on survey work.

Martin Wills was discharged from her in October 1838 and became an able seaman on *Terror*. He failed to satisfy his superiors and was discharged at St Helena. When he joined *Rattlesnake* in 1834 she was headed for the Far East, and from there she was sent to Hobart. She took the same route that seven years later the expedition would follow: from Hobart to Sydney, then on to the Bay of Islands. Her mission in New Zealand was to help protect the settlers from an imminent attack by Māori, who were hoping to regain control of the tribal lands they felt had been unfairly taken from them. After the emergency had passed, she returned to Britain in 1838.

Joseph Dayman, the mate on *Erebus*, joined *Rattlesnake* in 1845, just after his promotion to lieutenant. She had been converted to a survey ship, so was equipped with the extra boats needed for men to map and chart new waters and coastal features that the parent ship could not get close enough to. The commission that Dayman was involved in took *Rattlesnake* back down the other side of the world; she would be employed in charting the coasts of New Guinea and the northern coast of Australia. In May 1850 her commander, Captain Owen Stanley, died, and she returned to Britain in October.

A completely new venture was given to her in 1855 when she was despatched to Arctic waters to help search for a missing whaler out of New Bedford, Mass, captained by Jason Seabury. No trace was discovered, but many years later her nameboard, *Monongahela*, was found on a remote beach in the Aleutian Islands. An interesting story is attached to this ship and her master concerning a sea monster he is reputed to have slain, but positive evidence of this has never been found and only a vague story brought back by another ship said to have been given a written statement by Seabury describing his kill has survived the passage of time. Who will ever know?

Rattlesnake was one of many Royal Navy ships of that name, and this one finished up dismantled at Chatham in 1860.

HMS *San Josef*, 1797–1849, originally *San José*, had been built in 1793 for the Spanish navy and had been captured at the Battle of Cape St Vincent in 1797. Nelson had ordered his ship, HMS *Captain*, to close with the Spanish *San Nicolas*, in order to board her. At the same time *Captain* was being fired on by *San José*. But the wind carried *San José* too close to her sister ship; their rigging, already damaged by broadsides, became entangled – and Nelson, seizing his opportunity, led his men across the decks of *San Nicholas* onto *San José*. With the Spanish admiral badly wounded, both ships, as well as two more Spanish vessels, surrendered to the British.

With her 114 guns of various sizes on four decks *San Josef* proved to be a valuable prize, and continued in the service of the Royal Navy for over 50 years. Her full complement of officers and crew would have been well over 800 men.

Thomas Abernethy served as the gunner on *Erebus* after his discharge from *San Josef* in May 1839. His time on *San Josef*, which by that time had become a gunnery training establishment, was taken up with carrying out a gunnery course, but whether as instructor or student is not known.

HMS *Spartiate*,[37] 1798–1857, was equipped with a wide variety of weapons, including 32-pounder and 18-pounder guns, 32-pounder carronades and other smaller weapons spread over three decks: 74 guns all told. Her manning level was 640.

She had been won from the French in 1798 at Aboukir Bay, better known as the Battle of the Nile, only a year or so after she had been completed. By this time Nelson was commander of the British fleet, and by defeating the French navy he cut off the supply of men and materials supporting the French forces in Egypt, part of Napoleon's strategy to deny Britain its sources of wealth from India.

Spartiate also took part in the Battle of Trafalgar, suffering extensive damage, but after a lengthy refit resumed her duties harassing French shipping in the Mediterranean and the French ports on the Channel coast.

William Brimson was listed with *Spartiate* as his last ship before the expedition; he had seen service on her in the Mediterranean from 1827 until his discharge from her in 1829. He might then have been employed as a merchant seaman; this would account for the decade-long gap in his Royal Naval record. He joined *Erebus* in 1839 as an able seaman, and was promoted to captain of the hold on the death of Edward Bradley. His listing in the *Erebus* muster roll at age 27 means that on joining *Spartiate* he had been only 15.

Spartiate's capture back in 1798 certainly proved a valuable one, because she continued to serve in the Royal Navy for well over 40 years before meeting the inevitable end of so many of Her Majesty's ships: she was broken up in 1857, having been out of service for about 12 years.

HMS *Winchester*, 1822–1861, had originally been designed to take 60 guns but as her construction took place so modifications were carried out and her final tally was 30 × 24-pounder guns, 16 × 42-pounder carronades and 6 × 24-pounder guns. Built of wood, she took some six years to complete at Woolwich.

Four expedition sailors with connections with *Winchester* are:

Thomas Boddington, the captain's steward on *Erebus*. He had left *Winchester* in April 1839.

---

37 A spartiate was a member of the ruling class in ancient Laconia.

Samuel Glover, who was discharged from *Winchester* in June 1839 and became an able seaman on *Erebus*, but ran when she docked at Hobart.

William Perry, who became a sailmaker's mate on *Erebus*, was discharged from the expedition due to ill health when they sailed into Port Louis in the Falklands.

William Lewcock, who joined *Terror* at Simon's Town in 1843 as acting gunner. He then completed the expedition. The man he replaced had attempted suicide, citing 'drink and the devil', but he made a full recovery and was returned to Britain.

When Lewcock had been discharged from *Winchester* she had been on her way to the East Indies, and she completed that tour of duty. She then became another of Her Majesty's ships to see action in the Baltic, as part of the campaign to resist Russian expansionism in the area. In 1861 she was deemed too old for further service and, renamed *Conway*, replacing another vessel of that name, was used as a training ship. Her life was prolonged even further when, with another change of name, to *Mount Edgcumbe*, she was moved to the Tamar in south Devon to become a training ship for homeless boys from Plymouth. Her end came in 1920 when this last assignment was terminated. Her connection with all things naval had lasted 98 years; not quite a record, but one her builders would have been proud of.

HMS *Wolf*, 1826–1879, a sloop, was the leader in her class. Her armament consisted of just 14 guns, reduced from 18. Even with this reduced arsenal she still required 125 men to man her fully.

John Diggle left *Wolf* for *Erebus* in March 1839, to become her quartermaster. He had been on *Wolf* since December 1834 and during his term aboard her had seen much of the Far East. When *Wolf* reached Simon's Town, what was then known as the Kaffir Wars were still being waged; these had been going on since 1780 between the Boers and the British, and with more and more British settlers the pressures on the Xhosa tribes people built up, so conflicts occurred more frequently. The navy had been ordered to move troops by sea to strategic points along the coast, saving the several weeks and casualties that would have resulted from land columns.

On leaving the Cape Colony *Wolf* proceeded to Madras, then to the Strait of Singapore to search out pirates. She spent two years there, achieving a high level of success in her mission. After nearly five years away from home she docked at Portsmouth in February 1839.

In 1847 *Wolf*, accompanied by HMS *Iris*, set off once more for the East Indies station. This venture was to help establish a trading colony on the island of Labuan, close to Brunei; the Sultan of Brunei had signed a treaty whereby the British would operate as traders from this island, and it would, furthermore, provide the navy with fresh produce. An earlier survey of the island had shown that the soil was very fertile and it should sustain the colonists while they settled into their new environment.

As is so often the case when abroad, people fall victim to strange diseases; Captain Gordon of *Wolf* was stricken by one that the naval surgeons were powerless to treat. He died on 6 January 1848. As his death took place so were the men of the Franklin expedition dying, thousands of miles away in the Arctic. Among them was John Diggle, who had spent many years on *Wolf* in the waters near Labuan. Now he was cook on *Terror*, using foods preserved by the relatively new process of tinning, and the traditional meats and vegetables preserved in brine; all of these lacked vitamin C. To our 21st-century eyes, this seems particularly ironic, in that one of the reasons for the new colony at Labuan was to help prevent scurvy striking Royal Naval crews.

Wolf, like many other ships of the line when they had served their time, was reduced to being a coal tender to supply navy's new steam-powered ships. She was berthed at Queenstown (now Cobh) until 1879, when she was broken up.

POSTSCRIPT

Parts Two and Three list just a few of the men and the ships under commission at the time of the Ross expedition. During the 19th century about 1,000 ships were built for the Royal Navy; they were crewed by men from all walks of life, who by and large dedicated their lives to serving their country and have received very little credit, or even mention, in the many books about the exploits carried out by those vessels.

So it is my hope that this book will help to put some of those previously anonymous sailors back where they belong, in the limelight.

ACKNOWLEDGEMENTS

Over the years it has taken to put this book together and see the finished article many, many people have assisted in its production by providing contributions, and others have done their best to advise or support me in so many ways. I have to declare with some regret that a few of their names have slipped from my memory, and I must express my very sincere apologies for any omissions.

I could put all the names down alphabetically, or give them priority by a measure of importance according to their contribution. Neither of these ideas would do their owners justice, however, and could possibly cause offence. Every person and organisation mentioned below has helped, and I would like to thank you all for the help and encouragement I have received.

The only exception I am going to make is to thank first and foremost my wife, Cas, for her tolerance and support in high and low moments from beginning to end and beyond.

The names of organisations and individuals appear below in random order. All of them helped in small and large ways, and my inclusion of their names in this acknowledgement is my way of thanking them publicly.

Captain Richard Campbell RN, for loaning me his lengthy appraisal of Sergeant William Cunningham's diary put together while he served on *Terror* under Commander Crozier.

Philippa Ross, for her kindness in writing the foreword.

Philip MacDougall, for allowing me to use some of his prints about the early days of Chatham Royal Dockyard.

Ria Olivier of the South African National Antarctic Programme, for the help extended to me with this and my earlier book, *The Crossing*.

Dr Sydney Cullis, for the use of his photo of the plaque listing the exploring expeditions that visited Cape Town in the early years of polar exploration.

Judith Upton, co-ordinator of the Cornwall OPC Wills project. Her input allowed me to source the gravestone giving details about Thomas Honey which revealed exactly where he came from and when he was born.

.Glen Dunn, who allowed me to use John Stevens' picture of HMS *Challenger*.

George Landow of the Victorian Web, who entrusted the pictures of Victorian naval uniforms to me.

Robert Stephenson, who organises Antarctic Circle, a website devoted to publications and information relating to Antarctic exploration. He kindly allowed me to use a picture of *Erebus* and *Terror* in Antarctica.

Ann Kristin Balto, the photo librarian of the Norwegian Polar Institute, for the use of the photo, taken in 1900, of the first hut built in Antarctica at Cape Adare.

Rowland Rhodes of the Rountree Tryon Collection, who allowed me to use one of Keith Shackleton's paintings to illustrate my book and feature on the cover.

Daniel Hodges, who went to a great deal of trouble to source the panoramic picture of Chatham Dockyard.

Teena Ormond, who sent me numerous emails from the Falkland Islands Museum relating to the research into a picture of a wild cattle hunt, from when the expedition stayed there for the winter of 1842.

Brian Cooper, who has a website devoted to his collection of old surveying instruments, and has supplied me with the selection of pictures representing the type of navigational instruments used during the expedition.

Ralph Chou and Randall Rosenfeld, who helped me secure the use of the picture of the Old Observatory in Toronto held in the archives of the Royal Astronomical Society of Canada.

Paul Ward, who organises the Cool Antarctica website; he gave me permission to use a picture of the McMurdo Sound bases as they are at present.

Laurence, secretary of the Swiss Polar Institute, who promptly dealt with my request to use a picture of the Balleny Islands that I found on its website.

Becky Leach, from the Antarctic travel specialist company Swoop Antarctica, who granted me the use of Loli Figueroa's magnificent sunset, illustrating what the explorers must have often experienced in the Ross Sea.

The staff at the Tasmanian Museum and Art Gallery – Jacqui Ward, Jane Stewart and Paul Armstrong – who helped me locate the picture of the Rossbank Observatory that Ross set up when he visited Hobart in 1839.

The late Dr Andrew Lyall, who enlarged on the information I gleaned from the Linnean Society's magazine. It related to an article he wrote for them about David Lyall, the assistant surgeon on *Terror*. He also sent me two photos, one of David Lyall himself and the other showing his gravestone, which I have used in Part Two.

The Linnean Society furnished me with an extract from one of their magazines which was about David Lyall, and for that I would like to thank Andrea Deneau, the society's digital assets manager.

Carina Hibbert, of the Department of Conservation in New Zealand, who very kindly explained that the map of the Auckland Islands was in the public domain and I was free to make use of it. I had come across it on a website organised by John Vallentine, who had used the map to navigate a voyage from Hobart to Macquarie Island aboard his yacht *Tainui* in 2005.

Jenni Christoffels of the Alexander Turnbull Library in New Zealand, who responded so helpfully to my enquiry about the use of a picture in its archives that features Port Ross in the Auckland Islands.

Boris Kasinov, who has generously permitted me to use one of his excellent photographs from the website earthsisland.org. It features Cape Horn and clearly illustrates why this notorious geographic feature is often referred to as the 'Crouching Lion'.

Geoff Parselle, who took the photo of HMS *Victory* in dry dock at Portsmouth. I found it by searching the Defence Imagery website via commons.wikimedia.org.

The Wikipedia/wikimedia/commons websites, which are a veritable fountain of information, so a big thank you to all the contributors, and may you continue in such a valuable vein.

Ancestry.com, the incomparable site for family history and so much more, which made it practicable for me to research the stories I have produced in Parts 2 and 3.

Paul Benyon, who has collected an amazing amount of information about naval affairs of the Victorian period; the website that features this mountain of facts has been invaluable in putting the finishing touches to so many of the profiles I have given in Part Two.

David Taylor, who helped me fill in details of a distant relative of his, William Riggs, the armourer aboard *Terror*. David, having researched his family tree, had put it up on Ancestry.com, where I came across the connection.

Clare Hunt at the National Maritime RN Museum in Hartlepool, who sent me loads of information about its prized exhibit, HMS *Trincomalee*. Built in 1805, she is the oldest warship still in existence. The information helped me enormously when writing this book.

Nicola Holmes, who has some splendid photos on display in the Pictorial Collection of Antarctica, New Zealand. I was happy to choose the one of Possession Island when I could not find any comparable artist's impression of it from the period when Ross visited it.

Tim Ridge, who came forward with a surprising amount of information relating to Lieutenant James Woods of *Erebus*, and helped me to understand how his life developed after the expedition.

Simon Taylor, my close friend and neighbour, who very kindly spent many hours reading through the manuscripts and providing me with a list of corrections and guidance to greatly improve the text.

ILLUSTRATION ACKNOWLEDGEMENTS

Chapter 1 The Beginning
Panorama of Chatham Docks 1782. Painting by Joseph Farington. 1747 – 1821. Original held in the Royal Maritime Museum.
Courtesy of https://commons.wikimedia.org.
Early prints of Chatham Docks. Courtesy of Philip MacDougall (author of Chatham Dockyard Old Pictures)
HMS Victory in Portsmouth docks. https://commons.wikimedia.org. Attributed to Geoff Parselle. HPPO.DLO.Mod
HMS Ocelot, Chatham no 3 dry dock. https://commons.wikimedia.org. Photograph courtesy Mark.murphy.jpeg
Modifications to expedition ships. Extract from Ross's A Voyage of Discovery and Research vol. 1 (author's collection)
Gun deck with crew members. Courtesy of George Landow, Editor in Chief Victorianweb.org
Sailors' uniforms of 1850. Courtesy of George Landow, Editor in Chief Victorianweb.org
Officers' uniforms of 1850. Courtesy of George Landow, Editor in Chief Victorianweb.org

Chapter 2 Targets and Instructions
John Ross rescued by Isabella 1833. Painted by Edward Frances Finden. Courtesy of https://commons.wikimedia.org In the public domain, original held by Royal Museum Greenwich.
Troughton and Simms sextant (author's collection)
Scientific instruments. Courtesy of Brian Cooper, www.oldsurveyinstruments.com
Lieutenant D'Urville's Astrolabe and Zélée in Antarctica. Painted by A Meyer in 1838. Original in State library of N S Wales, public domain

Chapter 3 James Clark Ross and Francis Crozier
HMS Fury and HMS Hecla painted by Arthur Parsey. Courtesy of https://commons.wikimedia.org In the public domain, original held at National Maritime Museum.
Captain James Clark Ross painted by John Wildman. Courtesy of https://commons.wikimedia.org In public domain, original held at National Maritime Museum.
Captain Francis Crozier statue. Courtesy of https://commons.wikimedia.org. Photograph by Gina64
Memorial in Bainbridge church. Courtesy of https://commons.wikimedia.org. Photograph by Gina64

Chapter 4 Setting Sail
Funchal harbour in 1860. Courtesy of www.madeira-web.com
'Lady of the Mountain' church in Funchal. Photo by Barry Canuth. https://commons.wikimedia.org.
Mount Pico Ruivo. Courtesy of www.ocean-retreat.com/landmarks/pico-ruivo/
Map of Madeira. (author's collection)
Porto Praya , St Helena about 1800 painted by William Alexander. https://commons.wikimedia.org.
Longwood House on St Helena. Courtesy of www.memolands.com/St.Helena

Chapter 5 Cape Town and Beyond
Cape Town Observatory. Courtesy of https://commons.wikimedia.org
Hotel Plaque. Photo by Dr Sydney Cullis. Courtesy of Antarctic Society of South Africa
Christmas Harbour, Kerguelen painted by Joseph Dayman of HMS Erebus. Courtesy of www.en.wikisource.org
HMS Challenger in Royal Sound, Kerguelen. Courtesy of Glen Dunn representing Steven Dews the artist
Toronto Observatory in 1852, painted by William Armstrong. Courtesy of Toronto Magnetic and Meteorological Observatory
Joseph Hooker painted by G Richmond 1855. Courtesy of https://commons.wikimedia.org.
Chart of 1839-1843 Ross Expedition. (author's collection)

Chapter 6 Next stop, Hobart Tasmania
Rossbank Observatory. B & W scanned copy of Original painting by Thomas Bock in 1840. Courtesy of https://commons.wikimedia.org
Map of Tasmania as published in 1837 by John Dower. Courtesy of upload.wikimedia.org/commons.wikipedia
Franklin's statue in Spilsby (author's collection)

Chapter 7 First Taste of the Ice
Auckland Islands map. Creative Commons CC By licence. Courtesy of New Zealand Department of Conservation
Port Ross in the Auckland islands painted by Charles Enderby. Courtesy Alexander Turnbull Library in N Z
Ice berg in the Polar Sea painted by Keith Shackleton. Courtesy of Rountree Tryon Collection
Cape Adare huts 1900 expedition. Courtesy of Norwegian Polar Institute.
Possession Island, photo by Nicola Holmes in 1993. Courtesy of Antarctica New Zealand Pictorial collection.

Chapter 8 Amazing Discoveries and Wonders to Behold
Ross Ice Shelf /HMS Erebus and Terror. Courtesy of www.antarctic-circle.org / Rob Stephenson
Conquest of South Magnetic Pole in 1909 on Shackleton Expedition.Courtesy of https://commons.wikimedia.org.
Scott Base in McMurdo Sound. Courtesy of Paul Ward from www.coolAntarctica.com/bases/mcmurdo
Mount Heschel and Admiralty Range. Courtesy of https://commons.wikimedia.org.

Chapter 9 Turning North
Photo of Balleny Islands. Courtesy of the Swiss Polar Institute (Copyright – Parafilms/EPFL)
Erebus and Terror in the Antarctic by John Wilson Carmichael. Courtesy of https://commons.wikimedia.org. Original in N M Museum

Chapter 10 Australia and New Zealand
Parramatta Monument in Sydney. From www.sydney-city.blogspot.com
Erebus and Terror visiting Bay of Islands in New Zealand, painted by John Wilson Carmichael. Courtesy of www.Wikiart.org/JWCarmichael.com

Chapter 11 South again to the Great Ice Barrier
RRS James Clark Ross in Antarctic waters. Accredited to British Antarctic Survey Image collection

Chapter 12 Impending Disaster
Erebus and Terror escaping from ice bergs. Painted by J E Davis. Courtesy of N M Museum.

Chapter 13 Wild Cattle Hunt and Third Winter Away
Wild cattle hunt in the Falklands painted by Richard Wilson in 1820. Courtesy of Family of late R A Hooker
Stranding of D'Urville's Astrolabe and Zelee. Courtesy of https://commons.wikimedia.org.
Cape Horn, the sleeping (as on the page) lion. Courtesy of photographer Boris Kasimov and www.earthsisland.org
Replica of Yahgan canoe. Courtesy of https://commons.wikimedia.org.
HMS Beagle in Galapagos Islands. Courtesy of https://creativecommons.org and Licence CC BY-NC-SA2.0

Chapter 14 Return to Antarctica
Expedition's Antarctic route in 1842 (author's collection)
Cockburn Island. Courtesy of https://commons.wikimedia.org.
Antarctic sunset, Photographer Loli Figueroa a nd www.swoop-antarctica.com (Swoop Adventure Holidays)

Part 2 – Sailors' Stories
James Clark Ross' 2 volumes about his expedition (author's collection)
Chatham Dockyard Gateway. Courtesy Creative.commons.org, photo by Clem Rutter
Admiral Sir William Parry. Courtesy https://commons.wikimedia.org.
Burial place of Admiral Edward Bird. St Martin's Church, Little Waltham in Essex. Courtesy of www. achurchnearyou.com
Mendicity headquarters in Red Lion Square, London. Information found in www.londontraveller.org
HMS Dreadnought being used as a hospital ship. Courtesy of https://commons.wikimedia.org.
Edward Mann's will. Purchased from Public Record Office, ref ADM 45/36/863
Robert McCormick and Joseph Hooker, Surgeon and Assistant Surgeon on HMS Erebus. Courtesy of https:// commons.wikimedia.org.
Illustrations drawn by Joseph Hooker from his collection of plants. Courtesy of https://commons.wikimedia.org.
John Henry Lefroy, founder of Royal Canadian Institute in Toronto. Courtesy of https://commons.wikimedia.org.
David Lyall, Assistant Surgeon on HMS Terror. Courtesy of www.antartcic.circle.com
David Lyall's grave in Cheltenham Cemetery. Courtesy of Linnean Society and the late Dr Andrew Lyall
Facsimile of Margaret Honey's gravestone in Stoke Damerel cemetery. (author's collection)
HMS Heron and HMS Plover in Kotzebue Sound in Alaska in 1858. Original painting held by the British Library.Courtesy of www.commons.wikimedia.org/wiki/Files:Chimmo(1860)
Robert Chilcott's Mates certificate. (author's collection)
Map of King William Island where Franklin's 2 ships, HMS Erebus and HMS Terror, have been located. Courtesy of https://arcticnorthwestpassage.blogspot.com

MUSTER LIST FOR HMS *EREBUS*

Muster	Name	Age	Birth place	Rank	Joined	Left Expedition	Promotion and notes
1/1	James Clark Ross	39	London	Captain	April 1839	September 1843	Knighted
1/2	James F L Wood			Lieutenant	April 1839	September 1843	Completed journey
1/3	Edward J Bird	40		Lieutenant	April 1839	April 1842 Falklands	Invalided home
1/4	John Sibbald			Lieutenant	August 1839	September 1843	Trans to Terror in Falklands Aug 1842
2/1	George Grant			Gunner	April 1839	April 1839	Trans to HMS Poictiers
2/2	Thomas R Hallett			Purser	April 1839	September 1843	Completed journey
2/3	Robert McCormick	39	Gt Yarmouth	Surgeon	April 1839	September 1843	Completed journey
2/4	Alexander J Smith			First mate	April 1939	September 1843	Lieutenant
2/5	John Bromley			Carpenter	April 1839	September 1843	Completed journey
2/6	Henry Bradick Yule	28		2nd Master	April 1839	September 1843	Completed journey
2/7	John Roberts			Boatswain	May 1839	August 1840	Drowned near Kerguelen Island
2/8	Thomas Abernethy			Gunner	May 1839	September 1843	Completed journey
2/9	Joseph Dayman			Mate	May 1839	August 1840	Observatory in Hobart
2/10	Joseph D Hooker		Halesworth	Ass Surgeon	May 1839	September 1843	Completed journey
2/11	Henry Oakley	22		Mate	Sept 1839	September 1843	Trans to Terror in Falklands Aug 1842
2/12	Charles Tucker			Master & Pilot	Sept 1939	September 1843	Completed journey
2/13	Robert Beeman			Act Boatswain	August 1840	September 1843	Completed journey
3/1	Richard W Stebbing	33	Portsmouth	Armourer	April 1839	October 1840	Deserted in Hobart
3/2	William McDougal	26	Dundee	Able seaman	March 1839	September 1843	May/39 Caulker's mate. Dec1840 Caulker
3/3	John Steven	33	Isle of Stroma	Able seaman	March 1839	August 1839	Deserted in Chatham
3/4	Thomas Boddington	32	Whitchurch/Bucks	Capt's steward	April 1839	September 1843	Completed journey
3/5	John Watson	26	York	Purser's stewd	April 1839	April 1840	Deserted in Hobart
3/6	Edward Mann	29	Rochester	Bosun's mate	May 1839	September 1843	Trans to Terror Aug 1840
3/7	John Williams	26	London	Capt of F/top	May 1839	June 1839	Deserted in Chatham
3/8	James Rigden	28	Deal /Kent	Able seaman	May 1839	September 1843	May/39 Cap's cox--Sep/41 Cap M/ top--May/43 Q/Master
3/9	James Lewis	33	Jersey	Able seaman	May 1839	September 1843	Completed journey
3/10	William Simmonds	23	Canterbury	Able seaman	May 1839	September 1843	Completed journey
3/11	Jerimiah Quin	31	London	Gunner's mate	May 1839	September 1843	May/39 Q/Master
3/12	Robert Devese	25	Portsmouth	Able seaman	May 1839	September 1843	Completed journey
3/13	John Diggle	30	Westminster	Able seaman	May 1839	September 1843	July/39 Q/Master

	Rank	Name	Age	Place	Joined	Left	Notes
3/14	Able seaman	Henry Paradise	27	Chatham	May 1839	October 1840	Run in Hobart
3/15	Able seaman	John West	25	Dover	May 1839	September 1843	Completed journey
3/16	Able seaman	Edward Welch	36	Cork/Ireland	May 1839	September 1843	Completed journey
3/17	Able seaman	Edward Bradley	44	Stoke/Kent May 1839	October 1840	June/39 C of Hold.	Died in Hobart/ suffocated
3/18	Able seaman	William Watson	22	Sunderland	May 1839	September 1841	Unfit and left at own request
3/19	Able seaman	James Angeley	40	Alloway/Ayrshire	May 1839	April 1842	Oct/40 Q/Master. Drowned nr Falklands
3/20	Able seaman	Thomas Evans	36	Pembrokeshire	May 1839	September 1843	Completed journey
3/21	Able seaman	George Harris	40	Fishguard	May 1839	September 1843	Completed journey
3/22	Able seaman	George Scott	23	Hull	May 1839	September 1843	April/40 C M/top. Aug/41 Cap's cox
3/23	Able seaman	John Kerr	31	Dundee	May 1839	July 1839	Discharged
3/24	Able seaman	John Newman	31	Ireland	May 1839	September 1843	Completed journey
3/25	Able seaman	Thomas Elwood	34	Yorkshire	May 1839	September 1843	Completed journey
3/26	Able seaman	Samuel Glover	36	Malton	May 1839	October1840	Deserted in Hobart
3/27	Capt of F/top	James Woodward	39	Dartford	June 1839	September 1843	Aug/ 40 Boatswain
3/28	G/room stewd	John Lewis	22	London	June 1839	March 1840	Deserted in Hobart
3/29	Able seaman	Samuel Barber	29	Stoke/ Kent	June 1839	April 1840	Invalided in Simon's Town
3/30	Able seaman	Edward Fawcett	31	Stroud/Kent	June 1839	September 1843	Oct/40 C of F/castle
3/31	Able seaman	James Rogers	37	Boston	July 1839	September 1843	Sep/39 Q/ Master. Oct/41 AB
3/32	Cook	Richard Wall	40	Newcastle u Lyne	July 1839	September 1843	Completed journey
3/33	S/maker's mate	James Duffield	27	Gt Yarmouth	July 1839	October 1840	Hospital in Hobart
3/34	Able seaman	Alec Gunn	27	Portsmouth	July 1839	August 1939	Deserted in Chatham
3/35	Able seaman	Thomas Marshall	24	Shoreham/Sussex	July 1839	September 1843	June/39 C F/top. Apr/42 2nd Master. Jul/43 AB
3/36	Y/gents stewd	Edward Smith	21	Chatham	July 1839	November 1840	Hospital in Hobart
3/37	Able seaman	William Brimson	27	Gascombe/ I of W	July 1839	September 1843	Oct/40 Cap of hold
3/38	Blacksmith	Corneleis Sullivan	31	Killarny/Ireland	July 1839	September 1843	May/42 Ill. Oct/42 Armourer
3/39	Carp's mate	Joseph Barclay	36	Manchester	July 1839	October 1840	Deserted in Hobart
3/40	Quarter master	David Hennessey	48	Cork/Ireland	July 1839	September 1840	Discharged own request
3/41	Able seaman	William Waddup	26	Chatham	July 1839	September 1843	May/42 S/maker's mate. Jul/43 C F/top
3/42	Able seaman	Robert Bates	27	Chatham	July 1839	September 1843	Completed journey
3/43	Able seaman	Edward Lancefield	22	Chatham	Aug 1839	September 1843	Completed journey
3/44	Sail maker	William Turner	29	North Shields	Aug 1839	September 1839	Discharged at own request
3/45	Caulker's mate	Thomas Fant	22	Hull	Sept 1839	September 1839	Discharged to HMS Poictiers
3/46	Able seaman	John Collier	24	Dublin/Ireland	August 1839	September 1839	Discharged to HMS Poictiers
3/47	Able seaman	Joseph Smith	24	Portsmouth	Sept 1839	September 1843	Completed journey
3/48	Able seaman	James Wilson	34	Ayr/Scotland	Sept 1839	September 1843	Dec/40 Caulker's mate

Muster	Rank	Name	Age	Birth place	Joined	Left Expedition	Promotion and notes
3/49	Sailmaker	William E Greenstead	46	Brompton /Kent	Sept 1839	September 1843	Completed journey
3/50	Caulker	William Williamson	23	Hull	Sept 1839	September 1843	Oct/40 AB. Oct/41 Purser's steward
3/51	Purser's stewd	William Plunket	25	Houndsditch	April 1840 (S Town)	November 1840	Discharged at own request
3/52	G/room stewd	Henry Martin	41	Bath/Somerset	Aug 1840 (Hobart)	September 1843	Completed journey
3/53	Able seaman	Hugh Hughes	22	Caenarfon/Wales	Oct 1840 (Hobart)	September 1843	Completed journey
3/54	Carpent's mate	John Bennett	25	Dartmouth	Oct 1840 (Hobart)	September 1843	Completed journey
3/55	S/maker's mate	William Perry	31	Holyhead/Wales	Oct 1840 (Hobart)	March 1842	Discharged in Falklands. Unfit
3/56	Able seaman	Henry Sansom	28	Portsea	Oct 1840 (Hobart)	July 1841	Deserted in Hobart
3/57	Able seaman	Edward Baxter	29	Scarborough	Oct 1840 (Hobart)	November 1842	Q/Master Invalided in Falklands
3/58	Able seaman	Hugh McIntyre	23	Campbelltown	Oct 1840 (Hobart0	September 1843	Completed journey
3/59	Able seaman	Benjamin Golightly	27	South Shields	Oct 1839 (Hobart)	September 1843	Completed journey
3/60	Purser's stewd	Charles Patterson	20	Marylebone	Nov 1840 (Hobart)	March 1841	Discharged as unfit for service
3/61	Y/Gents stewd	George Pine	30	Tiverton	Apr 1841 (Hobart)	September 1843	Completed journey
3/62	Able seaman	James Savage	22	Brighton	June 1841 (Hobart)	September 1843	July/43 Cap M/top
3/63	Armourer	Joseph Fitton	29	Middleton/ Lancs	June 1841 (Hobart)	September 1843	May/42 Blacksmith
3/64	Able seaman	John Stewart	20	Dunfermline	July 1841 (Hobart)	September 1843	Nov/42 Q/ Master
3/65	Able seaman	Samuel Coffin	20	Aylsham/Hants	Sep 1841 (Bay of Is)	September 1843	Completed journey
3/66	Able seaman	John Hardy	28	Edinburgh	Oct 1841 (Bay of Is)	September 1843	Completed journey
3/67	Able seaman	William Hardy	24	Hull	Apr 1842 (Falklands)	September 1843	Completed journey
3/68	Capt F/Top	James Giles	41	Sheerness/Kent	May 1842 (Falklands)	September 1843	July/43 AB
3/69	Able seaman	William Holmes	23	Greenwich/Kent	Dec 1842 (Falklands)	September 1843	Completed journey
3/70	Able seaman	William Unwin	27	Hornden/Essex	Dec 1842 (Falklands)	September 1843	Completed journey

Marines

1	Sergeant	Samuel Baker	37	Waddington	Apr/39 Chatham	Sept/43 Woolwich	Completed journey
2	Private 1st	David Stratton	34	Dunbar	May/39 Chatham	Sept/43 Woolwich	Completed journey
3	Corporal	Robert Cuthbertson	28	Fenwick	Apr/39 Chatham	Sept/43 Woolwich	Completed journey
4	Private 3rd	William Pearsall	26	Oldburgh	Apr/39 Chatham	Sept/43 Woolwich	Completed journey
5	Private 3rd	Robert Eden	27	Thirkleby	Apr/39 Chatham	Sept/43 Woolwich	Completed journey
6	Private 3rd	George Parr	23	Hunston	Apr/39 Chatham	Sept/43 Woolwich	Completed journey
7	Private 3rd	George Baker	24	Coventry	Apr/39 Chatham	Sept/41 Bay of Islands	Drowned

MUSTER LIST FOR HMS *TERROR*

Muster	Rank	Name	Age	Birth place	Joined	Left Expedition	Promotion and notes
1/1	Commander	Francis Crozier			May/39 Chatham	Sept/43 Woolwich	Captain, Falklands 1842
1/2	Lieutenant	Joseph Kay			July/39 Chatham	August/40 Hobart	Command of Observatory
1/3	Lieutenant	Archibald McMurdo			Sept/39 Chatham	August/42 Falklands	Invalided to UK
1/4	Lieutenant	Charles G Philips			Sept/39 Chatham	Sept/43 Woolwich	Completed journey
1/5	Lieutenant	John Sibbald			Sept/39 Chatham	Sept/43 Woolwich	Erebus to Terror August/42 Falklands
2/1	Boatswain	Robert Beeman			May/39 Chatham	Sept/43 Woolwich	Terror to Erebus August/40 Hobart 1st
2/2	Carpenter	William Rich			May/39 Chatham	March/40 Woolwich	Invalided at Hobart 1st
2/3	Clerk in Charge	George H Moubray			May/39 Chatham	Sept/43 Woolwich	Completed journey
2/4	1st Mate	Peter Scott			May/39 Chatham	August/40 Woolwich	Hobart Observatory
2/5	Master	Pownall Powell Cotter			May/39 Chatham	Sept/43 Woolwich	Completed journey
2/6	Ass Surgeon	David Lyall			June/39 Chatham	Sept/43 Woolwich	Completed journey
2/7	Surgeon	John Robertson			June/39 Chatham	Sept/43 Woolwich	Completed journey
2/8	Acting Gunner	John Lumsden			July/39 Chatham	Aug/41 Hobart	Invalided Hobart 2nd
2/9	Mate	Thomas E L Moore			Aug/39 Chatham	Sept/43 Woolwich	Completed journey
2/10	2nd Master	John E Davis			Aug/39 Chatham	Sept/43 Woolwich	Completed journey
2/11	Mate	Charles E Molloy			Sept/39 Chatham	Oct/40 Hobart	Invalided Hobart 1st
2/12	Carpenter	Thomas Honey			March/40 Smn. Town	Sept/43 Woolwich	Completed journey
2/13	Act Boatswain	Edward Mann			Sept/39 Chatham	Sept/43 Woolwich	Erebus to Terror Aug/40 Hobart 1st
2/14	Act Gunner	James Cleat			Sept/39 Chatham	May/43 Simon's Town	Invalided at Simon's Town 2nd
2/16	Act Gunner	William Lewcock			April/43 Smn. Town	Sept/43 Woolwich	Completed journey
3/1	Armourer	William Riggs	34	Plymouth	May/39 Chatham	Sept/43 Woolwich	Completed journey
3/2	Capt's steward	John Bodman	42	Portsmouth	June/39 Chatham	Sept/39 Chatham	Discharged at Chatham
3/3	Capt of F/castle	Archibald Stewart	29	Cambletown	June/39 Chatham	Sept/43 Woolwich	Completed journey
3/4	Able seaman	Charles Levett		Plymouth			Deserted at Chatham
3/5	Able seaman	William Jerry	23	St Davids	June/39 Chatham	Sept/43 Woolwich	Completed journey
3/6	Able seaman	Henry Barnes	22	Stonehouse	June/39 Chatham	Oct/40 Hobart	Deserted at Hobart 1st
3/7	Able seaman	Thomas Farr	28	Milford	June/39 Chatham	Sept/40 Hobart	Rejoined as no 56 & 66
3/8	Able seaman	Theodore Bristow	25	Walmer Kent	June/39 Chatham	Sept/43 Woolwich	Capt's Cox then back to AB
3/9	Able seaman	Samuel Aldridge	26	Woodbridge	June/39 Chatham	Sept/39 Chatham	Dismissed at Chatham
3/10	Able seaman	Charles Gulliver	26	Norway	June/39 Chatham	Feb/40 St Helena	Dismissed at St Helena
3/11	Able seaman	Martin Wills	40	John's Town IRE	June/39 Chatham	Feb/40 St Helena	Dismissed at St Helena
3/12	Able seaman	Andrew Johnson	28	Guernsey	June/39 Chatham	Sept/43 Woolwich	Capt of F/top & Capt of Hold
3/13	Capt of Hold	James Mobbs	23	Guernsey	July/39 Chatham	Sept/43 Woolwich	Reduced to AB May/40
3/14	S/maker's mate	John Owens	30	Beaumaris	July/39 Chatham	Sept/43 Woolwich	Reduced to AB Jan/40

Muster	Name	Rank	Age	Birth place	Joined	Left Expedition	Promotion and notes
3/15	William Pennant	Able seaman	25	Unst Shetlands	July/39 Chatham	Sept/43 Woolwich	Drowned at Woolwich
3/16	William Briggs	Gunroom stewd	32	Orset Essex	July/39 Chatham	July/39 Woolwich	Dismissed
3/17	John Cummings	Able seaman	26	Arbroath	July/39 Chatham	Sept/43 Woolwich	Completed journey
3/18	Thomas Johnson	Capt m/top	22	Wisbeach	July/39 Chatham	Sept/43 Woolwich	Quartermaster 1840
3/19	Richard Parry	Able seaman	30	Liverpool	July/39 Chatham	Sept/43 Woolwich	Completed journey
3/20	William Evans	Able seaman	20	Holyhead	July/39 Chatham	Sept/40 Hobart	Deserted at Hobart 1st
3/21	Richard Evans	Able seaman	27	Quebec	July/39 Chatham	Sept/39 Woolwich	Dismissed Woolwich
3/22	Peter Wallace	Able Seaman	24	Quebec	July/39 Chatham	Oct/40 Hobart	Deserted Hobart 1st
3/23	James Harris	S/maker's mate	29	Milford	July/39 Chatham	Sept/43 Woolwich	Completed journey
3/24	William Beautyman	Capt f/top	26	N Shields	July/39 Chatham	Oct/40 Hobart	Deserted at Hobart 1st
3/25	Samuel Johns	Able seaman	25	Milford	July/39 Chatham	Sept/40 Hobart	Hospital Hobart 1st
3/26	Thomas Lee	Quartermaster	22	Camberwell	July/39 Chatham	Sept/43 Woolwich	Cook Feb/41
3/27	Thomas Chatworthy	Purser's stewd	31	Devonport	July/39 Chatham	July/39 Chatham	Dismissed Woolwich
3/28	Frederick Collins	Able Seaman	35	London	July/39 Chatham	Nov/40 Hobart	Deserted Hobart 1st
3/29	James Grimes	Quartermaster	23	Radcliffe	July/39 Chatham	Sept/43 Woolwich	Capt's Coxswain
3/30	James Wailing	Capt Main top	23	Radcliffe	July/39 Chatham	Sept/43 Woolwich	Completed journey
3/31	George Knight	Blacksmith	25	Braken Ash Norfolk	July/39 Chatham	Sept/43 Woolwich	Completed journey
3/32	Isaac D Munday	Gunroom stewd	21	Gosport	July/39 Chatham	Sept/43 Woolwich	Completed journey
3/33	Tilden Taylor	Y/ gents stewd	25	Milton Kent	July/39 Chatham	Feb/40 St Helena	Deserted St Helena
3/34	Alec Craig	Capt Foretop	22	Peterhead	July/39 Chatham	Sept/43 Woolwich	Quarter master Feb/41
3/35	William Abernethy	Able seaman	23	Peterhead	July/39 Chatham	Sept/43 Woolwich	Completed journey
3/36	Joseph Busbridge	Cook	40	Maidstone	July/39 Chatham	Sept/43 Woolwich	Demoted to AB Feb/41
3/37	Charles Gregory	Able seaman	32	Rochester	Aug/39 Chatham	March/40 Simon's Town	Transferred to HMS Melville
3/38	Edward Mitchell	Able seaman	26	London	Aug/39 Chatham	Sept/43 Woolwich	Completed journey
3/39	James Cleat	Quartermaster	32	Kirkwall Orkney	Aug/39 Chatham	April 43 Simon's Town	Promoted Act Gunner See record 2/14 above
3/40	William Tyler	Able seaman	21	Brentwood	Aug/39 Chatham	Oct/40 Hobart	Hospital at Hobart 1st
3/41	John Godfrey	Able seaman	32	Portsmouth	Aug/39 Chatham	Sept/43 Woolwich	Quartermaster July/41
3/42	William Smith	B/swain's mate	24	Portsmouth	Aug/39 Chatham	Sept/43 Woolwich	Completed journey
3/43	Robert Juck/Jack	Sail maker	22	Peterhead	Aug/39 Chatham	Sept/43 Woolwich	Completed journey
3/44	John Lane	Caulker's mate	28	Maidstone	Sept/39 Chatham	Sept/43 Woolwich	Carpenters Mate Oct/40
3/45	Alec Turriff	Carpenter mate	24	Aberdeen	Sept/39 Chatham	Oct/40 Hobart	Deserted Hobart 1st
3/46	Thomas Jopson	Captain's stewd	22	Middlesex	Sept/39 Chatham	Sept/43 Woolwich	Completed journey
3/47	John Wilkinson	Purser's stewd	28	Greenwich	Sept/39 Chatham	Sept/43 Woolwich	Completed journey
3/48	Samuel Johns	Able seaman	25	Milford	see record 25 above	Sept/43 Woolwich	C/f/top. C/f/castle. Q/master Feb/43
3/49	Alec Colston	Able seaman	34	Maidstone	Feb/40 St Helena	Sept/40 Hobart	Deserted Hobart 1st
3/50	James Hands	Able seaman	33	S Shields	Feb/40 St Helena	Oct/40 Hobart	Hospital Hobart 1st

No.	Name	Rating	Age	Birthplace	Joined	Left	Notes
3/51	Richard Roberts	Y/ Gents stewd	22	Biggleswade	Apr/40 Simon's Town	Sept/40 Hobart	Discharged own request
3/52	Thomas Roberts	Able seaman	31	Camberwell	Aug/40 Hobart 1st	May/41 Hobart	Deserted Hobart 2nd
3/53	John Barclay	Y/ Gent's stewd	22	Edinburgh	Sept/40 Hobart	Sept/43 Woolwich	Completed journey
3/54	John Robertson	Able seaman	30	Ayrshire	Oct/40 Hobart	May/41 Hobart	Deserted Hobart 2nd
3/55	John Irvine	Caulker	30	Whitehaven	Oct/40 Hobart	Sept/43 Woolwich	Down to AB Oct/41
3/56	Thomas Farr	Able seaman	29	Milford	Oct/40 Hobart	Nov/40 Hobart	See records 7 and 66
3/57	Richard Clark	Able seaman	30	Dublin	Oct/40 Hobart	May/41 Hobart	Deserted Hobart May/41
3/58	Thomas Jones	Able seaman	24	Liverpool	Oct/40 Hobart	June/43 Rio de Janeiro	Died in Rio de Janeiro
3/59	William Johnson	Able seaman	24	Shetlands	Oct/40 Hobart	Sept/43 Woolwich	Completed journey
3/60	Niel McBride	Able seaman	24	Greenock	Oct/40 Hobart	Sept/43 Woolwich	C/F/Top. Q/master. AB
3/61	Luke Smith	Able seaman	23	London	Oct/40 Hobart	Sept/43 Woolwich	Completed journey
3/62	Henry Harden	Able seaman	29	Beverley	Oct/40 Hobart	Sept/43 Woolwich	Completed journey
3/63	Charles Grimshaw	Able seaman	27	Manchester	Oct/40 Hobart	Sept/43 Woolwich	Completed journey
3/64	William Whateley	Able seaman	22	Wells	Oct/40 Hobart	Sept/43 Woolwich	Deserted Hobart 2nd
3/65	Francis Hardy	Able seaman	29	Dublin	Nov/40 Hobart	May/41 Hobart	Capt's Cox. C/F/Top
3/66	Thomas R Farr	Able seaman	27	Milford	Nov/40 Hobart	Sept/43 Woolwich	Completed journey
3/67	John Blyth	Able seaman	22	Edinburgh	June/41 Hobart	Sept/43 Woolwich	Completed journey
3/68	David H Sims	Able seaman	22	Lincolnshire	June/41 Hobart	Sept/43 Woolwich	Completed journey
3/69	Robert K Chilcott	Able seaman	22	Burton	June/41 Hobart	Sept/43 Woolwich	Completed journey
3/70	William Roell	Able seaman	22	Wiglow	June/41 Hobart	Sept/43 Woolwich	Completed journey
3/71	David Penivarden	Able seaman	25	Greenwich	June/41 Hobart	Sept/43 Woolwich	Completed journey
3/72	Peter McBride	Caulker's mate	23	Roxburgh	July/41 Hobart	Sept/43 Woolwich	Caulker. Oct/42 down to AB
3/73	Charles J Settle	Able seaman	24	West minster	Oct/42 E Falklands	Sept/43 Woolwich	Completed journey

Marines

No.	Name	Rating	Age	Birthplace	Joined	Left	Notes
1	W K Cunningham	Sergeant	30	London	June/39	Sept/43 Woolwich	Completed journey
2	Joseph Swain	Private	38	Chatham	June/39	Sept/43 Woolwich	Completed journey
3	William Ready	Private	33	St Giles, Camb.	June/39	Sept/43 Woolwich	Completed journey
4	William Stevenson	Private	35	St Marks, Notts.	Sept/39	Nov/40 Hobart	Joined Observatory
5	George Gren	Corporal	31	Hatfield	Oct/39	Sept/43 Woolwich	Completed journey
6	Michael Latouche	Private 3rd	19	unknown	June/39	Sept/39 Hobart	Hospitalised
7	John Ottley	Private 3rd	24	Braintree	June/39	Aug/42 Bay of Islands	Invalided
8	William Talbot	Private 3rd	29	Suffolk	June/39	Sept/43 Woolwich	Completed journey

ARRIVAL AND DEPARTURE DATES FROM PORTS OF CALL

Depart from Woolwich	25 September 1839
Call at Madeira	20 October
Tenerife visited	4 November
Cape Verde Islands visited	13 November
St Pauls Rock visited	29 November
Crossed Equator	3 December
Island of Trinidad visited	17 December
Arrive St Helena	31 January 1840
Depart St Helena	9 February
Arrive Simon's Town (1st visit)	17 March
Depart Simon's Town	6 April
Saw Prince Edward Island	22 April
Visited Crozet Islands with supplies	1 May
Arrive Kerguelen Island	12 May
Depart Kerguelen Island	20 July
Arrive Hobart (1st visit)	6 August
Depart Hobart for the South	12 November
Arrive Auckland Isles	25 November
Depart Auckland Isles	12 December
Arrive Campbell Island	13 December
Depart Campbell Island	17 December
Crossed Antarctic Circle	4 January 1841
Cross Antarctic Circle for first time	4 January
Took possession of Victoria Land	12 January
Sighted Mts Erebus and Terror	27 January
Sighted Great Ice Barrier	28 January
Furthest South	2 February
Arrive Hobart (2nd visit)	6 April
Depart Hobart for the South	7 July
Arrive at Sydney	11 July
Depart Sydney	5 August
Arrived at Bay of Islands	18 August
Depart Bay of Islands	24 November
Arrive Falklands (1st visit)	6 April 1842
Depart Falklands	6 September
Arrive Falklands (2nd visit)	12 November
Depart Falklands	17 November
Arrive Simon's Town (2nd visit)	4 April 1843
Depart Simon's Town	30 April
Arrive St Helena (2nd visit)	13 May
Depart St Helena	29 May
Arrive Rio de Janeiro	18 June
Depart Rio de Janeiro	24 June
Arrive Woolwich (Paid off)	23 September

BIBLIOGRAPHY

BOOKS

Buchan, Alex R. *A Grand Polar Veteran* (Peterhead: The Buchan Field Club, 2016)

Beals, Herbert, Campbell, R.J., Savours, Ann, and McConnell, Anita. *Four Travel Journals* (London: Hakluyt Society)

Campbell, Captain Richard, RN (Rtd). *The Diaries of Sgt William Cunningham* (London: Hakluyt Society)

Cyriax, Richard J. *Sir John Franklin's Last Arctic Expedition* (Plaistow: The Arctic Press, 1997)

Desmond, Ray. *Sir Joseph Walton Hooker* (Antique Collectors' Club, 2006)

Dodge, Ernest S. *The Polar Rosses* (London: Faber and Faber, 1973)

Edinger, Ray. *Fury Beach* (New York: Berkley Books, 2003)

Jarrett, Dudley. *British Naval Dress* (Letchworth: Aldine Press, 1960)

Kauffmann, Jean-Paul. *Voyage to Desolation Island* (London: The Harvell Press, 2000)

Lyon, David, and Winfield, R E. *The Sail and Steam Navy List* (London: Chatham Publishing, 2004)

McCormick, Robert. *Voyages of Discovery in Arctic and Antarctic Seas* (London: Sampson Low, Marston, Searle & Rivington, 1884)

MacDougall, Philip. *Chatham Dockyard* (Stroud: The History Press, 1988)

O'Brien, Patrick. *Desolation Island* (London: Harper Collins, 1996)

Palin, Michael. *Erebus: the Story of a Ship* (London: Hutchinson, 2018)

Palmer, Joseph. *Jane's Dictionary of Naval Terms* (Abingdon: Purnell Book Services, 1975)

Parry, Ann. *Parry of the Arctic, 1790 to 1855* (London: Chatto & Windus, 1963)

amsland, John. *From Antarctica to the Gold Rushes* (Melbourne: Brolga Publishing, 2011)

.ehbock, Philip E. *At Sea with the Scientifics* (USA: University of Hawaii Press, 1992)

Ross, Captain Sir James Clark. *A Voyage of Discovery and Research in the Southern and Antarctic Regions, 1839 to 1843*, two volumes (Newton Abbot: David & Charles reprint, 1969)

Ross, M.J., *Ross in the Antarctic* (Caedmon of Whitby, 1982)

Savours, Dr Ann, and McConnell, Anita. *The History of the Rossbank Observatory, Tasmania* (Taylor & Francis, 2006)

Smith, Michael. *Captain Francis Crozier, Last Man Standing* (Ireland: Collins Press, 2006)

Smucker, Samuel. *Arctic Explorations and Discoveries* (New York: Miller, Orton & Co., 1857)

Smythe, Admiral W.H. *The Sailor's Word Book* (London: Conway Maritime Press 1996, originally published 1867)

OTHER SOURCES

Ancestry.com, birth, marriage and death records, and census records.

Wikipedia Commons, https://commons.wikimedia.org. Information on personnel and illustrations.

National Maritime Museum, Greenwich, https://www.rmg.co.uk/national-maritime-museum. Naval records.

Victorian Web, www.victorianweb.org. Naval uniforms.